The
Strange
World of
Animals
and Pets

The Strange World of Animals and Pets

By Vincent and Margaret Gaddis

COWLES BOOK COMPANY, INC.
NEW YORK

Copyright 1970 by Vincent and Margaret Gaddis

SBN 402-12491-X

Library of Congress Catalog Card Number 75-108004

Cowles Book Company, Inc.
A subsidiary of Cowles Communications, Inc.

Published simultaneously in Canada by
General Publishing Company, Ltd., 30 Lesmill Road,
Don Mills, Toronto, Ontario

Printed in the United States of America

First Edition

Dedicated to all the pets, who rule us
with an iron paw—and especially
to Pooka-haunt-us, a fey white cat who
shed his grace—and fur—on us.

Contents

Japan; and Joker, who found his on a war-torn Pacific
Island • The pets who find their owners in distant hospitals • Those that show up at graves • How a dying mongrel sought out his onetime benefactor • Do plants have
emotions? Memories?

Introduction

On the surface the lives of animals seem simple—eating, sleeping, playing, occasional fighting. They may display such human vices as jealousy, and such virtues as loyalty. Some animals have a sense of humor; others, an astonishing sympathy for their fellow creatures. Between pets and their owners there is a special kind of love. That is the greatest gift of all.

This simple existence is the sum total of the lives of most animals and pets. Protected by human masters or in environments only mildly hostile, they never need to tap the deep inner resources that lie dormant. For pets especially, the sunshine and rain of the passing days are usually peaceful and gentle.

But there are the rare individual animals who, at certain times and under certain conditions, will use their latent supersenses. Subconsciously they can benefit from knowledge far greater than that of their conscious minds. They can contact a vast reality beyond the limited spectra of man's fallible senses: a mental reservoir linked strangely to the collective unconscious of mankind. Here, thoughts are *things;* and undefined natural laws regulate the empathies that began long ago when a brighter sun shone on a primeval earth.

No science in the foreseeable future will be able to do more than peer through small cracks into this great realm. "Our knowledge is a drop," wrote the great psychologist William James, "our ignorance a sea."

There are smart animals—scout dogs in Vietnam who can detect buried mines and grenade trip wires; baboons who drive tractors and operate the signals for speeding trains; Nick Carter, the bloodhound who could track a man's trail days after it had been left; and Rolf, the German shepherd who recovered lost articles valued at more than four hundred thousand dollars. There are also the wizards—the dogs and horses who understand amazing vocabularies and solve complex mathematical problems. They are all exceptional, of course, but that they existed at all indicates a potential that stuns us.

Animals, along with all living things, are affected by cosmic rhythms and celestial cycles. Snails and crabs live by the tides, even in laboratories. Biological clocks, nature's timing systems, regulate the behavior of all forms of life—from the simplest organism to man himself—as accurately as mechanical timepieces.

How does a tiny hummingbird fly over the Caribbean? And from what strange source does it derive its seemingly boundless energy? How does a robin return year after year to a certain backyard in Ohio? Without parental guidance, how does a young seabird fly thousands of miles to its winter range and back again? How does the golden plover streak two thousand miles nonstop from the Aleutians and hit Hawaii on the nose?

These are scientific problems, but there are also the mysteries of the heart. There are the good samaritans, pets who have saved the lives of their masters and animals that have rescued other animals. Dogs have returned to veterinarians who have treated them, bringing their ill or injured canine friends.

The voices of love are avenues of communication that the behaviorist will never know. How did Rags, the astonishing mongrel mascot of Sing Sing Prison, know that a certain inmate was planning to take his life one melancholy night; and why did she change the habit of a lifetime to save him? Pets have known when their owners were injured or killed in far-off accidents. Or, they can reverse this extrasensory communication. The great Polish pianist and statesman, Paderewski, knew ten days before the letter reached him in New York that his parrot, Cocky Roberts, had died in Switzerland. And the death struggles of Bob, a black retriever, were communicated to his master, Sir Rider Haggard, in a dream.

The love, devotion, and loyalty in the creatures we call pets cannot be measured. There was Bobbie, who found his way on bleeding paws three thousand miles across the U.S.A. to return home; and Tom, a cat who had never left St. Petersburg, Florida, but followed his folks to a totally unknown home in California. What strange affinities, what mysterious beacons, guided them across the plains, the desert, and the Rockies to the human beings they loved?

And, finally, there are the riddles that came at the end of life's trail. Nikola Tesla's pigeon flew into the electrical genius' hotel window to die. Pets sometimes die with their owners. When Red Skelton's son, Richard, died of leukemia, the boy's beloved white billy goat expired the next day. Skelton's white cockatoo and Gene Fowler, the writer, were buddies. A few days before Fowler's death, Red overheard him saying to the bird, "I'd need your wings to fly to where I want to go." When the Skeltons came home from Fowler's funeral, they found the cockatoo dead.

In some parts of the world, "telling the bees" is still a custom. *Is* there a "soul of the hive" or a "spirit of the colony," an intelligence made up of all the tiny minds of the individual insects, directing the bees to the graveside rites? What knowledge brings dogs, cats, pigeons, and even cattle to the funerals of their owners?

There are ghosts, too. Both sons of the noted psychologist, Dr. William McDougall, once heard a phantom horse in a deserted barn on a lonely New England farm. Albert Payson

Terhune had a ghost dog at his famed Sunnybank Kennels; and Pierre Van Paassen, the well-known correspondent, reported a frightening experience with a disappearing evil black dog in France. This is the wonder world—the mysterious magic—of animals.

In the accounts that follow, the cynical may see only stubborn stupidity, but I prefer to see bewildered pets whose love knew no boundaries or barriers.

Shep was a half-breed collie, the inseparable companion of a sheepherder in Montana's grazing country. He guided the herds and rounded up the strays. The bonds of affection linking dog and master were made all the stronger by their isolation. For years they lived and worked together beneath the big sky.

But, relentlessly, time passed and in 1936 there came a summer day when Shep's owner failed to emerge from the ranch house to perform the usual morning chores. Shep whined his bewilderment. Neighbors came and they carried his master away in a long black box. Shep followed the men to the railway station in Fort Benton and watched as the coffin was lifted into the baggage car of a train. The train pulled away and the dog was left whimpering on the station platform.

Shep didn't understand the finality of death, but he knew how to wait: Since his master had gone away on a train, he would return on a train. The collie never left the station. Every time a train stopped, he looked hopefully at each arriving passenger. During the day, between trains, he dozed in the sun; at night, he slept beneath the wooden platform.

The railroad men understood the dog's vigil and kept him fed and watered. The weeks became months, and summer and autumn were followed by the bitter Montana winter. Section Foreman McSweeney coaxed the dog into the warm freight house and made a small swinging door so Shep could come and go at will.

In time Shep became a local celebrity. People tried to adopt him, but he was strictly a one-owner dog. And day after day for five and a half years—he met every train that stopped at the station.

On January 12, 1942, he limped down the tracks as usual to meet an incoming train. He had grown old. His movements were slow and his joints were stiff. When he tried to leap out of the way of the locomotive, his feet slipped and he fell across a rail. Shep's long vigil was over.

The citizens of Fort Benton buried Shep with grief and honor. Station Agent Schanche made a wooden coffin and painted it black. Boy Scouts carried the coffin to the top of a bluff overlooking the station. Practically every resident of the town was present to listen as Pastor Underwood recited Senator Vest's "Eulogy on the Dog." A bugler played taps.

Today a stone monument, a profile statue of Shep, marks his grave. But the dog has another monument, a living one. A conductor named Ed Shields had a booklet printed about Shep for sale to the passengers. Shields decided to donate the modest profit to the Montana School for the Deaf and Blind at Great Falls. The first gift, a check for two hundred dollars was made on Christmas, 1946.

The "Shep Fund" idea caught on. Contributions, even legacies, enabled the school to buy badly needed equipment and to establish college scholarships for older students. "The Shep Fund," said Superintendent Glenn Harris, "helps make up for some of the love and security these deaf and blind children are deprived of by separation from their families."

So the dog that could not forget his beloved master has two monuments—one of stone, and the other, a growing one that lives to enrich the lives of handicapped children.[1]

Another dog named Shep, a Scotch shepherd, is well remembered at St. Anthony's Hospital in Rock Island, Illinois. Here, where the drama of life begins and ends, the story inspires courage and faith.

It all began in 1924 when Francis McMahon started down

the basement steps of his home, his puppy at his heels. Suddenly he slipped and fell headlong to the cellar floor where he lay unconscious. The puzzled Shep looked at his silent master, then began barking excitedly for help.

Neighbors heard and McMahon was rushed to the hospital. Shep went along. As the stretcher was wheeled into an elevator, the dog tried to follow but an interne pushed him aside. By this time McMahon was conscious and feebly stroked Shep's head.

"It's all right, Shep. I'll come back after they fix me up. Wait for me here!"

Shep knew what this meant. Often McMahon, going where the dog could not follow, had spoken these words and Shep had waited. The elevator doors closed and Shep lay down in the lobby.

His master never came back. Francis McMahon died of complications from a skull fracture and his body was removed by a rear entrance. After the funeral, members of the McMahon family located Shep but the dog refused to leave the lobby. The Franciscan sisters who ran the hospital saw to it that he had food and water and a soft mat to lie on. He became the institution's mascot, a friend to all the staff, but he had only one love, his master.

At first, when the elevator descended, he stood beside the doors, tail wagging, hope shining in his patient brown eyes. Occasionally he would venture outside by the front entrance or into a nearby corridor, but his ears were alert, listening, waiting for the familiar clash of the elevator doors. And when the sound came he would hurry back to the lobby. The months became years and after so many disappointments Shep would simply lie on his mat, watching, as the elevator doors opened.

He was kidnapped once, apparently by someone curious to see if his vigil could be broken, but he returned a day later, tired and dirty, his bruised footpads showing the evidence of weary miles. With this one exception, Shep never left the lobby for more than fifteen minutes at a time.

After awhile strange stories were told by the night workers

in the hospital. It was said that deep in the night, in the early hours before dawn, the dog would sometimes suddenly awaken and race to the elevator, whining softly, wagging his tail, and acting as if his master had returned at last.

"Sympathetic hallucinations," said the doctors. "Merely wish fulfillment. The dog lives with one hope, one desire, and when he sleeps he dreams that his wish has been realized and acts accordingly." But two of the sisters said they once heard the sound of an elevator when the carriage was motionless; and others told of seeing a faint bluish light appear beside the excited dog.

More years passed. Around the patient Shep the citizens of Rock Island lived through the carefree twenties, the tragic financial collapse, the frustrations of the Great Depression— but the dog was still waiting for his master. He was getting old now and very tired. His fame had spread widely. Letters of inquiry came from foreign countries, and many visitors came just to see and pet him. Motion picture companies filmed his vigil. Shep quietly accepted all these attentions but remained at his post. His master had told him to wait, and the people in this busy place looked after his needs. Twelve years and four months—that's a lifetime for a dog—a long time to remember and hope and wait.

In 1936, a few days before Christmas, the end came. Shep was outside the front entrance when a truck drove up. The driver didn't see the dog, and Shep, aged and infirm, could not move to safety in time. He was reverently buried, and his unshakable loyalty is memorialized in the hospital lobby, on a bronze plaque erected by the American Humane Association.[2] Another dog's faithfulness did not end in futility. Albert Payson Terhune who owned and wrote about the famous Sunnybank collies had a friend named Wilson. When Wilson moved to California, he left Jack, his collie, with a relative in Philadelphia.

But Jack refused to live in his new home. He remained at the old house, now closed, and spent his days on the porch.

Each evening he went down to the station to meet the trolley that Wilson had always taken home from work. After checking the departing passengers, he would return to the vacated house and grieve. Ignoring his food, he grew thin and gaunt and it seemed that his sorrow would end in death.

A neighbor, disturbed by the dog's condition, wired the facts to Wilson in California. Wilson took the next train east. When he reached Philadelphia he boarded the same trolley that he had always taken when he returned home from work.

Jack, as usual, had gone to the station to wait. Then, amazingly, it happened—his master got off the car at last!

The collie threw himself at his beloved owner. "He was sobbing almost like a child might sob," Wilson told Terhune later. "He was shivering all over as if he had a chill. And I? Well, I blew my nose hard and did a lot of fast winking."

Jack went to California with his master who had resolved that they would never be separated again.[3]

Cats, too, are capable of great devotion. England has had several historic prison cats of whom touching stories are told. The earliest goes back to the medieval Wars of the Roses, when the houses of York, and Lancaster fought back and forth for the throne for some thirty years. During the wars Richard III imprisoned Sir Henry Wyatt in an unheated room in the Tower of London. There a stray cat slipped through the bars and found a friend.

At first Sir Henry held her just to warm himself, but then grew fond of his only companion. She would catch pigeons and bring them to him for his jailer to cook each day. Wyatt suffered many hardships, including torture on the rack with mustard forced down his throat, but he managed to survive to return to royal favor after Richard was killed at Bosworth Field, and became rich and famous. The grateful knight had his portrait painted with his pet, showing him in the miserable dungeon with the stray cat climbing through the bars, a pigeon in her mouth.

At the bottom of the portrait are these lines:

"This Knight with hunger, cold and care neere starvd, pincht, pined away,
A sillie Beast did feed, heate, cheere with dyett, warmth & play."

No insult was intended to the cat by the word "sillie," which in the fifteenth-century English meant merely "weak."

Another cat was a true "homer" in the sense that she mysteriously found her own master, the Duke of Norfolk, wretchedly imprisoned in the historic tower by Elizabeth the First. The cat prowled the corridors, finally ascended to the roofs, and somehow found the right chimney. There he waited until there was no fire burning below, then scrambled down the bricks, landing covered with soot but happy beside the astonished nobleman. She stayed with him the remaining eight months of his imprisonment, until he was beheaded by order of the queen. We can hope that some of the duke's followers were sufficiently touched in that harsh era to carry the faithful pet to a new home far from blood and tragedy. The love between animals and men that can create such examples of devotion has been developing for many millenia, and human beings, too, can experience great depths of anguish when their pets die.

Novelist Sir Walter Scott erected a monument to the memory of his deerhound, Maida. When the dog died Scott wrote to a friend, "I have sometimes thought of the final cause of dogs having such short lives; for if we suffer so much in losing a dog after an acquaintance of ten or twelve years, what would it be if they were to live double that time?"

An unknown Greek in ancient Athens wrote this epitaph: "Laugh not, I pray thee, though this is a dog's grave; tears fell for me, and the dust was heaped above me by a master's hand."

Lord Byron had a Newfoundland named Boatswain. This flamboyant young nobleman—lame, vain, and tempestuous—had his troubles with his human associates, but he gave his unhappy heart to his dog. It is said that he eased some of his inner storms by swimming in the lake on his estate, where he would pretend to drown so that Boatswain could "save" him. The poet's grief was inconsolable when his dog died of rabies in his arms. Despite the terrible madness of the disease that parted them, Boatswain never bit his master.

A few days later Byron wrote:

> But the poor dog, in life the firmest friend,
> The first to welcome, foremost to defend,
> Whose honest heart is still his master's own,
> Who labors, fights, lives, breathes for him alone,
> Unhonored falls, unnoticed all his worth,
> Denied in heaven the soul he held on earth;
> While man, vain insect! hopes to be forgiven,
> And claims himself a sole exclusive heaven.
>
> To mark a friend's remains these stones arise;
> I never knew but one—and here he lies.

Occasionally men and their pets are buried together. The Scotch Kirk Sessions, touched by the fourteen-year vigil of Bobby at the grave of his master, "auld Jack," gave their consent to Bobby's burial beside "auld Jack" in consecrated soil.

At least one American cemetery—the Oakdale Cemetery at Wilmington, North Carolina—has permitted a heroic dog and his master to be buried together. In this case the dog died after he ran into a burning building in a hopeless attempt to save his owner and was buried lying in the arms of the man he tried to rescue.[4]

Eldon Roark, in his book *Just a Mutt,* tells of an elderly man whose dog was killed by a car. The man owned a cemetery lot, but the cemetery officials refused to permit the pet's burial. A pet cemetery welcomed the request, and when the man died some months later, he was, in accordance with his last will and testament, buried alongside his dog. And also in accordance with his dispositions, a stone was placed upon the grave bearing the inscription: "Here I am resting among friends."

The more we treat animals like friends, the more we talk to them and express our feelings toward them, the faster they develop their intelligence and heart instinct. At times they may teach us more than we teach them.

In a world where all of us are frail, who but our pets will look upon us with eyes that seem to say, "Thou art all fair, my love, there is no spot in thee"? We know very well how misplaced such worship is, and yet perhaps it makes us a little more disciplined so that the faith of a small, devoted creature will not be too shamefully abused. It has been said that the dog is the only animal that has seen his god, but this is true of all pets who have kind and loving owners.

Animals share with man the same emotions—elation and grief, passion and contentment, gratitude and affection. They, too, can know the heat of anger, the sting of rejection, and the pleasure of fellowship.

A former prisoner in the Pennsylvania State Prison tells of a fellow convict who found an English sparrow suffering from a broken wing. He took the bird to his cell, glued two matchsticks onto the wing to keep it spread and secured it to a cardboard device to keep her from fluttering about. He fed the sparrow wet crumbs for several days till the bird began to eat from his hand. In time the wing mended and the sparrow was released.

For two weeks the bird stayed around the prison. Then, after one day away, she appeared again at noon, circled over the heads of the thousand or so men marching from the dining hall, and finally settled on the shoulder of the man who had befriended her. These visits continued two or three times a week for several months. "Many of us grieved," the former inmate said, "when the bird finally failed to return."[5]

Alan Devoe, the naturalist, tells a similar story. He found a mourning dove disabled beside the road, took her home, and placed her in a bamboo cage with fresh water, seeds, and berries. Eight days later, he freed the bird, her health restored. One morning a week later the dove returned and perched on his forearm. "She stayed only a few seconds, close and comradely," Devoe said. "Then she was off. I never saw her again."

Are the beasts of field and jungle really inimical to man, or are they capable in their essential nature of responding to the same trust and love that provide the basis of friendship and affection between two human beings? Ernest Harold Baynes, the noted naturalist, believed that no animal in the world is incurably hostile to us. And after eighty-six years of outdoor adventure, Ernest Thompson Seton, who will always be remembered for his stories and paintings of wildlife, was convinced also that no animal is natively afraid of man. Animals have learned to fear us through bitter experience, and it is fear that causes hostility.

Thus the bond of brotherhood may extend beyond the limits of human fellowship and may even be universal in scope. Animals and birds are somewhat clairvoyant, and may sense the moral atmosphere that surrounds us. They may flee from the huntsman, but respond to the kindness of the harmless nature lover. Only in this way can the astonishing affinity of some persons for wild animals be explained.

Devoe tells of the experience of a man named Phil Traband who was out hiking through a woods. When he came to a clearing, he heard sounds behind him. He turned to find himself pursued by what he judged to be either a wildcat, or lynx, an animal considered mean and dangerous and hardly likely to turn trustfully to a human being.

Traband was frightened, but he stood still. As the big cat drew near, he could see in her eyes the unmistakable look of a kindred spirit appealing for help. The cat's mouth and muzzle were swollen, and as the man—almost instinctively—reached out a hand, the animal opened her mouth. In some manner one of the lynx's fangs had pierced the tongue and held it fast. The wound had become infected.

A groan of pain rumbled in the cat's throat as Traband held her mouth open and, as lightly as he could, worked the swollen tongue free from the impaling fang. The act required several long minutes and must have been very painful, but the wildcat stood quietly. When the tongue was free, the still-incredulous man patted the tawny back. A glow of thankfulness appeared in the cat's eyes and with a soft "mrroww," the lynx slipped away into the woods.[6]

If man could remove hate and fear from his heart, then might this fundamental bond of affinity and affection bring beneficent cooperation between all the kingdoms of life.

All living beings, including man, are prisoners of behavior patterns aeons old. A study of animal behavior will cause the student to wonder if indeed he has any real "control" over his own actions, for man, too, is a creature of instinct. Both physique and behavior are inherited from past ages of evolution and development. In each of us is a link from a chain that goes back, generation after generation, millenium after millenium, to the misty dawn of the beginning.

Late one night Loren Eiseley, professor of anthropology at the University of Pennsylvania, was working at his desk in his study. His dog, a big, ever friendly shepherd, was dozing on a rug in front of the fireplace. Outside a blizzard raged. Snow was falling and the wind moaned and rattled the windows.

Dr. Eiseley had before him relics of a greater winter of long ago when the vast arctic glaciers had moved far to the south. They were the flint lance points of Ice Age hunters and the fossilized leg bone of an ancient bison. The bone was so mineralized that it rang when struck. It had been more than ten thousand years since this bison had roamed the earth and since these flints had been chipped by men fighting to survive in a desolate, frigid world.

Removing the bone from his desk and placing it on the floor, the scientist continued his work. Suddenly he heard a rasping, grating sound. The dog had left the fireplace and was holding the bone between his jaws and mouthing it with a fierce intensity that he had never before exhibited. From his throat came a low rumbling.

"Wolf!" Eiseley called as he put out his hand. The shepherd backed away, still holding the bone between his jaws. The doctor arose from his chair and advanced. The dog's teeth gleamed as he wrinkled his nose, drew back his lips, and snarled a warning. He crouched, ready to spring. The scientist knew that if he took another step his dog would attack. And for a fleeting second he—the scholar—felt an urge to respond to the animal's challenge.

Suddenly, Eiseley understood and he retreated to his chair. Wolf became silent and dropped the bone, but placed a possessive paw on it. Moments passed and again the doctor arose, walked to the outside door, and asked, "Wolf, how about a walk in the snow?" The dog, quiet now, left the bone and eagerly accepted his leash as usual. And as they walked together through the wintry night, the master said to his pet, "We have been very far away. There is within us something that we had both better try to forget."

What had caused this dog who had never before displayed animosity, who had loved his master all his life, to act as he did? It was, Loren Eiseley tells us, shadows from the remote past that had echoed in the minds of the dog and even his owner. There had been nights on endless frozen wastes beneath cold stars when the spoils of the hunt had been few and no animal surrendered a bone that meant life itself.

The fossilized bone had no odor, no taste. What had evoked this long-buried ancestral memory? Could it have been the bone's large size, its shape, or was there about it an aura detectable by a supersense that could link it with ages of desperate struggle long vanished?[7]

There once was a time when many animals, including man, needed each other to survive the onslaughts of raging elements in a hostile world. Their affinity must have been very deep, involving senses and abilities long lost.

Dr. Eiseley says lingering legends indicate that the discovery of fire separated man from the animals. Fire may have marked the beginning of this separation, but as men organized into groups and tribes, the kinship continued with totems. The animals that symbolized the various totems were worshiped. There was a response to this outpouring of psychic energy. Strange bonds were forged.

Totemism as an effective psychic power exists among some primitive peoples today. Geoffrey Gorer, the anthropologist, gives new and striking evidence of the astonishing psychic kinship between West African tribes in his book, *Africa Dances*. And tribes around the Nyanza lakes of Central Africa have such animal kinships that should a boat be upset in crocodile-infested water, those who are of the crocodile totem swim slowly and unmolested to the shore; the others must beat off constant attacks at great peril.[8]

Ronald Rose, a scholar who lived for a time among the Australian aborigines, explains in his book, *Living Magic,* that among the more tribalized natives the totem is a mediating vehicle for information that is apparently acquired telepathically. The appearance of the totemic animal or bird announces an accident, the illness, or death of another member of the same totem clan. Sometimes the totem is observed by other persons and seemingly exists in reality; at other times it is an apparition observed only by the recipient; or, it may appear in a dream.[9]

As man developed his cultures, he lost his close contacts with nature and his animal brethren. He created communities for assistance in obtaining food, for protection, and for fellowship among his own kind. He lost the mystical powers he once needed to survive as he created the artificial environments of civilization. Today man stands apart from the natural world, and the chasm between ourselves and the rest of life is deep and wide.

We have a tendency to patronize animals, to limit their abilities, to compare adversely their physical forms, minds, and lives with our high estate. But animals live in realms of their own, realms totally different and far older than ours. They dwell within the earth, in jungles and deserts, in seas and the skies. They possess senses, and extensions of senses, we have lost or never attained. They see sights we shall never see. They hear sounds we shall never hear. They respond to terrestrial and cosmic rhythms and cycles that we have never charted. Perhaps, if these thoughts are kept in mind, some of the accounts that will appear later in this book will not seem so incredible.

As Henry Beston, a sensitive writer on Maine lore and observations of nature, says in his book, *The Outermost House,* the animal cannot be measured by man. In their own worlds they are finished and complete. They are not brethren or underlings, but "other nations, caught with ourselves in the net of life and time, fellow prisoners of the splendor and travail of the earth."[10]

2

Prima Donnas and Mascot Marvels

The dog's life led by the pampered pets of Francis Egerton, an eccentric British aristocrat, was the life of Riley. Few canines ever have had it so good. It's a shame it didn't last.

A well-educated nobleman, Francis Egerton had inherited three titles—he was the eighth Earl of Bridgewater, ninth Viscount Brackley, and Baron Ellesmere. He had also received great wealth. Unfortunately he was a snob and this disagreeable characteristic became more pronounced during his declining years. There were few he considered his equal and none his superior.

Driving about Paris, for which he had left England, he picked up fifteen stray dogs of assorted breeds and adopted them as companions. The dogs were given valets who dressed them in human-style clothes of finest quality, tailored to their measure. They were served gourmet food, and slept on beds of silk. Each day, half a dozen at a time, they were driven about the city on sight-seeing tours in the earl's luxurious four-horse coach with two liveried footmen perched behind. Two favorite dogs, in formal evening attire, ate with the earl at his dinner table. Such enchantment couldn't last! And it didn't!

When he died in 1829 Egerton was seventy-two. He left a will with bequests to persons and institutions, but somehow he forgot to make any provision for his four-footed friends. His hard-hearted executors turned the dogs out into the cold world where they would again lead dogs' lives.

It would seem, however, that more humans than canines lead dogs' lives. How many of us, for example, can yield to our wanderlust as did Hobo, a medium-sized brown mongrel, ownerless and homeless, who first appeared in the spring of 1957 at the railroad yards at Hopewell, Virginia? He began riding the switch engines, but soon was off on longer hauls. During the years that followed he traveled thousands of miles. Train crews told of seeing him as far south as Tampa and as far west as Cincinnati. But Hopewell was his home town and he always came back to the freight yards where he had started.

The railroad men took care of Hobo. They fed him scrambled eggs and bacon, his favorite dish, and permitted him to ride the diesel engines. In good weather the dog enjoyed riding outside on the catwalks, but when it was cold or rainy he'd curl up on the cab floor. Most of the time he rode the rails of the Seaboard and the Norfolk and Western lines. The end of the line approached for Hobo in 1963 when he began going blind. He died later, mourned by all the railroaders who had known him.[1]

But Owney, described by the U.S. Post Office as "the most traveled dog in history," made his first trip in forty years when he left Washington, D.C., for Toledo, Ohio, to attend a big convention. There he was one of the principal attractions, yet he didn't bark or even twitch a muscle.

These seeming contradictions are cleared up when we explain that it was Owney's shaggy hide prepared with the skill of taxidermy, together with his harness, medals, and tags, that were on display. The occasion was the convention of the National Federation of Postal Clerks in September, 1937. That Owney, four decades after his death, and remembered only by veteran postal employees, should receive such a posthumous honor was a tribute to his remarkable life. In a more romantic era the saga of this mongrel would have produced at least a ballad or two.

The story began one bitter wintry day in 1888 when a shivering little mutt crept out of the cold into the post office at Albany, New York, and fell asleep behind the mail sacks. When he was found the clerks shared their lunches with him and decided to adopt him as the post-office mascot. Since he apparently had no owner, they named him Owney.

The smart little dog was quick to prove that even an alley background is no handicap to fame if a fellow really applies himself. He soon learned the routine of the post office but probably found it rather dull. He saw the mail sacks being loaded into the railway cars and evidently decided that he was entitled to the same attention. Nobody knows just what day he took his first trip but he was gone for several weeks before he returned to Albany with a woof and a wag.

The postal clerks were afraid their pet would get lost so they bought him a collar with his identification on it and attached a tag asking other clerks to stamp the names of the places Owney went. Before long Owney spent more time on the road than off, traveling all over the United States as a welcome guest in the mail cars. He became so burdened with tags on his collar that he could hardly hold his head up.

The postmaster general presented him with a lifetime pass permitting him to travel in any U.S. mail car and a special harness that relieved the weight of his collar. By the time the harness was made, however, Owney had developed the ability to slip his collar off while traveling, and then pull it back on again with his paws before "making his entrance" at his stopovers.

In 1895 Owney went to Alaska. While returning down the Pacific Coast he visited Tacoma, Washington, where he followed the mail bags up the gangplank of the S. S. *Victoria,* outward bound for the Far East. He traveled first class, with the run of the ship.

In Japan he was taken to the mikado, who solemnly decorated him and presented him with an honorary passport
bearing the seal of the empire. Another medal and passport
were the gifts of the emperor of China. The perky pup continued his voyage around the world, passing through the Suez
Canal into the Mediterranean and across the Atlantic Ocean.
When he arrived in New York he had accumulated two
hundred medals, but reporters who "interviewed" him found
that he lacked one credential—a dog license!

The mayor of San Francisco gave Owney a custom kit
containing a dog blanket, a comb, and a brush. While in the
city by the Golden Gate, some wit entered him in a dog show
for purebreds. Despite his diverse ancestry he won a medal
and one well deserved—for being the most traveled dog in
the show.

Wherever Owney went he was welcomed and the railway
mail clerks he chose to ride with considered him a promise of
good luck. They believed that no accident could befall the car
in which their postal mascot decided to travel.

For more than nine years Owney trotted the earth. Perhaps
he had received too much attention, because in his old age he
became irritable and demanding. As to the manner of his
death, there are conflicting accounts, some possibly designed
to conceal the truth. When he died in August, 1897, the U. S.
Post Office Information Service Bulletin on Owney said that
he died of injuries received in a street fight with another dog.
The press relations director for the Smithsonian Institution, in
answer to a letter of inquiry, stated that the dog was shot by a
new postal clerk who thought he was a cranky stray. Still other
stories say he was "accidentally killed" or died of old age. But
however he met his end, little Owney was mourned by all the
men who had traveled with him.

His body was mounted and, together with his harness and
medals, displayed for some years in the Postal Museum in
Washington. Later it was moved to a glass case in the Smithsonian Institution, to which it was returned after the 1937

convention in Toledo. But the years, dust, possibly moths, took their toll and the body was removed from display. Today it rests somewhere in the vast, crowded storage vaults of the institution's basement along with other relics of America's past.

It seems unlikely that there will ever be another dog to compete with Owney as the Marco Polo of dogdom.[2]

There are, on the other hand, dogs who seem to sense that grim prison walls offer them refuge and care. At Sing Sing the men often deprived themselves of food to feed the strays, and on one occasion when the local dog catcher came to pick up animals without licenses, the prison grapevine was so efficient that before he could get inside the gates every dog had vanished into thin air.[3]

Perhaps the most remarkable mascot to brighten the dark days at Sing Sing was a small gray mongrel named Rags. She first appeared inside the walls on a chilly autumn day in 1929, squeezing her emaciated body through the iron picket fence above the Hudson River. A three-month-old pup, thin and unkempt, she acquired her name because she looked just like a shaggy bundle of rags.

Warden Lawes was a dog lover and he permitted the inmates to adopt her. Within a few weeks she was fat and sassy but by no means dignified. Possessing the stubby legs of a Scotty and the compact body of a wire-haired terrier, she had a comical fat-lady waddle. Moreover, she was a ham.

Rags moved about from group to group, putting on her acts as if she sensed that this was one place where amusement and laughs were needed. She would charge like a bull into a hedge with such force that she had to be pulled out. She would race across the exercise yard, holding grass in her mouth like a beard. Or, she would roll over and over, ending her acrobatics with a clumsy somersault and a violent wiggle of her rear end like a shimmy dancer.

At six thirty each morning she left the warm basement of the warden's home and joined the men as they marched from their cells to the mess hall. After breakfast she made her routine round of visits, first to the shops, then to the hospital where she entertained the patients, followed by passing through the gate and exercising with the gangs of trustees working outside the walls. During recreation periods she slept through lectures and motion pictures, listened politely at band concerts, and at baseball games barked and dashed back and forth in front of the grandstand every time the prison team scored.

Rags loved chocolate-coated raisins. Lonely prisoners, craving extra attention, would try to bribe her with this delicacy, but she was scrupulously impartial. After eating the raisins she would wag her appreciation, then trot away to pay her respects to another inmate. Rags knew she had to be the pet of all the men equally. Each day in the mess hall she stationed herself at the foot of a different table, carefully rotating as the weeks passed.

Intensely devoted to the convicts, Rags ignored visitors, treated the warden and his family with emotionless respect, and backed away and growled when the guards approached. And the inmates returned this devotion. They saved rare tidbits for her. If her nose seemed warm, they bundled her up in sweaters. When she was sick, their worry crowded out all other topics for conversation.

When the warden built a new home outside the walls, he ordered the guards to let her in and out of the gates whenever she wished. Rags was proud of this privilege. She would strut up to the south entrance each morning and bark imperiously for admittance. The guard on duty would press the button that rolled back the massive gate. Without a glance to right or left, Rags would prance through, her head held high.

The dog usually left the prison compound at lock-up time, but always returned if a show was scheduled to be held in the evening. One entertainer who heard about this was fascinated by the puzzle. "How can she know when there's going to be a performance?" he asked a lifer.

The prisoner shook his head. "Rags is a superdog," he replied. "She knows everything we know and maybe a lot more."

While entertainment had its value to imprisoned men, Rags had a far greater contribution to make toward the welfare of some of the convicts. They were the lonely and homesick, the men burdened with guilt, worry, or grief. They were the forgotten, rejected men who never received a letter or a visit.

When this remarkable dog noticed a prisoner sitting alone, brooding, she would gain his attention by rubbing her head against his knee. As he started to pet her, she would swing her tail like mad, go into a waddling dance, and move away a few feet. Usually the man would follow, the act would be repeated, and in a short time the inmate would find himself joining a group of his fellows where talk and banter would banish his blues.

One winter night Rags did something unprecedented. She followed a certain convict to his cell and remained in front of the cell door until morning. Only after she had followed the man to the mess hall for breakfast did she leave him.

"That dog saved my life," the inmate explained later. "When I didn't get that pardon I figured no one gave a damn about me and I had had enough. I was planning on hanging myself with a sheet. That dog never gave me a chance. Every time I got out of my bunk, Rags would growl soft-like, and I knew if I went ahead she would bark and bring the cellblock guard on the run. I figured that if the dog thought that much about me, I'd better give myself another chance. So I finally rolled over and went to sleep."

The years passed. Rags reached old age and its infirmities. She suffered from severe colds one after the other. Her eyesight became so poor that sometimes even the guards could pet her. But she still made her daily rounds, cheering lonely men, offering amusement and companionship.

One evening in May, 1941, Rags passed through the gate and started to trot to the warden's house. It was raining. Suddenly there was a vivid flash as lightning struck nearby, followed by the heavy crash of thunder. A tower guard who couldn't leave his post watched as the terrified dog sought shelter in the railway tunnel that bisects the prison. He telephoned the warden's family, but when rescuers arrived they found they were too late. The dog's wet body had touched the third rail.

Rags was buried in a grave beside the prison's walls. The grave is marked by a small mound and a stone slab bearing her name. As the writing team of Helen and Clem Wyle said in a magazine article about Rags, under this memorial stone lies a great deal more than an animal's dust.[4]

Rags' life was one of quiet heroism but Spot, a fox terrier, was a fire dog—the mascot of Headquarters Company Station at Camden, New Jersey. He lived with the horror created by smoke and flame. He rode the screaming red fire trucks and watched the long battles against blazing destruction. Then, one day, suddenly, Spot changed his sleeping quarters—from the fire station to the second-floor apartment of Mrs. Anna Souders, the widowed mother of his two playmates, eleven-year-old Nora and eight-year-old Maxwell. The fire house was across the street.

One cold night a few weeks later, Spot woke suddenly, his nostrils quivering. Smoke! He sprang to his feet and barked a frantic warning; then ran and threw his weight against the bedroom door of Mrs. Souders. The door flew open. Spot ran to the bed, seized the blankets in his jaws, and pulled them from the sleeping Mrs. Souders. Startled, she woke up, choking from the heavy smoke. Followed by the excited dog, she roused her children, flung open a window, and called for help. Then she collapsed, unconscious. But Spot remained at the window—barking.

A night patrolman heard him and investigated. He found the first floor a sea of flames, and ran across the street to the fire station. In a few minutes a ladder was under the window, and firemen had carried down the mother and her two children. All were overcome by smoke. Spot was the last to be saved, but he immediately took over his usual job of guarding the fire trucks while the blaze was extinguished.

Spot is only one of many fire dogs who have saved lives and property. They are the heroes among a group of mascots that originated at the very beginning of full-time organized fire departments. Sometimes they act as station watchdogs. At fires they protect the equipment from overly curious spectators. But most of all they serve as pets for the firemen during the dull hours of waiting between alarms.

Like their fire-fighting masters, the dogs occasionally work in cooperation with the police. There was Yaller, for example, who divided his allegiance between the Eldridge Street police station in New York and the nearby firehouse. He was credited with saving several lives during a tenement-house fire, but several times he helped in the capture of criminals.

Once Yaller was on patrol with an officer when two men were surprised while attempting a robbery. The officer apprehended one of the men, but the other fled. Yaller took after him, seized him by the leg, and held on until another patrolman arrived.

Later the dog took part in the pursuit of two robbers over the roofs of adjoining buildings. One of the fugitives managed to drop through a skylight and vanish. Yaller plunged after him, pursued the man through the darkened building until he was cornered, and then held him at bay until officers arrived.[5]

Not all firehouse mascots are dogs. The list includes cats, monkeys, raccoons, parrots, an eagle, and even a leopard. Most station-house cats become adept at sliding down the pole to the amusement of visitors, but the monkeys are the real clowns.

Two monkeys named Betsy and Bob created double trouble at one station house, however. The firemen began finding combs, compacts, brushes, and jewelry on their beds, in the lockers, and on piles of hose. Finally a lady's comb was found in the chief's car and embarrassing questions were asked.

One afternoon a fireman standing near a window noticed a flash of light. Startled, he saw Betsy climbing down the drain-pipe of a nearby house with a mirror in her hand. It was obvious that Betsy and Bob had been raiding homes in the neighborhood. The chief decided to take no more chances with the pair, and turned them over to the local zoo.

Another monkey, named Jenny, became a heroine when she saved her own firehouse. One night matches in the pocket of clothing drying on the second floor caught fire, and the flames spread to the woodwork. Jenny was chained up for the night not far away. The monkey seized several billiard balls, threw them down the stairway, and shrieked a warning. The man on watch heard the commotion, and the blaze was extinguished without serious damage.

The traditional fire dog, especially in the eastern cities, is the Dalmatian, a breed that originated in Slovakia and Dalmatia. Later it was introduced into Italy, Spain, and England, where it became the "carriage dog," "the plum-pudding dog," and finally "the English coach dog." They were trained to accompany the horse-drawn carriages of the wealthy and guard the stables. The spotted Dalmatians were brought to America by coachmen and grooms to carry on the tradition.

The Vanderbilt family is said to have presented New York's first Dalmatian to Hook and Ladder Number 1 in the City Hall about 1870. At any rate, the use of the breed soon spread —they were intelligent watchdogs and at ease around horses and wheeled vehicles.

When fire apparatus became motorized, they remained as the number one mascot. A decline in the number of dogs followed the change from horses to trucks, but about forty years ago the pets again became popular in eastern city fire departments. Today there are about 250 Dalmatians in New York City firehouses.

The dogs are devoted to their companions. Some years ago Bess, mascot of Engine Company 23 in New York, accompanied three firemen into a burning tenement house. A sudden wave of intense heat and smoke flared back, and one by one the men dropped to the floor unconscious. Bess ran from the building and summoned help by pulling other firemen into the blaze by their coats.

Another Dalmatian named Rex always stayed beside an injured man and would accompany him in the ambulance if he had to be taken to a hospital.

The firemen, too, are devoted to their pets. Many old fire stations bear stone memorials to their mascots. When Bulger, the pet of Engine Number 6 at Paterson, New Jersey, was killed by a neighbor, the department buried him with full honors and erected a large headstone in his memory.[6]

Not all fire dogs who deserved medals have received them, but Jack, the Dalmatian mascot of Engine Company 105, Brooklyn, New York, received a Medal of Valor from the Humane Society of New York. As the fire-fighters swung aboard their rig following an alarm, the heavy truck rolled toward the street, siren wailing.

Suddenly a little three-year-old boy dashed in front of them, then froze in fear as the huge red vehicle loomed over him. The driver jammed on his brakes but the weight of the truck was too great. Jack, sitting in his usual place beside the driver, leaped to the floor and shot ahead of the truck. Missing its front wheels by inches, he knocked the terrified child to safety.[7]

Jack won a medal. But truly there are no medals fine enough to reward the courage and loyalty of the fire dogs. The increasing adoption of the canine mascots in fire departments across the nation will continue to add stories of heroism to an already great tradition.

Individual dogs have won fame for many courageous acts, too, some of them most extraordinary. There was Tschlingel, mascot and honorary member of the Alpine Club, a mongrel who climbed the Alps' greatest mountains. From her collar dangled silver pendants inscribed with the names of thirty peaks and thirty-six passes that she had conquered. She was at the advanced age of ten years when, as incredulous observers watched through telescopes, she scaled Mont Blanc.

Pets of all varieties have gone off to battles with their masters, and have added a light and gentle touch to the grim business of war. During the Civil War, almost every outfit, Union and Confederate, had a mascot—among them raccoons, badgers, chameleons, white mice, and a tame squirrel that danced to martial music and spun like a top around the rim of the company's drum. But the most famous mascot in the Union Army was a bald eagle, Old Abe, of the Eighth Wisconsin Regiment.

The winged warrior was originally an eaglet that a Chippewa Indian named Chief Sky found when he cut down a tree in the Flambeau River country. The chief traded the fledgling to a farmer, Dan McCann, for a bushel of corn and McCann took it to his home near Eau Claire, Wisconsin. In April, 1861, as the Eighth Wisconsin was being organized, McCann was in Eau Claire while the new recruits swarmed into the town. The soldiers crowded around the bird and one man shouted, "Let the eagle enlist, too! He'll lick the Rebs!"

The troops of Company C scraped together five dollars and purchased the mascot that was to give the nickname "Eagle Regiment" to the Eighth Wisconsin. As the men cheered, the eagle—with red, white, and blue ribbons tied around his neck—was sworn into service.

A five-foot length of pipe topped by a brightly painted metal Union shield was the bird's perch. Old Abe immediately joined in the spirit of the occasion. It is said that as the soldiers marched through Madison on the way to Camp Randall to the beat of drums and with colors flying, the eagle leaped from his perch on the metal standard, seized a corner of the flag in his beak, and helped carry it through the crowded streets.

The Eighth Wisconsin had its baptism of fire at Farmington, Missouri. Old Abe broke the cord that bound him to the standard and with shrill screams flew above the embattled men. The regiment's commanding officer, Captain John Perkins, was killed, but the eagle's bravery even under heavy artillery fire helped to restore the unit's morale.

As the war continued, Old Abe flew and screamed over the thickest of the fighting in many battles. He escaped injury at Corinth, but during the siege of Vicksburg a spent bullet struck his chest, and another passed through his left wing. Several times his tail feathers were shot off, but he was never seriously injured and none of the eleven standard bearers who carried him into battle was killed or captured.

This is all the more remarkable since the Confederates had developed a superstitious dread of the fighting eagle and he had become a hunted bird. There was a price on his head, and often the Confederates concentrated their fire on Old Abe, now known to them as the "Yankee Buzzard." One artillery shell aimed at him killed a dozen men and tore the flag to shreds. Frustrated General Sterling Price said, "I would rather capture or kill that eagle than take a whole brigade."

In more than three years of war this remarkable eagle led the regiment in thirty-six battles and fifty skirmishes. Between such excitements he marched and paraded with his fellow soldiers, came to "attention" during inspections, and squawked his accompaniment to his favorite tunes, "Yankee Doodle" and "John Brown's Body." If he were close to a river or lake, he fished for his own living.

In 1864 the Eighth Wisconsin and Old Abe were recalled for recruiting duty. During this period the bird was the guest of honor at what may have been the only banquet ever held for a bird. When the regiment headed back to Memphis and the war, a railroad conductor almost started another war by insisting that the rate schedule called for a double fare for the eagle. When the angry soldiers encircled the trainman and began closing in, the conductor decided quickly that Old Abe was indeed a hero who could ride free.

After the winged warrior's final battle at Hurricane Creek, Louisiana, he returned home with the twenty-six remaining members of the regiment. In peace his fame continued to grow. He toured the country several times, raising more than eighteen thousand dollars for wounded veterans, and receiving over twenty-five thousand letters containing additional contributions. He appeared at fairs and at servicemen's reunions in many states.

His quills were in demand for the signing of state documents. He was the subject of a bronze statue and many portraits. P. T. Barnum offered twenty thousand dollars to add the bird to his circus, but the priceless eagle made his headquarters in a large cage in the basement of the Wisconsin State Capitol at Madison, where he received visitors from all over the world.

In March, 1881, a smoldering fire broke out in the basement and smoke enveloped the cage. Old Abe was rescued, but he died from the effects of the smoke a few days later. His body was mounted and placed on display. In 1904 another fire swept the State Capitol and destroyed the body, but visitors to Memorial Hall in the Capitol will find on exhibit a replica and a portrait of Wisconsin's winged warrior.[8]

Another unlikely animal who has captured the public's heart is the elephant, a huge and heavy beast who nevertheless possesses grace and has a remarkable sense of balance.

The most beloved of all elephants as well as the largest ever seen in captivity was Jumbo, hailed by the great Barnum as "The Only Mastodon on Earth." He was slightly over a yard high when he was captured in Ethiopia in 1861, but at the age of seven, his appetite and size suddenly increased. He ate two hundred pounds of hay each day. When he attained his maximum, this colossal pachyderm stood eleven and a half feet in height at the shoulder, and weighed six and a half tons. He consumed tons of apples and bonbons. For dinner alone he could put away fifteen loaves of bread, a barrel of potatoes, four quarts of onions, and occasionally a keg of beer.

Matthew Scott was Jumbo's keeper. He was a lanky man with a handle-bar moustache and a bowler hat, who lived alone in a room at the zoo and often slept with Jumbo. Between man and beast a deep love developed. "Scotty" shared all his treats with Jumbo, even to whisky and chewing tobacco.

Untold thousands of delighted adults and shouting children rode around London's Zoological Gardens on Jumbo's back, the adults including Queen Victoria and the Prince of Wales. He became the most popular animal in the vast zoo, and perhaps all this attention caused his outbreaks of temper when he reached the age of twenty-one. For years the American showman, P. T. Barnum, had been trying unsuccessfully to buy the elephant. Now he told his London agents to offer ten thousand dollars. To Barnum's surprise the offer was accepted.

When news of the sale reached the public, a storm of protest swept Great Britain. There were mass meetings, parades with signs, and thousands of letters of objection, including one from the queen. The *New York Herald,* with tongue in cheek, declared that war was imminent. A large fund was raised to buy the animal and an injunction was sought, but the court ruled in Barnum's favor.

On Jumbo's last day at the zoo, a huge crowd came to bid him farewell. The line was half a mile long and the zoo took in fifty thousand dollars. Spectators wore Jumbo hats, ties, and jewelry. Restaurants featured Jumbo pies, salads, and ice creams. Along with thousands of farewell messages came hundreds of gifts, including many dolls, games, books, and similar articles useless to even an intelligent elephant such as Jumbo.

Only Scotty could lure Jumbo into his traveling crate after several days of stubborn refusal. The elephant arrived in New York April 9, 1882, aboard a freighter. With his crate on a flatbed wagon pulled by twenty-two horses, Jumbo moved from the dock up Broadway to the old Madison Square Garden, preceded by clowns, dancers, and a brass band. Ten days later he had earned more than his purchase price and transportation, and in the first month alone he brought in over three hundred thousand dollars.

During the next three years Jumbo toured the United States and Canada in a private railroad car with the faithful

Scotty sleeping in a berth just above the elephant's head. Much to Scotty's annoyance Jumbo developed the mischievous habit of pulling the blankets off his sleeping keeper. And in the meantime Jumbo's name became known and loved throughout North America as he headlined the Barnum and Bailey Circus.

Jumbo's final public appearance was on September 15, 1885, at St. Thomas, Ontario, Canada. In the evening the circus was being loaded on cars on a railroad siding. As Scotty was leading his charge from the circus grounds to the cars along the tracks in a narrow defile, a freight train appeared from around a curve and bore down on them. With dirt embankments on both sides of the defile, there was no place for the colossal beast to find safety.

Scotty slapped the elephant on the rump and shouted, "Run, Jumbo, run!" At the same time the engineer applied the brakes. But it was too late. As Jumbo shuddered out his final gasps, Scotty flung his own body across the crushed victim and wept.

Jumbo's skeleton is on exhibit at the American Museum of Natural History in New York. The mounted hide may be seen in the Barnum Museum at Tufts University, Medford, Massachusetts. During the few years of his life that remained, Scotty could frequently be found in the university museum standing in front of the mounted elephant, talking to it quietly, and patting the lifeless hulk.[9]

3

Pets Who Earn Their Keep

There's a Menomini Indian legend that long ago, when the deserts were green and the mountains were hills, the animals and man spoke the same language. Then the Great Spirit looked into the hearts of men and saw selfishness and greed, and he warned the animals that if they did not adopt languages of their own man would enslave them.

Man has indeed enslaved some animals, while others have been made employees paid in the coin of their particular realm. As for slavery, at least some of the cruelties of the past no longer exist. Although dogs in some parts of Europe are still being made to pull heavy carts, we doubt if those other dogs, unfortunate enough to be born low-slung and bandy-legged, are still being forced to run in circular treadmill cages to turn roasting spits, churn butter, or raise buckets of water from wells.

Animals can perform certain uncomplicated tasks as well as man or machine, and they work contentedly for peanuts, chicken feed, or bananas, as the case may be. And there are psychologists who foresee a time when animals will displace men in certain tedious jobs. To a limited extent that time has already arrived.

Geese are useful birds. They weed peppermint fields in Oregon and Washington. They waddle through cotton fields in the Southern States, destroying weeds more efficiently than herbicides or mechanical weeders. In fact they are credited with reducing the cost of growing an acre of cotton from $124 to $98.

Gaggles of geese in Scotland guard the sheds where thousands of barrels of aging whisky are stored. When thirsty intruders appear, they start cackling and armed human guards come on the run.

In France trained pigs snuffle out underground truffles, the small black fungi considered table delicacies. The female pigs have a keener sense of smell than their mates, and pregnant sows the sharpest of all. They are rewarded with beans, corn, or acorns.

Monkeys in Malaysia scramble up coconut trees and throw down the fruit. They are paid with soda pop. In Thailand a bank employs a monkey to bite coins suspected of being counterfeit. When a leak developed in a Canadian dam, and engineers couldn't locate it, a pair of beavers were turned loose. They found the leak and repaired it in less than a week.

Railroads use trained dogs to keep their rights-of-way clear of sheep, tramps, and carcasses. Utility companies have found them efficient in finding gas leaks, and country clubs have used them to locate lost golf balls. The Ainus of Japan and the Portuguese in coastal villages use trained dogs for fishing. The Ainus drive the fish shoreward by having the dogs swim in a double formation; the Portuguese teach them to dive for gear and nets, and to swim with messages back and forth within the fishing fleet.[1]

Lindsay Schmidt, an Australian sheep rancher, has as his only permanent farmhand a monkey named Johnnie. Johnnie's classification as a full-time employee has been granted a ninety-dollar-a-year tax deduction. In 1955 the rancher was given the monkey, then only a few weeks old, by a traveling circus in appreciation for putting out a truck fire. Immediately man and monkey became buddies.

Johnnie opens up bales of hay to spread around for the sheep, manhandles bales on and off the tractor, scatters feed for the chickens, helps herd the sheep, and removes burrs from the sheep wool at shearing time. But his most remarkable feat is operating the tractor. At first he only steered the vehicle, in straight or curved paths as instructed, and around rocks and trees. Schmidt could then stand on the wagon and pitch out fodder.

By the time the monkey was nine years old, he had completely mastered tractor operation. Not only does he start the engine after making certain it is in neutral, but he can shift gears and apply the brakes. At noon when the rancher and Johnnie knock off for lunch, they sit together in the shade of the tractor and enjoy sandwiches, fruit, and soda from their individual lunch bags. When it's time to go back to work, Johnnie tidily picks up the scraps and litter and places them in his bag for later disposal.[2]

Baboons are exceptionally intelligent members of the simian kingdom. One, separated from her parents in South Africa's bush country, wandered onto a farm operated by a German woman named Hedwig Aston. There, in a herd of about a hundred goats, she found companionship, an endless supply of milk, and a job. Without human supervision she took complete charge of the herd—brought them back and forth to pasture, picked off fleas and ticks, saw that each kid was with its own mama at chow time, and at night was ready to raise a clatter for help if a jackal or leopard came around. Other baboons have successfully shepherded sheep.[3]

Perhaps the most astonishing example of a baboon's intelligence is the story of Jack, whose life of devotion is memorialized in the museum at Port Elizabeth, South Africa. Jack lived with his master, James Wide, a signalman at the Uitenhage Tower on the Johannesburg-Pretoria Railway. Wide had lost both his legs in an accident, and would probably have become dependent on charity without the help of his pet. Instead, man and baboon lived together in a small cottage with a garden where Jack performed many of the necessary duties such as pumping water from the well, keeping the house clean, and weeding and watering the vegetables.

Each morning after breakfast Jack locked the house, gave Wide the key, and pushed his master to work in a small carriage designed to run on rails. Formerly he had pulled the cart assisted by Wide's dog, but after the dog was killed by a passing train, he found that if he pushed instead of pulled he could manage the task alone.

What really brought Jack fame was his ability to operate properly the sets of levers in the tower. He came to know every one of the various block system signals, and as the trains sped by, he pushed or pulled the levers that set the signals. In addition, when it was required, he operated the tower controls that opened or closed the switches on a siding. Truly an anthropoid genius. For nine years Wide permitted his simian assistant to operate the levers, and during that time Jack never made an error that caused a mishap![4]

Professor William W. Cumming, a psychologist at Columbia University, is working on the theory that even pigeons can replace people. In his laboratory he has taught them to detect infinitesimal flaws in tiny electronics parts. After some fifty to eighty hours of training, the beady-eyed birds were 99-percent accurate. They were also taught to find improperly coated drug capsules.

Dr. Cumming placed each bird in its own compartment with two windows—one a square pane of clear glass, and the other, round and frosted. As the parts came into sight, the pigeon would reject defective parts by pecking at the clear window. If it made a mistake, the light went out, and the pigeon was "punished" by a twenty-second wait before it could earn more food.

In the beginning Dr. Cumming's birds were rewarded with

food when they struck with their beaks on the window to signal that they had found an imperfection. But in the course of time his birds kept right on working without any reward at all. With automation, labor unions, and an expanding labor pool, it is unlikely that trained pigeons will ever serve as assembly-line inspectors outside laboratories. However, Dr. Cumming pointed out that his birds would not cost more than one dollar apiece, eat only about a dollar's worth of food a month, work long hours without a complaint or a coffee break, and live for years.[5]

Pigeons have had a venerable history of service to man. About A.D. 980 the Caliph Aziz of Cairo, who had a passion for cherries, is thought to have invented the airlift with the birds' help. The luscious fruit grew in the orchards of Baalbek, some four hundred miles away in Syria. So at the beginning of the season huge flocks of pigeons were sent from Egypt to the slaves working in the orchards. They fastened tiny bags holding a choice ripe cherry to each of the birds' feet. The task completed, a thousand carrier pigeons soared aloft, bearing the finest of the fruit to the banquet on the Nile.[6]

For many centuries carrier pigeons have earned their board, but those used by the French Post Office during the Franco-Prussian War made a fortune for the government. When Paris was beseiged during the fall and winter of 1870, the mail had to be brought into the isolated city by homing pigeons.

Months before, the French had taken the precaution of removing about 250 of these birds to a safe distance. To get the mail through, the messages were set in type, photographed in microscopic size, and then printed on thin films of collodian to keep them as small in size and weight as possible.

Each day two birds were dispatched. By this method they could carry up to eight thousand letters a day. As the fee for this pigeon-post was ten cents per word, wartime postal revenues averaged around $112,000, a big factor in helping the French to hold out against the enemy.[7]

During World War II, pigeons were so valuable as message carriers that several received citations for outstanding service. Many got through, although seriously wounded by enemy gunfire. In fact "GI Joe," a dark, mottled pigeon kept for emergency use by the British 56th Infantry Division in Italy, saved a thousand men from massacre by their own planes.

On October 18, 1943, after requesting an air attack to break the stubborn German line at Calvi Vecchia, Italy, the resistance suddenly collapsed, and the British troops swarmed into the town. In the frenzy their communications had completely broken down. Only a few pigeons were available to transmit messages. GI Joe fulfilled the desperate trust and flew the twenty dangerous miles to the airfield through the shellfire arriving just as the Allied planes were warming up on the runways for the takeoff.

GI Joe had quite a history. He was hatched at the U. S. Army Pigeon Section in Algiers, served on the Tunisian front, then finally in Calvi Vecchia. He won the famous Dickin Medal, presented to him by the Lord Mayor of London in 1946, for courage under fire; and later he received a reward from Congress. When the war was over, GI Joe was kept in the Army's Churchill loft at Fort Monmouth, New Jersey, built for famous war pigeons. Later, in 1957, the fifteen birds in the Churchill loft were given to zoos, where they could have until death the fame that they deserved. GI Joe was on display as an honored inmate of the Detroit Zoo until his death in June, 1961.[8]

Pigeons were the carriers for the very first United States "air mail" route, established in 1894. The birds flew a thirty-five-mile route from Los Angeles to Catalina Island in less than an hour. In those days before the invention of the wireless, the fifty birds of this special Carrier Pigeon Service were very important to the island's winter residents. They had a regular and rigid schedule for the messages, which were printed on onionskin paper and left at a drop station on the island.

Hawks, eagles, and hunters were a hazard, as were the storms and heavy fogs of the Pacific Coast. But for three seasons the pigeons did their part—bringing medical aid, letters, and various announcements to and from the mainland. They flew to a loft in Los Angeles, where the messages were examined and either delivered by boys or telegraphed from that point. The fee averaged about seventy-five cents each to many satisfied customers.[9]

In at least one case a man has built up a big business based on his hobby of breeding carrier pigeons. One enterprising hobbyist owned a brick-manufacturing plant in Pennsylvania that he wanted to expand. Finally he decided that his birds gave him a novel advertising approach. Whenever he heard of a building going up within his territory, he shipped one of his homers to the contractor. Fastened to the pigeon would be a sales promotion letter giving information on his bricks, prices, and terms. Very few could hold out against such a novelty. Almost always the bird returned if not with an order, at least with an invitation for a salesman to call. Once an especially irresistible bird carried back an order for seven hundred thousand bricks.[10]

There have been many other animals who have brought to their owners objects of value and even great fortunes. There was Mrs. Winifred Mansell, of Keston, England, whose ginger cat, Ginnie, came limping home one afternoon in 1955 from an excursion. When Mrs. Mansell examined the cat's left forepaw, two small bits that looked like glass fell out.

"Could these be diamonds?" she asked her husband.

Mr. Mansell chortled at the naïveté of women. But his more optimistic wife took the shiny bits to a jeweler who told her they were not only diamonds but well-cut small stones worth at least one hundred dollars apiece. Being an honest soul she turned them over to the police, who when no one claimed the jewels gave them back to Mrs. Mansell. Ginnie's paws were examined daily thereafter, but the pet never retrieved more jewels from the mysterious cache.

John Thorburn Williamson went to Tanganyika from Canada years ago and unsuccessfully prospected for diamonds for five years. He was practically penniless when he took over the care of a stray dog of uncertain ancestry. One day man and dog were out walking when the dog sniffed around the base of a tree, began scratching, and tossed out a rough diamond. That same patch yielded the fifty-four-carat pink diamond that Williamson later presented to Queen Elizabeth. In time he owned six hundred acres, which are still being mined today and are estimated to hold stones worth a total of $6 billion.

A hound in Montana investigating a badger hole is credited with the discovery of one of the richest sapphire ledges in America. Another badger hunting dog in Alaska trotted up to his owner with a gold nugget caught between his toes. The claim that followed eventually produced gold valued at a million dollars.

Pets may not always reward their owners with jewels or mines, but even a small negotiable token is appreciated. Mr. and Mrs. Dan Rice took their Irish retriever with them on a visit to the Hialeah Race Track. The dog romped around, then ran up and dropped a slightly chewed piece of cardboard at the couple's feet. It was a hundred-dollar ticket on a horse that had just won a race with the odds six to one.

There are other dogs who earn their keep by performing unusual tasks. An account in the *American Kennel Gazette* tells of a collie at a kennel in Ohio who took care of his fellow canines. Each afternoon at four o'clock he carried the food pans from the kennel to his owner's house to be refilled, then returned them to the kennel. His final act was to turn on the faucets above the fixed water pans in the kennel runs and to trot back down the line turning the faucets off.

The Bowser Inn near Vancouver, British Columbia, once had a waiter who was a dog. Mike, half shepherd and half wire-haired terrier, could have given lessons on the greeting of guests to many formidable *maitres d'hotel*. He played no favorites. When a patron sat down, Mike trotted up and waited for the order with his owner, Charles Winfield, listening behind the bar. Then he went to the bar and returned, holding the bottle right side up in his teeth.

The dog waited until the patron reached into his pocket for money, then he came back to the table and barked. As soon as the coins were placed on the table's edge, Mike nuzzled them off into his mouth, took them to his boss, and brought back any change.[11]

The ways in which pets have earned their keep seem almost as diverse as human occupations.

There's Nicodemus who, writes Eleanor Harris, in her book *Career Cat*, "has worked his way up from cat-rags to cat-riches—honorably!"[12] As the most highly paid cat model in the business, Nicky is a languid-eyed, glamorous, snowy-white Persian who advertises furs, cosmetics, and jewels—at the rate of fifty dollars an hour!

As Nicodemus Enterprises, he is probably the only incorporated cat in the world with a corporate seal and his own paw mark on contracts. As such he was the subject of an illustrated story on the financial page of *The New York Times* in May, 1960.

Originally the unwanted runt of a pedigreed litter, Nicky was finally given to Loiselle Adams, a lonely girl in the big city who kept afloat by taking part-time jobs. In the beginning Miss Adams and her cat were equally timid, but she began carrying him to work just for company, hiding him in a desk drawer during working hours.

One day she was being interviewed at Revlon Cosmetics by the personnel director. Nicodemus, who was in her tote bag, raised his head up and winked at the receptionist, who burst out laughing. That was the beginning of his career as a popular model.

In addition to his commercial work, Nicky has posed for charity, been on the reviewing stand in front of St. Patrick's Cathedral during the Easter parade, and in the arms of the pastor of the Broadway Presbyterian Church during a children's sermon. He has been a guest on the *Today Show, Captain Kangaroo, Play Your Hunch,* and many other TV shows. John Frederick, famed hat designer, made him an Easter bonnet, and he has a lavish wardrobe of sequinned and velvet harnesses, opera coats, and castle-shaped carriers, jeweled and turreted.

When the husband-wife team, the Gordon Gordons (who write under the name of The Gordons) moved into their hill-top home in Encino, California, they put up a plaque at the entrance that reads: "This home was bought and endowed by a cat." The cat referred to was the inspiration and hero of a humorous mystery titled *Undercover Cat* that sold more than a million copies and earned his owners $200,000. The book became a Walt Disney movie, *That Darn Cat,* starring Hayley Mills and Dean Jones.

D. C., as the cat is called (the initials stand for Damn Cat in the book and Darn Cat in the film) was a twenty-five pound black tom that the Gordons bought for two dollars at the Los Angeles S. P. C. A. Since release of the movie, D. C. has inspired another book, a sequel titled *Undercover Cat Prowls Again.*

"And to think," says Mildred Gordon, "that we used to complain about how much he was costing us for food, trips to the vet, and all that. Why, D. C. must be the most valuable cat in history!"[13]

In filming *That Darn Cat, Incredible Journey,* and other stories, a cat star was required. So Al Koehler, a veteran animal trainer, went to the Chafee Humane Association Pound in Ontario near Los Angeles, and bought a Siamese. The late Walt Disney named him Syn Cat "because he synchronizes so well with everything."

To train a cat at all is a remarkable feat. Cats are independent individualists in business for themselves. As a rule they are emotionally unstable, frighten easily in strange environments, and have no sense of responsibility. Most cats are selfish, predatory, and haven't the slightest desire to learn. But there are the rare exceptions, and Syn Cat is one.

Koehler, who has trained animals for forty years, says he is convinced "that Syn Cat is the smartest, most sociable, most emotionally stable cat in the world. A cat like Syn comes along once or twice in a lifetime."

Syn Cat isn't bothered by the confusion that surrounds a movie set. He doesn't bolt and run when an actress screams, a horn is blown, or a gun is fired. He remains easygoing, cooperative, unspoiled, and friendly. In front of the cameras he's a real ham. Syn Cat is insured for two thousand dollars—the maximum accorded cats—and his owner receives $1000 a week for his services.

Koehler reads the movie scripts carefully and rehearses the cat to accustom him to particular noises such as door knocks, police sirens, and automobile backfires. Next he teaches Syn to walk, run, jump, climb, lead, or remain stationary—not only by command but also by ringing bells in sequence. The animal is conditioned to search for the bell.

Al Koehler usually records the ringing bells on tape. Miniature speakers are placed in strategic spots, and the cat's performance is directed by the successive sounds as he tries to locate the bells.

Unfortunately there are very few movie scripts starring cats, and although Syn Cat has earned a small fortune for his owner, he's unemployed most of the time.

Although Syn has an eight-foot pen in the yard equipped with a tree and a luxurious bed box, he prefers to roam inside the Koehler house. Here he has found love and returned it ever since he was brought from the shelter in 1963.[14]

4

The Warriors and the Sleuths

Among wild animals killing is necessary for the hunt and at times for defense. There is fighting between members of a species to establish leadership, ownership of a mate, or hunting territory, and sometimes there are fatalities. But the object of this fighting is to overcome, not to destroy. With captivity, however, the unnatural state of confinement disturbs the behavior controls for some species, and a father, for example, may even destroy his offspring.

Civilization, too, creates artificial, unnatural environments. Dr. Konrad Lorenz, in his book, *On Aggression,* suggests that a cosmic slip in evolution caused man to lose his automatic control against killing. Whatever the answer, man has slaughtered nearly 60 million of his own kind in the past century alone. Old cruelties have been abolished and humanitarian activities have girdled the globe but wars have steadily increased. Even now, as man challenges outer space, his gamut of weapons threatens planet-wide annihilation.

The use of animals, particularly dogs, in warfare goes back beyond the beginning of recorded history. Entire packs of savage dogs, specially trained for attack and equipped with spike collars and armor, were unleashed against enemy forces by the Roman legions. Napoleon used dogs in some of his battles. But it was not until World War I that they were used on a large scale. It is estimated that when the Armistice was signed in 1918 the Allied forces had about ten thousand dogs at the front, serving as messengers, ammo carriers, and belligerent scouts.[1]

The number of dog warriors increased tremendously during World War II. Estimates by both the Allied and Axis powers place the total well beyond the 250,000 mark. Approximately ten thousand dogs were trained in the U. S. Army's K-9 Corps, and a number were cited for outstanding valor during combat operations. Of these the greatest was Chips, part collie and part husky.

Chips' career is the subject of various legends. It is said that Chips bit so many mailmen and meter readers that his master decided to let him exercise his aggressions in warfare. Following K-9 training, he went overseas in 1943 and received his baptism of fire in North Africa. On July 10 of that year, he was one of three dogs with the Third Division Infantry Regiment of General George S. Patton's Seventh Army when the Allies made their landing in Sicily. Opposition was intense. While Italian soldiers fired from pillboxes, the crack Hermann Goering and Fifteenth Armored Division of the Germans launched a tank attack that threatened the entire operation.

Heavy machine-gun fire shot up miniature geysers of sand like rain as Chips and his handler, Pfc. John Roswell, hit the beach. Man and dog dug in. Roswell determined that the fire in his immediate vicinity was coming from a peasant's hut that was obviously a camouflaged gun emplacement, but before he could inform his fellow infantrymen in surrounding foxholes of his discovery, Chips broke away and raced to the phony hut.

"There was an awful lot of noise and the firing stopped," Roswell said later. "Then I saw one Italian soldier come out of the door, Chips at his throat. I called him off before he could kill the man." So unexpected and savage had been the dog's attack that the other three machine gunners surrendered in a state of shock. Chips received only a minor scalp wound and some powder burns.

Captain Edward Paar wanted Chips to get the Distinguished Service Cross. "The dog's courageous action in single-handedly eliminating a dangerous machine-gun nest and causing the surrender of its crew reflects the highest credit on himself and the military service," his recommendation read.

Expressing doubts that a dog should receive one of the Army's top decorations, Maj. Gen. Lucian K. Truscott, Jr., commander of the Third Division, did award Chips the Silver Star in a ceremony on October 24, 1943, "for bravery in action against the enemy." You won't find the award listed, however, in the official records. There were frowns in Washington and an order was issued stating, "Awards of War Department decorations to other than persons, that is, human beings, is prohibited."

Perhaps the affair was a thorn in Chips' sensitive pride. Or, it may have been because the Allied commander in chief was clad in civvies with high-cuts and no tie. At any rate, when Gen. Dwight Eisenhower visited Allied Headquarters in Italy and bent down to pat our hero, he was neatly nipped in the leg. With eight battle stars to his credit, Chips was returned to his original owners, the Wren family of Pleasantville, New York, after the war. He died in 1947.[2]

During the Korean War in the early 1950s a fundamental change was made in training scout dogs. They were trained for more than attack; they were expected to locate the enemy and alert their handlers, who in turn would notify the patrol leaders. The change reduced casualty rates as much as 65 percent among night patrols accompanied by dogs.

The most outstanding dog of the Korean conflict was a member of the Twenty-Sixth Infantry Scout Dog Platoon—the Army's oldest active canine unit—named York. He led 148 patrols—alerting his companions to ambushes—and never lost a single man to enemy fire.

In Vietnam this special training has developed supersensory heights as astonishing as the coat-hanger dowsing rods used by the Marines to locate tunnels, land mines, booby traps, communication wires, and food and arms cached underground. Past wars have been won by taking and holding enemy positions, but the unique war in Vietnam has forced the mastery of new skills and unconventional techniques.

The fighting on the part of the Vietcong and North Vietnamese has consisted principally of ambushes and hit-and-run guerrilla tactics. The South Vietnamese, the United States, and their allies, on the other hand, have engaged in search-and-destroy missions and aerial bombing. There is no conventional way of measuring victory there such as taking and holding land. Friends and enemies are identical in appearance. Armed bands on both sides have tramped over the same highland and waded through the same rice paddies over and over again in seesaw captures and recaptures. The only measure of victories has been the "body count."

After preliminary tests with dogs in Vietnam proved successful, an accelerated training program was launched in 1965. German shepherds, both males and females, make the best scouts. Physical examinations by trainers and medical experts are rigorous. The dogs must be alert and aggressive, measure at least twenty-three inches at the shoulder, be about two and a half years old, and have exceptional vision, hearing, and scent. Since smaller dogs do not tire quickly and can move better through dense jungle, the scouts usually do not weigh more than sixty pounds.

The soldiers or marines chosen as handlers are men who love dogs. Once a man and an animal are teamed together, they are almost never switched around. They work together, eat together, and develop a teamwork and rapport that is astonishing. As one trainer said, between man and dog "there is a kind of loyalty that is almost beyond belief."

Cpl. John C. Keith, of Allendale Estates, Georgia, received personal congratulations from Gen. Omar Bradley when the famed World War II officer was visiting Vietnam. His tour of duty completed, Keith was preparing to return to the States when he realized that he couldn't just pack up and leave Anzio, his German shepherd. So he signed up for another tour of combat duty.

Trainers and handlers estimate that the scout dogs can hear twenty times, smell forty times, see ten times better than a human being, and have saved thousands of lives.

Satan, a dog of German shepherd and Labrador retriever ancestry, has been one of the best canine scouts during the Vietnam conflict. On his first combat mission—a night patrol in the Tuy Hoa sector in November, 1966—he froze into an alert. His handler, Sgt. Edward Kozub, thought the animal was confused by the sound of troopers coming up from behind. He prodded the dog on as the patrol advanced about two hundred yards. Again Satan stiffened and an almost inaudible growl rose from his throat. Kozub sent word back to the platoon leader that something could be moving toward them along the trail. The men began to walk slowly and quietly.

From ahead came the pitter-patter of sandals and around a turn in the trail appeared the point man for a VC column. He stopped in startled surprise and was dead before he could raise his rifle to his shoulder. The troopers fanned out quickly and stabbed the jungle with withering fire as they advanced. With the exception of the dead and badly wounded, the Vietcong fled—abandoning automatic weapons, large quantities of food, medical supplies, and pouches containing secret documents.

Scout-dog team rapport increases with experience. On a later occasion Sergeant Kozub and Satan were ahead of a small patrol when the dog froze, then leaned forward against the leash. This meant he had detected a live scent. "Must be a small patrol up ahead," Kozub told the commanding officer. "Maybe we can flush him out."

Agreeing, the officer issued the orders to fan out. Satan, his body stationary in his alert, continued to sniff the air and then point his nose in the opposite direction. "Something's wrong," the sergeant said. "I think he's trying to tell us to clear out! Anyway, that's the way I read it."

"Okay, he's a smart dog. We'll just take his advice!"

The men took cover in the jungle along the trail. Within a few minutes they heard voices and the tramp of feet, and instead of a patrol, an entire company of North Vietnamese regulars marched by. Radio contacts alerted the nearest troop concentration, and in the battle that followed, the North Vietnamese suffered forty casualties before they scattered.

"If Satan hadn't told us to pull back," Kozub said later, "we would probably have been wiped out."

Early in this tragic conflict, the VC would conceal themselves inside the banks along traffic-laden rivers, with only a small air vent just above the water line. From here they observed troop and supply movements for Intelligence or sniped at servicemen with almost no chance of detection. When South Vietnamese soldiers sought to locate these pockets by driving poles into the earth, they were exposed to fire from similar hiding places on the opposite bank.

Finally someone thought of using the dogs. No matter how tiny the air holes were, the dogs found them by picking up the human scent. In a matter of weeks the river banks were cleared of these hidden snipers, for if the wind is blowing in the dogs' direction, they can spot traps at distances up to three hundred yards either by odor or by hearing the faint hum of the trip wires vibrating in the breeze.

Captured documents and the testimony of prisoners reveal that enemy snipers have been instructed to make scout dogs and their handlers prime targets. They are to aim low and hit the dog first, then fire at the handler.

One such sacrifice on the altar of war was Tiger, a German shepherd, who with his handler, Sp. 4/c Jerry L. Brown of McComb, Mississippi, was assigned to a First Cavalry unit.

One hot afternoon in the Ira Drang Valley they were leading a search-and-destroy mission. In the dangerous point position alongside man and dog, two crack riflemen stood ready to respond to any sniper fire. From time to time Tiger would stop, raise his muzzle into the wind and sniff, then move on.

Suddenly the dog froze. From the animal's position Brown knew he had detected a live scent. A second later, reacting to a subconscious warning, Brown whirled and shoved the dog and his two riflemen to the ground just as automatic weapons opened up from an ambush. After the initial burst of fire, Brown and his companions began crawling back out of range.

Tiger, who scrambled up to go ahead of the men, was suddenly struck by a bullet. The impact threw him into the air, and he was hit again and again by purposeful fire until his coat was streaked with red. Brown, crawling on his belly, pulled the wounded dog out of the line of fire, but a bullet struck him in the hip and flipped him over on his back. Tiger died beside him, his furry body riddled with seven bullets.

The ambush was a battalion-sized force of more than three hundred men. It had been set up to attack the two hundred soldiers who were coming up behind Brown and Tiger. Not only did the dog prevent the ambush attack, but his warning led to the Vietcong's rout. Within minutes a strike force of fighter-bombers and helicopters were raking the VC position with rockets and bombs. Twenty minutes later the surviving Communists had fled into the jungle, leaving their dead and their possessions behind.

Today Tiger sleeps in the scout-dog cemetery at Phan Rang. The headstone on his grave is decorated with a Silver Star. Other dog heroes lie in similar cemeteries in Guam, Okinawa, the Philippines, South Korea, and elsewhere throughout the world. They, too, were skilled, faithful, and devoted, loved and were beloved, and died in the service of the country of their masters. They live on in the memory of those men who shared with them the perils and hardships of war.[3]

Rolf, an extraordinary German shepherd, lived on the Danish island of Funen during the 1950s. Over a seven-year period he recovered lost articles with an estimated value of more than four hundred thousand dollars. Rolf proudly traveled about in a panel truck proclaiming his name and business —*Sporhunden* (Tracking Dog) *Rolf*—followed by his telephone number. His pride was justified, for he had found objects encased in ice, buried in swamps, and hidden in manure piles.

Svend Andersen, his owner, kept a second-hand store, but as the dog's fame grew he employed an assistant to mind the shop. They answered between six hundred and seven hundred calls for help yearly, and four out of five times succeeded in finding the missing articles. Andersen told Robert Littell, a writer for the Copenhagen publication *Dansk Familieblad,* that he would repeat over and over the name of the lost article as they drove to the site. There Rolf would circle and backtrack "until he picked up the faint scent of an object lying in a spot where it didn't belong, out of its proper place or context."

A farmer at a cattle show lost a gold filling from a tooth when he sneezed. Rolf found it several yards away from where the man had been sitting, trampled into the soil by the feet of many spectators. A man's wallet disappeared while he was driving a hay-kicker. Rolf paid no attention to the hay field, but trotted across two adjoining fields to where the machinery stood. There, impaled on the tines of the hay-kicker, was the wallet.

Once the dog was summoned to find an heirloom watch lost by a child playing in a straw rick. Fifty children searched with no luck. The police came twice with different dogs but both failed. More than a week later Rolf was brought to the scene. He ignored the rick and nosed about in a root pit some distance away. Within minutes he had found the watch. Someone had pitched a forkful of straw from the rick into the pit.

Feats of this type involve more than following a scent. Once again we have a strange rapport between a man and an animal, a partnership that demands more than the usual five senses. A police expert who served as a judge at some official trials in which Rolf was tested said that what impressed him was the "fantastic cooperation between dog and guide." He added that Andersen's skill in keeping up the dog's interest by quiet remarks seemed to him "like the conversation of two friends."

Robert Littell noticed that sometimes Andersen would stand tense, motionless, and obviously concentrating "as if giving orders only Rolf could hear." He writes:

> Between Andersen and Rolf there is a deep and subtle sympathy. But there is also something mysterious, beyond rational explanation. If Andersen is tired, Rolf is less efficient. Andersen believes his own concentration helps Rolf in his search. When Rolf fails on a job, Andersen lies awake that night, going over and over the ground in his mind. Often he gets out of bed and drives with Rolf to the scene of their failure, where they go hunting again by flashlight. He says that the night is quiet and it is a good time to hunt for what is lost. Often they find it.[4]

Once Rolf, in his desire to make good, exhibited sticky jaws. Andersen had scolded him sharply for failing to find a lost watch, and the dog had left sheepishly, tail between his legs. Soon he returned in triumph with a watch in his mouth, but followed by an angry, half-dressed man shouting: "Your damn *Spornhunden* stole my watch! I was getting dressed when he poked his head in the door, took my watch from the table, and made off with it!"

Another dog, appropriately named Nick Carter, found wanted men instead of objects. During the decade from 1900 to 1910 he followed some five hundred trails and brought about the conviction of more than six hundred criminals. In the Kentucky and West Virginia mountains he took trails so rough that his feet bled as he walked; he followed others over city streets where hundreds of other persons had passed meanwhile. An all-time record was set when he tracked a trail four days and nine hours old. Very probably Nick was the greatest blood-hound that ever lived.

Much of Nick's greatness must be credited to his owner, Capt. Volney G. Mullikan, a man almost as astonishing as the dog he had trained. He was as instinctive and relentless a man-hunter as Nick. Mullikan began his career as a private detective and trainer of bloodhounds at seventeen when he captured his first criminal, a horse thief. Born in the eastern Kentucky mountains where feuds were commonplace, he was hardened and totally without fear. When he finally retired he stated that, as a conservative estimate, he had brought twenty-five hundred criminals to justice.

The captain had bought Nick as a puppy, selecting him from a pure-bred litter because of his eagerness to trail. He believed that this strong desire to hunt, rather than a more sensitive nose, made one bloodhound superior to another.

The determination and stamina of this man-dog pair were almost incredible. Seldom if ever did they abandon a trail without running their quarry down. One morning they began the cross-country trailing of a village store burglar. Four hours later they spotted the fugitive in a valley below them—at the very moment he caught sight of them. Although blood-hounds are kindly dogs despite their chilling name, the burglar accepted the common misbelief that if caught he would be chewed to bits. He dropped his loot and fled for the wilds.

The chase continued throughout the afternoon and evening. Night came, but Mullikan and Nick Carter kept on, stumbling up hills, across streams, and through wooded valleys, aided only by bright moonlight. At last dawn was followed by day-light. Still the chase went on. Blisters on the captain's feet had broken into raw sores and pain marked each step. Nick's feet were bleeding, and his ears were torn by rocks and bushes. Finally, as noon approached, they found their man. He had collapsed and lay sprawled on the ground, semiconscious from exhaustion. They had trailed him for forty-eight hours over fifty-five miles of rough mountain country.

Trails cannot always be followed. A strong wind can blow one away or a hard rain can wash out a scent. Unknown factors may intervene. Under almost ideal conditions Nick once started on a trail only a few hours old, and lost it twenty feet away. On the other hand, when conditions were good—the air cool and moist and still—Nick could easily track down a man on horseback.

On one occasion Nick was beaten by a mentally disturbed woman who had been setting her neighbors' barns on fire. When he tried to take the trail, he was halted by convulsive sneezing and in obvious pain refused to continue. The woman had covered her tracks with large amounts of pepper. But this was her undoing, for inquiry at the local grocer disclosed that she had been buying pepper in ten-pound bags.

Yet what made Nick Carter the best of them all was his ability to track old trails. He set a record on another barn burner in southern Ohio. When word came from the Ohio sheriff, Mullikan and Nick were in West Virginia running down a murderer. One hundred and five hours had passed since the barn had been destroyed when man and dog arrived at the scene. Atmospheric conditions were good, and the sheriff had thoughtfully kept the barn roped off and under guard. But the captain believed too much time had passed. There was no hope in his voice when he told Nick to seek the trail.

Nick began circling the barn foundation, nose to the ground, head swinging slowly from side to side. Several times he looked back at his master as if puzzled, but Mullikan encouraged him to continue. Suddenly the dog raised his tail and lunged into his harness. It was a difficult trail and time after time Nick lost it. Finally, after darkness had fallen, he led the captain into the yard of a farmhouse just a little over a mile from the barn.

Mullikan knocked, and a man opened the door. With a startled cry, the man jumped back; Nick, in the darkness below, had licked his hand. The detective took advantage of the man's surprise and pulled a trick that has been successful many times.

"When you burned that barn," he said quietly and quickly, "you didn't count on the dog, did you?"

"Hell, no," the arsonist replied. "Who would—after four and a half days?"

In another case the time lapse was so great that Mullikan refused to take credit for the solution. An old man had vanished from his home. When the captain and Nick were asked to look for him, the man had been gone for a week, and dozens of persons had been in and out of the house and through the yard. The detective was certain no trail could be followed after so long a time.

But Nick sniffed some of the missing man's clothing, and vainly roamed the yard trying to pick up a trail. After a bit he trotted down a hill toward a lake. For several hundred feet the bloodhound moved along the lake's edge, then stopped and poised his head out over the surface. When Mullikan released him from his leash, Nick entered the water and swam around. The captain could not believe the dog had actually found a scent.

"Okay, boys," the missing man's son shouted, "this must be the place. Let's start dragging!"

As Mullikan told a friend years later, "There wasn't anybody in that crowd more surprised than I was when they found the body. I still don't know if Nick had actually found a scent, or if it was sheer accident."

Another attribute that made Nick Carter so great was his ability to follow an individual scent among many through the welter of odors on a city street. This, according to Captain Mullikan, was his dog's most incredible skill, and he doubted if any other bloodhound in history could have solved one memorable case.

Master and dog were living in Wilmore, Kentucky, when they were invited by a wealthy citizen to Petersburg, Indiana. Some malcontent had taken to throwing rocks through the windows of the more substantial residents' homes and the authorities were baffled. The railroad trip, which required seven changes, took a full day in those days. There had been no rain for days. The rocks had been thrown from the side-walks where thousands of persons had already passed back and forth.

After a quick search the captain found a rock that had rolled under a couch and had been left untouched. Nick was permitted to sniff the stone and then was taken out on the sidewalk. Within minutes he picked up the scent, then led the way through all the mingled odors of a dry, warm day. The trail passed through the town and out into the country and finally to the rear door of a farmhouse. The door opened and a weeping teen-ager emerged.

"I heard Nick Carter was in town," the youth said between sobs. "I've been waiting here because I knew you'd find me."

After Nick died, his master mourned his passing for the rest of his days. Captain Mullikan trained many bloodhounds, in-cluding Nick's mate, the remarkable Ivy Bell, but neither he nor any other trainer has ever found a canine genius to equal Nick Carter.[6]

Police dogs are taught to patrol, stand guard, trail, pursue, attack upon command and hold but not seriously injure cap-tives. However, there are rare police dogs who, like the blood-hound Nick, belong in the genius class. The greatest detective in dogdom was Dox, who along with his many other accom-plishments actually solved crimes.

In Europe's annual police-dog matches, Dox won the crown in 1953 and successfully defended his title for years thereafter against such seasoned dogs as Rex of Scotland Yard and Xorro of the Paris Police. In 1960 when he was fourteen years old (allowing seven human years to a dog year, this would make him ninety-eight), Dox was considered the world champion of police dogs, with four gold medals and twenty-seven silver ones to prove it. He also possessed the scars of seven bullet wounds acquired in line of duty in his native Italy.

Among this German shepherd's specialized feats was his ability to untie a man bound in a chair, no matter how complicated the knots. He could also unload a pistol without firing it by nudging the safety catch into position and removing the clip with his paws and teeth.

"Dox may have been born a dog, but he is no longer just a dog," declared Dr. Carmelo Marzano, commanding officer of Rome's police department. "He has probably cracked more cases than any other detective on the force. We consider him one of our best men." He added that the dog's exploits with Rome's mobile squadron alone had resulted in the arrest of some four hundred criminals.

Once more we have that mysterious rapport, that team relationship between man and animal that leads to the extraordinary. Dox performed his feats while in the company of his master, Police Sergeant Giovanni Maimone, who had acquired Dox in Germany as a forty-day old pup, trained the dog himself, and over the years they were inseparable. They shared the same room in the police barracks overlooking the Tiber.

Dox's memory was phenomenal. One afternoon in Rome, Maimone and his big German shepherd entered a restaurant and the dog suddenly pounced on a customer enjoying a plate of spaghetti. It turned out that the man whose dinner was so rudely interrupted was a fugitive who had eluded the law—and Dox—in a police case six years earlier in Turin.

Italy's canine cop once kept twelve suspects standing with raised arms while Maimone left the room to telephone for assistance. The sergeant kept an account of his dog's career in five huge scrapbooks. They contained news clippings telling of the time Dox saved a little girl's life by butting her out of the path of a speeding car; the time he found a lost skier in the Subiaco mountains after a posse of men and dogs had ended their search; and the time when, with his leg broken by a burglar's bullet, he caught the culprit after a five-mile chase on his three good legs.

One day while master and dog were patroling a slum district on foot, two men on a motorcycle noticed the pair and immediately abandoned their vehicle and fled. Dox got the scent from the motorcycle seats, and he and Maimone took off in pursuit. The trail led through alleys, up stairways, across rooftops, and finally to a dingy apartment.

A woman opened the door. She denied knowing anything about the two men, but Dox began barking at a very large sofa. The officer ordered whoever was hidden behind it to come out, hands first, and one of the fugitives slowly arose, his hands above his head. At the same instant his companion crept out of a closet behind Maimone's back with a knife in his raised hand.

Seconds later the would-be assailant was wishing with all his heart that he had chosen "the straight and narrow." On top of him were 140 pounds of raging fury with muscles of steel. Clamped to his wrist were fangs that bit deep to tortured nerves until the knife spun harmlessly across the room. The pair had committed a string of unsolved burglaries, with the value of the loot totaling thousands of dollars.

But it was Dox's almost incredible ability to actually solve a crime by himself that made him the world champion. The case of the missing button is an example:

One night a burglar remained hidden in the basement of Rome's Principe Theater after it closed, then chipped an opening through the wall into a jewelry store next door. Discovered by a night watchman, he escaped after a brief struggle. Since it was after midnight with few persons on the streets, the time was favorable for trailing. Dox was brought to the theater, where he picked up the scent from the watchman's clothing and an abandoned chisel.

The dog led the officers a number of blocks away to a cellar apartment. The occupant, a man who had previously been arrested for larceny, was awakened but succeeded in convincing the policemen that this time he was innocent.

"Even I believed the man, especially after the night watchman who had joined us said he did not recognize him," Sergeant Maimone confessed. "I shook my finger at Dox as I told him to be more careful. But his answer was to bark at me and lope off, so we followed."

Back at the jewelry store the dog wandered about, then entered a rear storeroom where he picked up a button and dropped it in his master's hand. He gave another sharp bark to indicate he wanted to be followed, and led them back to the cellar of the suspect.

There Dox sniffed at the opening to a closet. When the door was opened, he pulled a raincoat with one button missing off a hanger and deposited it at Maimone's feet. The button he had just found at the jeweler's matched those on the coat. The suspect confessed.[7]

Dogs like Rolf, Nick Carter, and Dox are rare but there will be others like them—geniuses because they have uncommon masters, and because between dogs and men there exist strange bonds and a mysterious rapport.

5

Good Samaritans

To the vagabond cats roaming Lawrence, Massachusetts, elderly Mrs. Nina Sweeney was what we call "a soft touch." No stray ever left her door hungry. When the blizzards howled she gave them shelter. Thus on a certain January day in 1953 she had six cats as house guests in addition to her own pet cat and dog.

It was a day of whirling and bitter wind. When night came and she went to bed, she was suddenly stricken with a paralyzing illness that left her helpless. Unable to leave her bed, she listened as her windows rattled and the fire in her stove went out. Outside the temperature dropped below zero, and the numbing chill began penetrating the house. Mrs. Sweeney prayed and shivered beneath her blankets. But not for long!

When the neighbors missed her a day later and investigated, they found that Mrs. Sweeney's bed was a warm haven. One cat was purring on either side of her head. Another was draped like a fur piece on her neck. Two more nestled on her chest, and under her armpits beneath the covers were two other cats. Her dog lay across her stomach. The strays she had befriended had kept Mrs. Sweeney from freezing to death.[1]

The realists will point out that the pets did not act to protect their benefactress, but to save their own skins. As the temperature dropped they sought the only remaining sources of heat—their own bodies and that of Mrs. Sweeney. Since our own cat insists on joining us in our warm, comfortable bed, this is logic that we will not assail with fanciful notions about pets and prayer.

However, tough-skinned and weather-hardened wild animals do not seek human stoves on cold nights. Nature has given them protection against low temperatures and bitter winds, and they have no need to cuddle close. What then motivated the animals in the following incident reported by the Central Press of Canada in November, 1956?

Twelve-year-old Rheal Guindon, of Opatsitka, Ontario, went with his parents on a fishing trip. From the shore, the boy watched the boat overturn and his parents drown. Grief-stricken, lonely, and frightened, he set out for Kapuskasing, the nearest town. It was bitterly cold and when night came the temperature fell below zero. Finally, exhausted and chilled to the bone, he lay down on the ground and he prayed.

Suddenly he felt something furry against him. In the dark he couldn't tell what kind of animal it was, but it was warm so he put his arm around it and huddled close, then cried himself to sleep. When he woke it was morning. Three beavers were lying against him and across his body. They had kept him from freezing to death. Late that morning he arrived in Kapuskasing with his feet cut and bleeding but alive—thanks to the strange sheltering of three wild animals.

Animal good samaritans perform their kindly deeds in ways as varied as life itself. Dr. Gustav Eckstein, in his book *Everyday Miracle,* tells of a spitz dog who served as night nurse for a diabetic mistress. Sleeping in the crook of her arm, he would awaken instantly if her breathing rhythm changed, a sign that she might be slipping into a coma. Then the dog would dash into the adjoining room to wake the patient's daughter. A dog would be quicker than a physician, Dr. Eckstein wrote, in detecting the advance of coma from the breathing.[2]

A special class of good samaritans are seeing-eye dogs, but other animals have served as pilots for the blind. Back in the nineteenth century in a German village there was a devout elderly peasant woman who had lost her sight. Every Sunday she was led to church by her gander, who guided the blind woman by holding a fold of her skirt in his beak. During the service the gander grazed among the graves in the churchyard.

The Reverend O. F. Robertson, who lived near Hartsville, Tennessee, had a seeing-eye cow. When the minister's sight failed to the point of almost total blindness, it became very difficult for him to get about on his little hill farm. One day he was walking slowly home when he felt a gentle push. It was Mary, his cow, trying to help him up the slope. She seemed to know that he needed her eyes, and from then on she accompanied him whenever he walked around the farm.[3]

Oddly enough we have run across a genuine listening-ear dog. He was a collie named Don, owned by David Bingham, of Somerville, Massachusetts. Mrs. Bingham was deaf, and Don in some manner found out about this handicap while still a pup. From then on, whenever the telephone or doorbell rang, he ran to his mistress, caught hold of her dress, and led her to the phone or door. If it was the doorbell he stood on guard, ramrod stiff, while she opened it, ready to growl if the caller was a stranger unless she told him it was all right.

"Don is buried in a pet cemetery now," Mr. Bingham wrote, "but for thirteen loyal years an understanding male collie made himself the indispensable ears in a house of silence."[4]

The other animals who have saved human lives include a monkey, a parrot, and even a canary. In 1959 *The Burman,* an Indian publication, reported the monkey rescue from New Delhi. A native mother was walking along the bank of the Payaswami River when she accidentally dropped her baby into the water. Unable to swim, the woman began screaming until one of a group of monkeys in the trees plunged into the river and deposited the infant at the mother's feet. Then it leaped back to its tree, jabbering—probably telling her in monkey talk to be more careful in the future.

Mrs. Leslie Smith, of Ward, New Zealand, one afternoon noticed that her cat kept racing up to her in the yard, then back behind the house. She followed and found her two-and-a-half year old son floating face down in a pond several hundred yards from the house. She was able to save the child's life by artificial respiration.[5]

It was raining so hard one night in 1954 that Mrs. Rosa Daigle, eighty-three years old, of Meridian, Mississippi, closed the windows and turned on an electric fan. She didn't know that a gas appliance in the next room had sprung a leak. With the fan pulling the gas into her bedroom, she went to sleep.

But Minnie, her Maltese cat, knew that the odor in the air meant danger. She carried all her kittens out of the bedroom to safety and then came back to land with all her weight upon on her mistress, working her sharp claws in and out of Mrs. Daigle's arm. She succeeded in rousing the elderly lady, who staggered to a telephone in another room and called the police. Thanks to Minnie, Mrs. Daigle recovered in Rush Memorial Hospital.[6]

For our parrot story we go to the town of Lentino, Italy, where one morning three-year-old Palma Marletta darted into the path of a truck. Bystanders froze but the parrot flew from its perch on the porch and fluttered madly in front of the windshield. The startled driver applied the brakes and the vehicle came to a stop a few feet from the child.

Again, our realists will tell us that dogs who arouse families in burning houses bark to save their own hides. But one day in 1953 Mrs. James Stimson heard the family's German shepherd barking in a frenzied manner at her home in Mendon, Massachusetts. When she opened the door, the dog raced to the bedroom and dragged nine-month-old Billie Jean outdoors. The house was on fire.[7]

Dogs understand simple words, such as commands, especially when the tone of voice and an accompanying gesture adds emphasis, but do they understand sentences with comparatively complicated meanings? The story of Ringing Bells, an English setter, as told by naturalist Archibald Rutledge, indicates that some dogs can.

Bells and her master enjoyed nothing better than duck hunting in the great delta of the Santee River in South Carolina. One cold day after rains had flooded the marshes and swamps, the two were in a canoe near the middle of the submerged area when a sudden severe storm swept in from the sea. As the rain slashed down in a relentless deluge, the wind whipped the river into a choppy cauldron. A wave caught the frail canoe broadside and overturned it.

Man and dog swam to a tiny islet some fifty yards away. No other land in the expanse of river remained above the surface and the rapidly rising water would soon submerge their foothold. The hunter turned to his dog.

"Bells, I want you to swim to shore and go to my brother Ben's. Don't go home and stay there. Go on to Ben's. Bring him here. Bring Ben to help me! You understand?"

Ringing Bells did understand. She wagged her tail and took off. She swam to the mainland, and made her way to Ben's home. Soaked and shivering, she refused to enter the house and thaw out. With a whine she caught Ben's coat and led him to the river bank where she began to bark. Then she jumped into the river, swam out, came back and tugged again.

Ben knew dogs and guessed that something had happened to his brother. He and three other men followed Ringing Bells by boat. The islet had disappeared, and the marooned man was standing in three feet of swirling water, barely able to keep his footing. They had arrived just in time.[8]

Mrs. E. W. Smith, of Hermitage, Tennessee, had a remarkable experience with a canary. Her Aunt Tess was an independent old lady, eighty years old, who refused to leave her nearby house and move in with them. She had her canary and her cat, and she liked things the way they were.

One rainy November night in 1950, Mr. and Mrs. Smith were relaxing before the fire at home. As she drew the curtains Mrs. Smith looked through the woods rather anxiously to see if the light was on in Aunt Tess's house. The old lady had grown more feeble since Uncle Jeb's death the year before. She had no telephone and there were no other close neighbors.

But tonight there was a light in her window so Mrs. Smith picked up a book and settled down near her dozing husband. About an hour later something began rapping on the window. The wind was rising—it was probably a branch. But the sound, which grew louder and more insistent, was followed by an almost human cry.

She ran to the window and threw back the curtains. The small bird beating frantically against the glass, suddenly fell to the sill, totally exhausted. She opened the window and picked up Aunt Tess's canary, Bibs. The little bird was dead.

Mrs. Smith awakened her husband and showed him the small feathered body in her hand. "Something's wrong, Ed! Aunt Tess must have sent Bibs to call us!"

"Don't be silly! The bird got out and headed for our lights, that's all."

"But the blinds were drawn and the curtains closed."

At her insistence they drove over to her aunt's. They found the old lady lying on the floor in a pool of blood. Her head had struck the corner of the table as she fell. Fortunately, Aunt Tess recovered and came to live with them.

Nobody knew how Bibs got out of the house to help, beating out his little life as if he were really trying to save his mistress.

"God gave him the power," said Aunt Tess.[9]

Despite the fact that life feeds upon life for survival, thus maintaining a biological balance, there is an underlying kinship among animals that often surprises naturalists. Even today this incongruity in nature produces some strange bed-fellows. One wonders if, as Isaiah prophesied, there shall come a time when the wolf "shall dwell with the lamb, and the leopard shall lie down with the kid; and the calf and the young lion and the fatling together. . . ."

The late J. Frank Dobie, beloved Texas professor, historian, and wanderer among the far, quiet places in America's South-west, author of *Coronado's Children* and *The Longhorns,* wrote: "It would not startle me to see a lion and a lamb lying down together—provided each had been cut off from its kind, and the lion had made the acquaintance of the lamb while not hungry." He adds that nearly all animals yearn for companion-ship, and when they cannot consort with their own kind they sometimes form devoted attachments to creatures utterly foreign.[10]

Dobie's speculation became reality in 1962 when Dr. Wada, director of Japan's Osaka Zoo, reported that a threesome con-sisting of a lion, a sheep and a goat were living peacefully to-gether in the same cage. After he was rejected by his mother at birth, the lion's diet consisted principally of milk and vege-tables. Unusually gentle, he became a favorite with zoo em-ployees and was taught to walk on a leash. Dr. Wada first placed the goat in the cage and then weeks later moved in the sheep. The coexistence that resulted was not a wary truce, but perfect harmony. They not only ate and slept together, but enjoyed play periods that often began with the goat butting the lion into action.[11]

Dobie, writing in *Nature Magazine,* told of relationships between deer and dogs, puppies and squirrels, buffalo and mustangs, quail and chickens, and fawn and kittens. Tradi-tional enemies can become happy playmates. Cats have nursed infant mice and rats. Mules have raised foals; and moose, calves. In England a greyhound adopted a rabbit, although nightly he chased a mechanical rabbit that he would have torn to pieces if he could have caught it.

Among the bizarre friendships on record is one between a monkey and a hippo in an Indiana zoo. Bashful, the monkey, discovered that Hippy ate great quantities of food, and left many unchewed tidbits in his cavernous mouth. In some strange manner Bashful got Hippy's consent to take care of the situation. So Hippy, after consuming his meal of fruit and grain, would swim to the tank's edge, open his huge mouth, and patiently permit the monkey to poke around for the left-overs.[12]

In Mill Valley, California, the J. R. Rowntrees reported that in 1957 they were the proud owners of a very rare type of good samaritan. Their cocker spaniel, Duke, slowly went blind from cataracts, and finally began bumping into objects. One day Mrs. Rowntree saw from a window that Duke had wandered some distance away and was swinging his head back and forth in confusion, uncertain how to return to the house.

She called out to guide him and was surprised when Bos'n, her gray tomcat, ran out of the house and headed for the troubled dog. She watched Bos'n nudge Duke on either side to lead him home. After that the cat took over the job of watching out for the dog. He not only guided Duke about, but would shove him away from the edge of the porch and from other dangerous places where he might fall.[13]

Down under in Melbourne, Australia, Mrs. Irene Hughes raised thoroughbred collies. One day in the spring of 1954 she reported to the police that two of her most valuable dogs had been stolen. Two weeks later she saw a third collie trotting away from the house with a piece of meat in his mouth. She followed. To her amazement he went straight to an abandoned mine shaft where he dropped the meat. There, fifteen feet below, were her lost dogs, who had been kept alive by their faithful pal.[14]

Sometimes dogs are as heroic where their mates are concerned as any human lover. Mooch, for example, had a good thing going as mascot of Fire Engine Company No. 11,

Newark, New Jersey, but he was strictly a station-house pet. His fear of fires was a joke among the men. He offered his companionship and he'd entertain with tricks, but ride to a fire? Not on your life!

That's the way it was until the day his lady friend Winkie was trapped in a blaze near the station. Then Mooch forgot his pyrophobia. He raced into the flaming house, found Winkie dazed by heat and smoke, and dragged her out to safety. For this act of true heroism, the men of Engine No. 11 gave him a medal of honor that he wore on his collar to the end of his days.[15]

In New York City a man named Eldon Bisbee owned an aging miniature French poodle. One night a blizzard swept into the city and the dog disappeared in the storm. In the chill wind Bisbee trudged through the snowy streets for hours, calling for his pet. Finally he returned helplessly to the home that was so silent, so empty.

The thought of his little poodle alone out in the cold and the darkness banished sleep, so Bisbee sat waiting impatiently for morning. Around 3 A.M. the doorbell rang. The caller was a taxi driver. "Are you the owner of a dog, a poodle?" he asked.

Bisbee nodded.

"I have her out in my cab. Got your address from the collar. She's been hurt, has a broken leg and bruises. I'll go get her."

Bisbee cared for the dog while the taxi driver drank a cup of coffee and told what had happened. He had been driving cautiously through the storm when suddenly a German police dog appeared in the light of the headlights and planted himself squarely in front of the cab. He brought the vehicle to a stop and blew his horn, but the big dog wouldn't budge. When he leaned out and shouted, the dog came to the window and whined, then ran to the snow bank along the curb, looking back coaxingly.

The driver got out and followed the dog. Almost buried in the snowy bank lay the white poodle where she had apparently been thrown by a snow plow. The police dog stood above her, thumping his tail for joy that help had come.

"I tried every way I could to locate that police dog," Bisbee said, "but I had no success. I wanted to shake his paw."[16]

Katie, a Weimaraner who lived in San Diego, California, dearly loved her little friend Taco, a mixture of Pomeranian and Chihuahua. Late one day the two dogs were trapped by Mission Bay's incoming tide beyond the wildlife refuge fence. Soon exhausted little Taco began to sink. Katie dived for him and supported him with her jaws but the struggling little dog got away from her and Katie had to repeat the maneuver.

A passerby named Warren Mooers came to the rescue. He swam out and brought Taco to shore while Katie rested her paws on the fence and kept her head above water. Mooers went back for Katie, then took both dogs to a vet. But Katie didn't survive.

"She died of overexertion and shock," the veterinarian explained. "Katie literally gave out completely in trying to save her little pal."[17]

Smart dogs seem to know that medical aid is meant to help even though it sometimes hurts. And they remember. Sometimes they bring their canine friends to the pet hospital or office where they received treatment.

Dr. W. F. Sturgill was a physician and surgeon for the Norfolk and Western Railroad. He was also owner of several English setters and foxhounds, and president of the National Foxhunters' Association. When a friend's hound was injured by a barbed wire, he brought the dog to Dr. Sturgill for treatment.

About a year later the doctor heard a scratching at his office door. There was his friend's dog and beside him another dog whose paws were cut and bleeding. Dr. Sturgill dressed the second dog's wounds and the two trotted off together.[18]

Two veterinarians in Birmingham, Alabama—the Thompson brothers—also had a canine visitor who came on his own seeking help for a mangled paw. They did not recognize the big black collarless dog. But as Andrew Thompson said, "Any dog with enough sense to know where to come for treatment is entitled to care."[19]

In March, 1954, Suzi, a rare Japanese spaniel owned by Mr. and Mrs. Raiberto Comini, of Dallas, Texas, was expecting puppies. One Sunday she left home, crossed a busy six-lane intersection, trotted two miles, and scratched on the door of the J. N. Holt Animal Clinic, which she had visited before only rarely. Before Dr. James Conley could lift her to the table, Suzi had given birth to a pup. Later at the doctor's home she gave birth to two more puppies. Dr. Conley said he had heard of injured dogs seeking out a vet, but this was the first time, to his knowledge, that a pregnant dog had sought medical assistance.[20]

During the summer of 1962 a bighorn sheep came down from the mountains into the village of Mt. Baldy, California. Sick and almost blind, the ewe was found and nursed back to health by a local doctor. When the animal was well, she returned to the wilderness. Two months later, she brought her ailing newborn lamb to the doctor's home. Unable to heal it herself, she had found her way back to the man she knew could help.

6

Bridges Over
the Border

"Unlike circus trainers," says Ivan Tors, "I don't believe in the old 'whip and chair' fear methods. You never get trust with punishment. Instead, we practice a method I call affection training. I believe you get the best from animals by loving and petting them."

Tors has proved that "affection training" works. He has trained the four-footed stars of such TV programs as *Daktari, Gentle Ben, Cowboy in Africa,* and *Clarence the Cross-Eyed Lion.* His 260-acre ranch, Africa, U.S.A., in Soledad Canyon near Los Angeles is the training ground for some six hundred animals used in motion pictures.

Affection-trained lions won't bite even if you put your hand in their mouths. When you see a lion or tiger wrestle with a man in a movie, they are only playing. The growls and snarls have to be dubbed into the sound tracks to create the illusion of conflict.

In addition to love, language bridges the realms of man and the more intelligent animals. Judy, the chimp in TV's *Daktari* series, can obey 125 verbal commands.[1]

Dr. Wilfred J. Funk, the noted lexicographer, once made an

intensive study of the ability of dogs to understand human speech. He decided that the average pet has an understanding vocabulary of about sixty words, while some highly trained ones comprehend perhaps two hundred and fifty.

Fellow, a German shepherd, was tested by professors at Columbia and New York Universities and found to have an understanding vocabulary of around three hundred words. And it was the actual words, not the tone of voice or similar clues that he grasped, for when they rearranged familiar commands into other phrases, he still obeyed. His owner, Jacob Herbert, in describing his training methods, said: "I never said anything to Fellow without a purpose. I never rewarded or punished him except by saying 'Good dog' or 'What a shame!' "[2]

The higher animals communicate with one another by sounds, and in the case of apes, these sounds reach the level of words. At the Yerkes Laboratories of Primate Biology in Orange Park, Florida, Blanche W. Learned discovered thirty-two chimpanzee words associated with food, drink, other animals, or persons. Similar anthropoid vocabularies have been reported by Dr. R. L. Garner and the German scientist, Georg Schwidetsky. In fact Schwidetsky believes that certain of the anthropoid words are identical to root words used by the Bushmen of South Africa and found in ancient Chinese. Some African jungle natives believe gorillas talk just as well as we do when they are alone, but conceal this ability when humans are around so they won't be enslaved or forced to pay taxes![3]

With the exception of certain birds, the animal most frequently taught to talk human style is the dog. Here in a majority of cases we must allow for imagination and exaggeration on the part of proud owners, but even the worst of these canines are probably as understandable as the growls of some cabbies and bus drivers!

Back in the 1940s there was a talking dog in the Bronx named Blitz. He was "interviewed" by Paul Phelan of the former New York *Sun,* at Public School 48 where his owner, Arthur J. Devlin, was custodian. Phelan did a triple-take when from the mouth of the eighty-pound shepherd-plus-mongrel came the words, "Good morning, I want my mommie."

Devlin said he discovered his dog's conversational ability in 1942 when, after asking him for the thousandth time, "Do you want to go out?" Blitz looked at him and aarfed, "Want out!"

Devlin couldn't believe it. "I was afraid I was going nuts," he admitted. But when he called in a neighbor, Blitz repeated his performance.

We suspect that Devlin had his fingers crossed when he told the reporter that Blitz sometimes had other things to say. "Once I had him in a tavern in Bay Ridge," he said. "I gave him a quarter and he put his paws upon the bar, laid the quarter down, and said, 'I want a hamburger.' The bartender dropped a glass of beer and went into shock."

Fox terrier Joe was owned by Mr. and Mrs. D. O. Ball, of Traverse City, Michigan. Mr. Ball, as president of that city's Cherryland Animal Society, first ran into Joe at the animal shelter. Joe didn't talk in the beginning. He crowed! He had been taught to crow by a man, not by a rooster. The Balls adopted Joe. Mrs. Ball's twin sister Irene came by almost every afternoon, and Mrs. Ball often talked to Joe about her in a chummy way.

"One day a car door slammed outside," said Mr. Ball. "I looked at Joe and he looked at me. Before I could say a word, he said very plainly, 'Aunt Irene.' "

Joe sang, too, certainly not in a fashion that would appeal to music critics, but it was very pleasing to the Balls.[4]

Mr. Lucky was a Boston terrier with a vocabulary of twenty words. Dr. William Perkins of the University of Southern California's Speech Clinic accepted the invitation of the dog's owner, Mrs. J. T. Davis, of Midvale, Utah, to record Mr. Lucky's speaking voice. It was thin and high, similar to a talking doll's, although his natural bark and growl came out deep. The dog had difficulty in pronouncing the letters *s* and *r*, but his speech was still understandable.

In 1953 reporters from the Salt Lake City *Deseret News* interviewed Mr. Lucky. They came back convinced that he could talk. Newsman Jack E. Jarrard stated, "He doesn't talk just unintelligible gruntings that can be interpreted as words, but makes recognizable words and sentences."

Like other talking dogs, Mr. Lucky was fond of saying, "I want my mommie." Perhaps a canine twist on the Oedipus complex? He also said, "I want 'ome," if someone else was drinking pop, or if his ball was lost. He could say "I will" and "I won't," and "Oh, dear, oh, dear," if shut up in the basement. If he wanted a ride, he said, "Wide, wide." He hated to be left alone.

Each time, before he could get real words out, Mr. Lucky had to moan and grunt for a bit. Then the speaking voice would come out. Another sentence he could produce was, "Give me my mirror," but the *r's* didn't sound right. Mrs. Davis found out he could talk when one day she stayed too long next door chatting with a neighbor. Mr. Lucky gave her a bored look, and like many another male, came up with, "Aw, come on home!"[5]

Several species of birds can mimic human speech but it is seldom that the individual birds have any comprehension of the meaning of the words. We once lived next door to a mynah who constantly startled us and passing females with his wolf whistles. And we knew a little parakeet who would light on our shoulders with unnerving frequency and ask, "Why don't you talk to me, precious?"

In Uganda, Africa, there was once a raven who was taught by teetotaling missionaries to frighten imbibing natives by croaking out, "Go and sign the pledge." It was said that over a two-decade period the raven's unwitting temperance campaign resulted in two thousand five hundred converts.[6]

And there was the parrot who gave police the clue that solved the murder of his owner.

On July 12, 1942, Max Geller, the owner of the Green Parrot Restaurant in New York City's Harlem, was fatally shot by a quarrelsome drunk who fled the scene. Although over twenty persons were in the establishment at the time, all claimed to have been in the restrooms at the time of the murder.

Geller had named the café after his large green parrot, a touchy old bird with a sulphurous vocabulary. From its perch above the bar it greeted patrons with salty oaths, and occasionally with the startling announcement, "It's murder!" Although the slayer hadn't rifled the cash register, detectives noticed that the parrot frequently screamed, "It's murder, robber, robber!" followed by some choice words from his repertoire of profanity.

After days of frustration, Detective John J. Morrisey told his superiors that he thought the parrot might have been naming the murderer right along. "I found out that some of the bar's regular customers had taught the bird to announce their names when they entered the place," he explained. "I also found out from the old-timers that before the crime they never heard the bird shout 'robber.' That bird is smart, but not smart enough to look at a hold-up and immediately start yelling 'robber'! What's more, I've noticed that when the parrot calls out the name of some customer, he always follows it with the same string of oaths. When he shouts 'robber' he uses these same phrases, so I think what he's really saying is 'Robert! Robert!' "

There were a number of Roberts on the Green Parrot customer list, but with one exception all were able to account for their whereabouts the evening of the murder. The exception was a Robert Butler who had vanished from the neighborhood at the time of the crime. A year passed by, then detectives learned that a friend of Butler's had received a letter from Baltimore that might have been written by the fugitive. Officers picked up the friend as an alleged robbery suspect, read the letter without his knowledge while he was being searched, then released him.

On the following day two New York detectives arrested Butler as he was leaving his job at the Bethlehem Steel plant in Baltimore. When he was told that the parrot had fingered him, Butler said, "The bird was just too damn smart, and I never did like him." He also said that on the night of the murder he had entered the café intoxicated, and had shot Geller in anger when Geller refused to serve him. On February 10, 1944, Robert Butler was sentenced to Sing Sing.[7]

Eliminating a possible contact with extraterrestrials, man's first conversation with nonhumans will probably take place with one of the brainy, bottle-nosed dolphins.

The dolphin's swift and efficient skill in swimming originally launched the U.S. Navy's special study of the mammals at its Communications Research Institute in the Virgin Islands. Dr. John C. Lilly, a neurophysiologist, was placed in charge of the project, which, it was hoped, would lead to improved submarine design. As the research progressed, however, startling discoveries were made.

For one thing, the dolphin is by far the most intelligent animal other than man; his brain power in some respects might even be superior to man's. Not only is the dolphin's brain 40 percent larger than man's, but the cortex, the layer of gray matter, is just as convoluted and has as many brain cells per unit area.

Dr. Lilly had to program a computer to keep up with his dolphins because, he said, their brains work so incredibly fast compared with humans'. Another scientist, Colin Taylor, curator of the Port Elizabeth Oceanarium, South Africa, estimates that dolphins' brains work sixteen times as fast as a man's brain, but he doesn't believe they retain as much information. In one experiment Dr. Lilly placed an electrode in the "pleasure center" of a dolphin's brain. The dolphin learned in one try to turn on the switch producing the current whereas monkeys generally have to make three hundred or more tries to learn this technique.

Navy scientists have taught dolphins to pick out a plastic-encased panel of copper from identical panels of aluminum and other metals, but they do not know how the mammals detect the copper. As a result, they hope the animals can eventually be trained to locate valuable, recoverable underwater minerals, and to detect and identify submarines, mines, and missile installations. Special metallic plates would identify friendly submarines and mines. Some of these scientists (who strike us as far more cold-blooded than fish) suggest a kind of involuntary hari-kari, in which their dolphins might be trained to destroy enemy submarines with explosives carried in body harnesses. Already some can perform simple chores like Sealab's messenger Tuffy.

But it was the accidental discovery that dolphins mimic human speech that has created the hope of eventual communication. One day a dolphin began making a series of sounds in imitation of laboratory equipment. Dr. Lilly made a tape at one quarter its normal speed. He heard his own voice giving the tape footage, "three-two-eight," and the dolphin immediately and clearly repeated the words in high-pitched whistles. Other tape recordings of what had seemed to be an unintelligible series of squawks and quacks were played at quarter-speed with the sound volume lowered to confirm the discovery. Sometimes the dolphins even mimicked the laughter in the laboratory.

These dolphins were distinctly imitating the human words they heard, but telescoping the sounds. They were talking at a rate eight times faster than human speech. Incidentally, they vocalize through their blowholes, not their mouths.

Dolphins talk almost constantly and give every indication of conveying information to each other. At least a part of their chatter has to do with their sonar sounding, which is far more efficient than man's finest electronic equipment. By sending out sounds and picking up the echoes, the animals can tell the direction of oncoming objects as well as their size, shape, texture, and even density.

Their distress call is an undulating whistle. One of Dr. Lilly's dolphins had been kept under restraint in a small tank for a special experiment. When it was taken back to the large tank and the other dolphins, it couldn't swim or move its flukes properly, and had developed an S-curve along its back. Its distress call was answered by two companions who raised its head above water so it could breathe. Next the pair of good samaritans took turns swimming under the stricken animal's anal region, which was raked with their dorsal fins. This caused a muscular reflex that in turn automatically activated the dolphin's flukes and drove the animal to the surface for breathing. The guardian dolphins kept up their therapy for several hours.

Dr. Lilly has taught dolphins to pronounce equivalents of certain English words. In Hawaii Dr. Dwight W. Batteau has invented a device that translates spoken Hawaiian words into whistled tones like those used by dolphins, and has trained a pair to respond and answer several commands vocally.

Colin Taylor, the South African curator, also created a device that converts English words electronically into dolphin-like sounds. He believes that dolphins mainly hear variations of timing and intensity. With his device, he says, he has taught one dolphin a dozen basic command words.

Taylor has compiled a "vocabulary" of several hundred sounds that dolphins emit under certain stimuli and circumstances, but has not yet deciphered their meanings. He suggests that certain nuances of sound are not caught by electronic recording equipment. Both of his dolphins, for example, consistently make the same sound when making a left-hand turn as they circle the pool. Yet they do not respond to his recording of this sound.[8]

Another communication problem has been the fact that many dolphin noises are of too high frequency to be heard by human ears. The animals can hear and "speak" in our spectrum of sound, but we can do so only within a small portion of their spectrum. The International Oceanographic Foundation, however, reported in December, 1967, that a dolphin-to-man translator had been developed by a private firm at the United States Biological Facility at Point Mugu, California. Using an intermediate language designed for the purpose, a man's words are translated into a frequency-modulated whistle within the range that dolphins use. Dolphin sounds are picked up by under-water microphones and converted by electronic circuitry into sounds similar to those of the intermediate language.[9]

Cataloguing dolphin sounds and teaching the mammals human words are only preliminary steps toward the huge hurdle of relating meanings to the sounds. This will be difficult and time-consuming, and only the astonishing intelligence of the dolphin offers hope of success.

How this intelligence developed is a puzzle, for the dolphin lives in a watery world where all the mentally stimulating aspects that have favored man's progress are unknown. The dolphin lacks hands and fingers for manipulating objects. Yet he lives in social groups dominated by a leader, has a sense of humor, can learn at a fantastic rate, and even originate playful games with humans.

Arthur C. Clarke, the well-known science writer, has suggested that since dolphins have no written records, they could have an oral history passed down from generation to generation. Since the mother dolphin nurses her baby for eighteen to twenty-one months and they remain close during this period, Dr. Lilly speculates on whether the mother teaches her baby the sum total of dolphin knowledge and legends.

Solving the problem of conversational contact with another species will provide a basis for developing communication techniques that will be of value should man eventually confront other alien intelligences in space. If dolphins offer this breakthrough, there is a background of lore that may be symbolically significant. There have been mystical bonds between men and dolphins.

Sailors in all ages have welcomed their appearance as a sign of good luck and a successful voyage. The sea gods of antiquity either rode on dolphins or had groups of them in attendance. According to Pliny, they were attracted by music and the sound of human voices, and enjoyed playing with children.

There was Pelorus Jack, the famous dolphin who accompanied ships from 1888 to 1911 passing through Cook Strait between the two main islands of New Zealand. He is said to have guided the vessels along the six-mile stretch between Pelorus Sound and French Pass. Today Jack is remembered with a monument and statue erected on the beach at Wellington.

There are several cases on record in which dolphins have saved human lives. *Natural History* Magazine in 1949 told of a dolphin who pushed a semiconscious woman to the beach after she had been caught in the undertow while swimming.

Dr. Winthrop N. Kellogg, in his book *Porpoises and Sonar,* reports the story of Mrs. Yvonne M. Bliss, of Stuart, Florida, who fell overboard off the coast of Grand Bahama Island in 1960. After some moments of swimming and floating she felt something touch her. At first she thought it was a shark but then recognized a dolphin.

The animal shoved her into a new direction so she was no longer bucking a cross tide with waves washing over her head. Next the creature moved behind and around to her other side and again nudged her along. If the dolphin hadn't done this, she would have been going into deeper and faster-moving waters, but she had been guided to the section along the shore where the water was most shallow. As her feet touched land, her rescuer "took off like a streak down the channel."[10]

It is easy to be overly sentimental about animals, for human vanity enjoys imagining manlike characteristics in them. But we must not read our thoughts and actions into theirs, for they move in realms that the human consciousness has not yet penetrated and cannot fully comprehend. Ernest Thompson Seton's animals were fictional characters.

Yet it is just as easy to go too far in the other direction, to believe that all of the higher animals live behavioristic, mechanical and instinctive lives, with no complimentary humanlike characteristics at all. We should remember that all higher life is linked in an evolutionary stream; that there is a creative brotherhood. Within all of us is something of the same mind and heart. It is this truth that permits bridges, however narrow, to cross the border between man and the animal domains.

The emotions that govern, and sometimes plague, human lives are also known to our pets.

A jealous female German shepherd named Chiquita who lived in Los Angeles had a pal named Wimpy until Wimpy had a litter of puppies and at once lost all interest in Chiquita. The unhappy, neglected shepherd decided she would have her own litter. She picked up things and took them to her kennel for solace. Soon she had a bizarre collection—a teddy bear, a stuffed spotted dog, a pair of galoshes, and a torn glove. She mothered them with steadfast devotion, just as Wimpy mothered her pups. They were not alive. They were not even identical. They were symbols. Man alone is supposed to use symbols.[11]

Timothy was a wise and trusted cat. His favorite spot to sun himself was the dining-room window where the canary's cage hung. He paid no attention to the bird, and so every day the cage was opened for awhile and the canary flew about the dining room.

The day came when Timothy did pay attention to the bird. Instinct and temptation proved overpowering. He ate the canary. For his crime he was painfully punished and driven out of the house in disgrace. Several hours later, Timothy returned. In his mouth he carried, unharmed, a nestling sparrow which he deposited at the feet of his mistress.[12]

Some years ago in the fishing village of Letite, New Brunswick, lived a dog named Bosco. He was a friendly canine, owned and fed by all the citizens, loved by the children. Occasionally he would disappear for a few days, but he always came back as friendly as ever. Meanwhile the villagers were disturbed. Valuable objects were vanishing. Neighbor watched neighbor with suspicion.

One afternoon two men, Tom Harris and Earl Dupré, were

rabbit hunting in a wooded area. Below a bluff they noticed the mouth of a small cave. As they approached, a fierce wild dog burst out with an ominous growl and attacked them. Harris took quick aim and shot the animal as it leaped for his companion's throat. Only then did they recognize the dog as Bosco. Inside the cave were the stolen objects, including a Bible. Did Bosco have a conscience?

The courtship techniques of some animals are akin to those of human swains. Penguins, wrens, and waxwings present gifts to their lady loves. Fiddler crabs and scorpions dance. Lobsters and crayfish sing. Hummingbirds dramatize their love with exhibitions of flying skill. Elephants kiss.

Male Australian bower birds build elaborate bowers, sometimes several feet high and as much as fourteen feet long, to which they invite the hen-birds of their hearts' desire. With remarkable artistic sensibility, they decorate the bowers with bright flowers and berries, and even mix paints and apply them with homemade bark brushes. The female satin bower bird has blue eyes, and her wooer brings her gifts of berries, colored pebbles, and the like—all blue!

So astonishing are the five-day "honeymoons" of egrets that Dr. Julian Huxley, the English scientist, couldn't believe they occurred until he actually witnessed one. After the big birds pair off, they withdraw to a chosen nesting site. Hour after hour they perch motionless, the female resting her head against her mate's body. This content is interrupted now and then by surges of ecstacy. Both birds then raise their wings with an outburst of love cries. Raising their heads, they intertwine their necks together in a true lover's knot.

At other times each will take the plumes of the other in its beak, nibble them lovingly, and give each plume a long sliding kiss from tip to base. When passion subsides, they again rest side by side in quiet delight ,their bodies touching.

Is sexual attraction the trigger reaction between the male and female of a given species that behaviorists would have us believe? In general this may be true, but among the higher animals there are exceptions and even animal romance can contain its mysterious ingredients.

Boo-Boo was a winsome young female chimpanzee in the London Zoo. Her keepers had an excellent reason for their determination to find a mate for her. So from public and private zoos throughout Great Britain and from abroad came young and handsome male suitors. Boo-Boo ignored them. The Zoological Society directors became desperate, so much so that they finally permitted the Bristol Zoo to send Koko.

Koko was middle-aged, paunchy, and seedy-looking, with scraggly hair and a bristling windblown bob. His cries were hoarse and his gait was shambling. But Boo-Boo took one look and it was love at first sight. Within minutes they had their arms around each other. And the next year Boo-Boo and Koko became the proud parents of Jubilee—the first chimpanzee ever born in captivity in London.

Love among many animals is not confined to carnality and is greater than the sex drive. Alan Devoe tells of seeing a pair of elderly apes, long past the days of passion, sitting by the hour "with their arms around each other, petting, comforting, in the quiet joy of togetherness."[13]

In sordid sexual activities, it is men who are the "beasts," not animals. Love among nature's creatures can be grace, devotion, tenderness, and the warm fire of creation. We recall our yellow tomcat, Butch, long deceased, who brought his first lady love to call. He came with her ceremoniously to the front door, not the kitchen as was his custom, led her proudly through his human domain, and watched with fond eyes while she consumed his lunch.

As among humans, animal insecurity may manifest itself in ill health, aggression, timidity, or as excessive affection for a parental figure. Like children, animals can sulk and have tantrums when they feel frustrated. Vance Packard, in his book *Animal I. Q.,* tells of chimpanzee frustration reactions of indigestion and violent itching; of a baby chick reared in solitary who became wildly eccentric; of a rat, forced by constant jets of air to jump, that had a nervous breakdown; and of a dethroned cow-queen who first became a stubborn malcontent, then went insane, after she lost her regal place in cow society.

Some monkeys scream in anger when their unfinished efforts at art work are taken away, but they do not object to losing their finished paintings. Monkeys scratch their heads when puzzled. So do men. Belligerent bullfrogs inflate their chests. So do army sergeants.

Naturalist Sally Carrighar in her book *Wild Heritage* points out that many animals understand property values and some have a sense of justice or at least of order. A bird will wait his turn to bathe. Many animals are industrious and cooperative. They queue up for carrion feasts—wolverines first, then wolves, then foxes, and ravens last.[14]

The honey guide, an East African bird resembling a robin, likes honey but cannot rob the bee tree itself. So the clever little bird has learned to enlist the aid of natives in the Wandorobo tribe. After locating a hollow tree containing wild honey, the bird scouts around until it finds men, then introduces itself by excited chattering. The natives whistle an acknowledgment. The honey guide leads them by flitting ahead from tree to tree, chattering all the while, while the natives answer with low whistles. When it reaches the bee tree, its notes climb several decibels.

The Wandorobo build a smoky fire to drive away most of the angry bees, then open up the tree's trunk, extract the honey, and lay aside an offering for the bird. At this point the bird's mate arrives to share in the feast. In reporting on this strange partnership, the November, 1952 issue of *Natural History,* published by the American Museum of Natural History, editorializes that behavior psychologists will find this difficult to explain on their terms.

Early in the nineteenth century Charles Darwin visited the remote Galapagos Islands on his famous cruise around the world. There he identified a subspecies of the woodpecker finch, now called the Darwin finch, that was a seed-eater in those days. In 1965, however, naturalists discovered that the Darwin finch has learned to use cactus spines as tools to impale grubs deep inside the hollows of trees. And with this newly acquired ability, the little bird has changed from a vegetarian to a meat-eater.

Anthropomorphism—the attribution of human characteristics to things not human—should have, perhaps, a reverse meaning. We seek to know how animals resemble us, but we should observe how we resemble them.

Perhaps this was why the feats of wild-horse trainer John Solomon Rarey have never been equaled. At a period when most training of animals was based on cruelty and fear, Rarey said he mixed kindness, patience, and firmness. Ralph Waldo Emerson wrote of him: "John Rarey has turned a new leaf for civilization." His exact methods were secret since he insisted on being left alone with the horses he tamed.

John discovered his talent when he was twelve years old and his father, Adam Rarey, brought an incorrigible colt to his farm near Columbus, Ohio. The previous owner had hired a dozen professional horse-breakers to tame the animal, and all had given up. Adam got him at a bargain. The first step, he thought, was to show the colt who was boss. He struck a sharp blow with the whip. With an angry leap the animal snapped the halter rope and slammed Adam into the fence with such violence that his leg was broken. Neighbors carried him into the house and called a doctor.

"That colt is mad—insane," Adam said. "Bargain or not, you men will have to kill him. He's too dangerous to have around. Take my rifle. It's standing by the kitchen door."

When the neighbors reached the corral, the colt was gone. They started for the barn and then heard a shout: "Don't shoot, men! It's all right! I've already gentled him!" And out through the barn door came the horse that had crippled its owner only minutes before. Riding the horse was young John Rarey.

"You can't hurt horses like this when you tame them," John

told the silent, awe-stricken men. "They've got spirit and pride. I told this colt that if he calmed down we wouldn't hurt him."

From that time on, John Rarey's fame spread. Wild, vicious horses from all over the Midwest were brought to the Rarey farm for the boy to gentle. He not only never failed, but if the horse was kept at the farm for several days he would teach it to bow, kneel, and canter.

When John was nineteen he went to Texas, where he was really challenged. The Texans, who were betting heavily against Rarey, had assembled five of the most vicious equines in the state. Four of them had killed one man each; the fifth had crippled two men.

Six thousand spectators, including many newspapermen, were present to watch John Rarey meet his Waterloo. The youth ignored his hostile audience, quietly walked across the corral, entered a huge box stall that housed one of the killer horses, and closed the door. During the next forty minutes the odds favoring the horse rose as it seemed apparent that Rarey was either dead or maimed. Then, just as the spectators began demanding that authorities investigate, the stall door opened.

John rode the horse to the center of the corral as the audience roared its astonishment. Dismounting, he had the erstwhile killer kneel on command, then lie on its side. Finally he removed his hat and bowed.

His Texas performance brought John Rarey national fame. He trained a pair of elk, hitched them to a buggy, and drove about the country, giving lectures on kindness to animals. Meanwhile he continued to prove his claim that there was no horse so vicious that he could not make it as tame as a housecat in six hours—and usually in much less time.

In 1868 John went to England where more challengers and skeptics sought the most dangerous horse they could find. They decided upon Lord Dorchester's former racing stallion, Cruiser, who for four years had apparently been insane. The horse had spells so violent that he would bite chunks out of his own flanks and legs, and tear up a wooden stall in minutes. John agreed to go to Murrell's Green where Cruiser was kept in a special brick and steel reinforced stall.

A party of titled gentlemen, sportsmen, and reporters accompanied the trainer to the stall. The horse was throwing himself against the door in maniacal frenzy, with an impact that shook the entire structure. Lord Dorchester suddenly realized that he might be an accomplice to murder. He glanced at John Rarey, a small, frail man. The stall, which was only slightly larger than the infuriated horse, seemed to contain a nightmare of flying hooves. "I cannot permit you to enter the stall," he told Rarey regretfully. "I withdraw the challenge and I will reimburse you for your trip from London."

"You needn't worry," John said. "All I ask is to borrow a halter and a body belt." He waited until Cruiser was momentarily dazed from striking his head against the wall, stepped inside, quickly slipped a halter on the horse, and leaped out. Now the maddened animal expended its energy on the halter, which was secured to a ring on the wall, until he finally dropped from exhaustion.

Again Rarey entered the stall, snapped the heavy leather body belt around the horse's middle, then threaded two smaller leather straps through a brass ring in the belt's center so arranged that by pulling on the straps he could cause the horse's front legs to buckle. For three hours he sat beside the horse, stroking its neck and talking to it softly. Whenever it struggled he gently pulled on the straps.

The next day John Rarey rode Cruiser through the streets of London, enjoying the cheers of spectators and the jingle of gold coins in his pockets. He had won some sizable wagers. A week later there was a command performance before Queen Victoria at Windsor Castle, where he gentled an unbroken stallion in the royal stables.

From England, John Rarey went to France, Germany, Egypt, Spain, and Sweden, taming the worst horses the local citizens could find without a single failure. In 1860 he returned to the United States in triumph and toured the great cities in the East and Midwest. John Rarey died at the early age of thirty-eight. His honors may seem strange today, but a century ago the horse was the most important animal in captivity and essential to most transportation.[15]

There was another man who developed a rapport with an animal much farther removed from humankind. He was Leonard Dubkin, a self-taught naturalist, the author of several books and many *Chicago Tribune* features on nature and wild life.

One summer evening, exploring a clump of trees in a weed-grown Chicago lot, he discovered a dome-shaped structure formed by entwined vines hanging from the lower branches of a tree. The foliage was almost impenetrable and rose to a height of about eighteen feet. Its only entry was an opening about two feet in diameter.

Inside this grotto Dubkin discovered around two hundred bats sleeping head downward. As dusk approached they began to stretch and squeak. At first Dubkin's presence excited them but when he remained quiet they ignored him. With the coming of darkness they began flying around the tree trunk, their numbers increasing until all the adults were in the flock. Then, responding to some secret signal, they swarmed out of the small opening at the top of the grotto like a cloud of smoke.

That summer and fall Dubkin often returned to visit the bat colony. In mid-October the bats all left for some unknown place of hibernation. There while winter winds chilled the air and snow shrouded the earth, their tiny lives were suspended in the total darkness of unconsciousness.

Spring came again and the bats, restless and excitable, returned to the grotto. It was the time for giving birth to the young. One day late in May, Dubkin watched with fascination the birth of a rare albino bat. The completely white infant was as conspicuous in the grotto as a light in a cave. Dubkin would be able to observe its individual development.

When the baby was slightly over a day old, he examined her

while her mother and several other bats flew nervously around his head. She crawled across his hand, her eyes still closed, her folded wings trailing like silken garments, and when she reached the end of his little finger she tightened her feet on it and swung head downward.

"Little white lady," he whispered, "you are a very rare creature." Then, with a sudden flash of wings, the mother swooped down and recovered her baby.

When the white lady was several weeks old, Dubkin began taking her home in a cigar box after the adults had left for their night of hunting. There he placed her in a canary cage surrounded with screen wire. After exploring the cage bottom, she would climb up on the perch and hang downward, wide awake, her eyes following his every movement.

Later she learned how to escape from her cage. When morning came the naturalist had to search for her, and this could be difficult when she was hanging from a white wall fixture or white curtain. He would return her to the grotto on his way to work. When freed from the box she would utter a faint cry and instantly her mother would snatch up her daughter with a lightning swoop.

When the white lady was twenty-three days old, she flew for the first time. Dubkin entered the grotto and watched for two hours as she developed her skill. She made certain her huge, strange friend was admiring her. She would brush her wings against his face as if to say, "Look at me, look at what I can do." And the next night she flew away with the adults for the first time.

As the days passed, the narrow span of friendship between man and tiny mammal was strengthened. Dubkin visited the grotto daily. If the bats were outside when he walked across the lot, the white lady would welcome him by diving and flashing her wings near his face. He discovered that he could feed her. He would place an insect on his open palm and she would take it from his hand in a dive.

One evening he took her to his apartment and released her.

As she was flitting about, she suddenly flew directly toward the revolving blades of an electric fan. But as Dubkin watched in horror, the white lady flew into the fan and came out the other side as easily as a child skipping rope. She enjoyed performing this feat again and again, but if the fan was revolving at a high speed she would not go through but over the top of the fan. Somehow she knew when it wasn't safe.

Dubkin tested her homing ability by releasing her at various places in Chicago. Finally, in September, he took her along on a business trip to Milwaukee. As he started back, he released her, and drove directly to the grotto. And there she was already in her usual place, after flying ninety miles over unfamiliar territory in slightly over two hours.

Soon winter was approaching again, and the bats became more and more lethargic. They slept longer and more deeply, and some did not even leave the grotto at night. And so there again came a day in mid-October when the naturalist found the grotto silent and deserted. The white lady and her companions had gone to their secret retreat to sleep the winter away.

Impatiently Leonard Dubkin waited for spring. On the first Sunday in May as a soft breeze from off the lake foretold the coming summer, he drove out to see if the bats had returned. With a shock that stabbed his heart he looked upon a scene of desolation.

Where there had been a large weed-grown lot with a clump of trees, only a bare, muddy plain remained. A steam shovel, its jaws open like those of a Mesozoic dinosaur, stood where the grotto had been. "Now I would never know whether the white lady had a baby, or how long she would live, or what happened to her," Dubkin wrote.[16]

And we have our own thoughts about the white lady. Did she, in her wild life, ever recall the odd giant creature who admired her and fed her? Did she remember the strange place with walls, a cage, curtains, and a fan she could fly through?

When, snug and content in some hidden haven as rains fell and winds moaned, did she remember days of sunshine when once she had known the affection of an alien being? In fact, how great was the white lady's memory, and did she remember the past in pictures as humans do?

7

Animal Supersenses

When George E. "Murphy" Adle, Jr., of San Lorenzo, California, left for Vietnam in August, 1967, to serve with an armored regiment, Candy, his German shepherd, went on a hunger strike and barely ate for several weeks. The dog happened to be near the mail box when Murphy's first letter arrived. She perked up immediately, sniffed, nuzzled the various pieces of mail with her nose, then picked up one single envelope—the letter from Vietnam. Thereafter Candy examined the mail daily, and if there was a letter from her master she always separated it from the rest with barks and whines of delight. She was successful despite the fact that the envelope may have been handled by dozens of persons and taken weeks to be delivered.[1]

A highly acute sense of smell may be the solution to some mysteries in the animal kingdom. It now appears that this is the answer to the question of how salmon return from the sea to spawn in precisely the stream in which they were reared. Experiments in which the olfactory nerve has been cut or the nasal-sac opening plugged have supported the theory of scent guidance. And since salmon fingerlings can discriminate be-

tween the odors of two different streams, zoologists suspect
that young salmon are "imprinted" by some volatile organic
substance in the home stream.

Writing in *Science,* Toshiaki J. Hara, Kazuo Ueda, and
Aubrey Gorbman of the University of Washington, Seattle,
told of experiments using electroencephalography. They found
that when spawning salmon arrived at the home pond, the
olfactory bulbs and posterior cerebellum exhibited considerable electrical activity. When waters from other nearby
sources were infused into the olfactory sacs, there was little
or no change in the bio-electrical patterns. This sense guidance
would only be effective in the final stages of the homeward
migration in fresh water. It is believed that salmon navigate
by a sun-compass mechanism in the open sea.

The determination of a salmon to return to its original body
of water for spawning is awesome. In 1962 a silver salmon
was hatched at the Prairie Creek Hatchery near Eureka, California, and reared in a spawning tank. When it reached
fingerling size, it was transferred to other tanks. Along with
thousands of others, it was marked by the removal of the
adipose fin when a year old, then taken in a tank truck and
released into a stream flowing into the ocean. This was a
different stream than the one flowing through the hatchery.

In December, 1964, our salmon, now fourteen inches in
size, came home. To do so, he had to locate the mouth of
Redwood Creek, swim up this stream to Prairie Creek, go up
several drainage canals, pass through a culvert under U. S.
Route 101, and then go straight up a four-inch pipe with a
ninety-degree turn in it. This pipe was one of five; the other
four had dead ends. At the end of this pipe he had to knock
a wire screen cover off a 2½-foot-high standpipe. After leaping
through this standpipe, he went over a two-foot-high wire net
and dropped down into the very spawning tank where he was
born. His only injury was a sore nose, suffered when he
rammed the wire screen off the standpipe.

The hatchery workers named the fish "Indomitable." Said

Kenneth Johnson, hatchery manager, "Indomitable has completed the most amazing spawning journey known to world fish history."[2]

For most animals their sense of hearing is not only extremely sensitive, but has a greater range than that of man. A sound that a man with good hearing can detect at 175 yards, a dog can easily hear at a full mile. Studies at the Berlin Physiological Laboratory have proved that dogs, cats, and even chickens can determine the exact sources of sounds far more accurately than sharp-eared humans.[3]

The German scientists also found that dogs and especially cats have remarkable tonal senses. In one experiment the dog could distinguish between two notes separated by one-fourth the range that separates two piano notes. And cats, too, can detect the delicate difference between almost similar sounds such as halftones.

According to Ida M. Mellen in *The Science and the Mystery of the Cat,* several famous musicians have credited some of their success to their critical cats. Cats are supersensitive to discords and cannot endure shrill off-key notes or poor singing. They appreciate good music. Some learn to pluck guitar strings. Others enjoy the sounds of gentle bells, violins, and harps. Most cats enjoy walking over piano keyboards, a practice that has inspired such compositions as Domenico Scarlatti's "Cat's Fugue" and Chopin's "Valse Brilliante."

Cats catch mice. Is it because mice sing? Their sounds resemble the chirping and twittering of small birds, in a fluty vocalizing with more variety and individuality than most bird songs. A Detroit musician had a mouse with a range of two octaves and a tempo that varied between two and six notes per second. A New York resident reported that he watched three mice in his apartment sitting upright and singing together in different pitches with fair harmony. Several singing mice have entertained TV and radio audiences.

Biologists suspect that all mice sing, but that usually their sounds—like the hypersonic twitterings of flying bats—are pitched too high for human ears. Perhaps, to attract our notice, a singing mouse must be a rare *basso profundo* of the rodent world, with his companions warbling far up the scale in soprano inaudible to us. Again, there are a few persons with unusual auditory endowments that permit them to hear little mouse melodies.[4]

It is curious that all around us are songs and sounds, lights and colors, that we human beings never hear or see because of our limited spectra. Animals, however, hear some of these sounds and see some of these lights that exist just beyond our limitations. Occasionally this is responsible for some odd incidents.

In 1963 a U. S. military attaché moved into a new home in a foreign country. Immediately he noticed that at certain times his dog seemed to be battling an invisible enemy in a corner of his study. Not believing in ghosts, he asked for an investigation by security officers.

A high-frequency listening device that could transmit any conversation held in the room was found under the flooring. An examination revealed that it was turned on and off by a high-pitched tone inaudible to humans but very disturbing to dogs.

What we call light, or the visible band, extends apparently indefinitely beyond both the violet and red edges of the spectrum, but human eyes cannot see beyond those limits. There are many animals, however, who not only can detect waves beyond these limits, but apparently can sometimes actually see by them.

We marvel that an owl in almost pitch darkness, on the high limb of a tree and over a field of tall, matted grass, can see the stirring of a field mouse. Some zoologists now believe that the owl's eyes are sensitive to the infrared heat waves radiating from the warm-blooded body of the wee mouse. Thus they see the mouse as a streak of reddish light moving within the mass of cool grasses and can dive in an accurate strike.

This same principle in a different manner is used by pit

viper snakes in seeking their mammalian prey. They have pit-like organs on the sides of their muzzles in front of their eyes that are highly sensitive to heat or infrared radiations. The reptiles use these organs as direction finders to lead them to their food.

Nor is this principle limited to the appeasement of hunger. There are certain moths that mate after dark. While the females appear to sit doing nothing, the males locate them unerringly in total darkness over great distances, regardless of wind direction. This was a puzzle until a spectroscopist discovered that the females were broadcasting a mating call over infrared wavelengths.

It's difficult to think of any of man's practical inventions that nature didn't have first. Tailor birds use needles and thread, and wasps make paper from wood pulp. Water spiders use diving bells, and the barrel cactus stores cool water like a refrigerator. Now it's infrared broadcasting, sonar, and radar.

Until recent years the ability of an eel-like fish, *Gymnarchus niloticas,* in the Nile River to dart backward at great speed in and around objects without the use of eyes was a mystery. Now we know it uses a radar principle, discharging electricity into the water in controlled bursts. It can pick up or receive these impulses from others of its species or from its own broadcasting, by reflection from solid objects. Again we have a principle in natural operation for millions of years, yet man only discovered it during the Second World War.

There are mysteries in the animal kingdom that conceal from man great discoveries he will make in the future. There may be some surprising and desirable dividends for man himself when he learns how crabs can predict hurricanes, lost pets can find their masters across a continent, and horses can solve mathematical problems.

Earlier we told the story of Rolf, the tracking dog that recovered over four hundred thousand dollars worth of lost articles, but there are human trackers, too. Science writer Rutherford Platt tells of a friend who has this ability but cannot say how she does it. If someone has lost a bracelet on a mile of sandy beach, she will find it within minutes. She is a biologist by training, the wife of a physician, and a person of high integrity. She says she must be rested and relaxed in order to demonstrate this talent, and that it works best in a foreign country where she does not understand the language.[5]

Apparently under certain circumstances our well-known five senses can be developed far beyond the normal. This should be equally true of the lesser-known senses. When this happens we have "wild talents"—human trackers or finders, dowsers; human compasses, sensitives, and psychometrists.

The evidence is that some of these senses were faculties developed by primitive man for survival in a hostile world. Today they are atrophied or dormant in most of us. The seat of these senses may be man's inner brain, the thalamus, which he has inherited from his animal ancestors. About the size of the little finger, it is the message center, the receiver of incoming impressions. From the depths of this primitive brain come dreams, visions, and instincts.

As we have noted, the primitives in today's world exhibit some of these visionary, directional, and telepathic senses. Some aborigines possess amazingly developed senses among the basic five. Ron Anderson, of the Copley News Service, in a dispatch from Johannesburg, South Africa, dated October 23, 1966, tells of studies of African bushmen made by scientists from the University of Witwatersrand. For ten years teams of investigators have been studying these little people (the adult men never grow taller than five feet, two inches) who eke out a precarious existence in Bechuanaland, Angola, and Southwest Africa. They are, however, gradually mingling with other tribes and losing their old identity.

In a special study conducted by researcher George Silberbauer it was found that on a clear night the Bechuanaland bushmen could see the four major moons of the planet Jupiter with the naked eye. On quiet days it is commonplace for them to hear a twin-engined aircraft landing forty-five miles

distant. As an example of their phenomenal physical development and endurance, Silberbauer cited one man's thirty-four-
mile run through heavy desert sand in midsummer, in only
five hours.

Some civilized persons are born with extraordinary sight—
like Mrs. Janet Hitchman, thirty-seven, of Newmarket, Suffolk,
England. In 1954 the London Refraction Hospital called her
eyes "among the most remarkable in the world." She could
read a newspaper ten feet away and see the phases of Venus
and the major moons of Jupiter.

Primitive men and wild animals possess phenomenal senses
to aid them in finding food, to be on their guard against preda-
tors, and to make other decisions vital to survival. This acute-
ness disappears as man creates the artificial environment of
civilization and as animals become domesticated. Over the
generations and through natural selection, the brains of domesticated animals have been reduced in size from 10 to 30
percent. "This has been established," writes Carleton S. Coon,
in his book *The Origin of Races,* "in the case of dogs, ferrets,
pigs, ducks and cats. When house cats become feral, larger
brains reappear."[6]

Many wild animals become pathetic neurotics in captivity.
In zoos they are deprived of the environments they require for
normal behavior. They often react to monotony and frustration
with violence; others suffer chronic depressions, sexual ob-
sessions or inhibitions, and emotional ills that cause physical
damage and even death.

To attempt to make intelligence tests of wild creatures after
they are imprisoned and their behavor patterns shattered, their
senses torpid, and their minds sluggish, is ridiculous. Only in
their natural habitat does their natural brilliance shine forth.

It is also a mistake to believe that animals think in the same
manner as civilized man. Says Ralph Helfer, the Hollywood
animal trainer: "People mistakenly rate the intelligence of
animals by their own. There is a wild intelligence in a tiger
that is top rate, but which is different from our thinking."[7]

There are more than a million known kinds of animals in the world and many more still to be discovered. Each one lives in its own special niche, behaves in its own individual style, and thus presents a different problem to those who seek to understand it.

We define intelligence as the capacity to learn. Obviously the general intelligence level of an animal depends on the complexity of its body organization and the relative size and specialization of its brain. The amoeba, having a very limited sense of responses, can learn only simple acts such as turning away from an annoying light. The primates, on the other hand, with their specialized sense organs and complex nervous systems and brains, are at the top of the animal intelligence scale.

Laboratory experimenters seeking to determine animal intelligence use mazes or puzzle boxes, or have their subjects push or peck the right symbol to obtain a food reward. These methods and similar ones are unsatisfactory, and at best may rate only the intelligence level and response time of the individual subject. For not only do the levels between various species vary, but there can be great differences between individuals within each species. There are smart cats and there are stupid cats. This explains why zoologists cannot agree on a specific intelligence scale.

Scientists at Columbia University's Animal Laboratory list the animals behind man as follows: the great apes (with the chimpanzee at the top), monkeys; the carnivores, which include the dog, cat, fox, raccoon, lion, tiger, and bear; the ungulates, or grazing animals, among which are the elephant, horse, pig, cow, deer, and zebra; followed by birds, reptiles, amphibians, and fishes.[8]

Studies at the University of Georgia resulted in a different scale. They place the pig just below the fox and raccoon and ahead of the dog, followed by sheep, birds, rats, rabbits, cats, horses, and guinea pigs. The Georgia report adds that man is probably more to blame for the poor intelligence showings of the dog, cat, and horse than the animals themselves. "It seems that in our desire to care for them by supplying food and shelter, we have at the same time eliminated that threat to their existence which would have kept them more alert," the report concludes. "Domesticated life has dulled their natural curiosity and prowess."[9]

And so it goes. The intelligence of various animals is rated variously in different tests. Doubtless, in the animal domain, tests could be devised to prove that they are more intelligent than we are.

But there is another intelligence, independent of individual intellect—a wisdom of the wild that is as old and strange as life, intuitive and subconscious, what the Indians call "deep-knowing." It is the hidden heart of nature. As naturalist John Burroughs said, the animals know, but they know without knowing that they know.

This is the hypothesis of Carl Gustav Jung's great collective unconscious, a mental reservoir, the depository of all memories, thoughts and knowledge of life past and present, space-less and timeless. Unlike the individual unconscious, the collective unconscious is one and the same everywhere, in all individuals, just as all instincts are the same in all members of the same species. Like trees rooted in the common soil, so individual minds at their deeper levels enter this mental medium and are in rapport with one another.

It is this well of instinctive knowledge that guides animals and birds to the proper herbs to cure their ills. Naturalist Archibald Rutledge tells us that the Indians and our pioneer ancestors learned the rudiments of medicine by observing what plants were sought out by animals suffering from wounds, fever, infections, and other disturbances. A wolf, bitten by a rattler, chews snakeroot; bears eat fern roots that are cathartic in their effect; during rainy spells the wild turkey compels her little ones to eat spicebush leaves.

Bears smear their wounds with spruce or hemlock resin and sometimes clay. A muskrat uses hemlock gum, which does not dissolve in water. Apes, when wounded, will attempt to stanch the flow of blood with their hands, and then will close the wounds with packings of astringent aromatic leaves. A woodcock with a broken leg will apply a splint of clay to the injured member, usually reinforced by fibrous roots.

Instinct causes animals to change their diets when their systems require certain adjustments with the changing seasons. During the mating period female birds need lime to form eggshells, so they fly to places where shellfish are found. Phosphate mining in the South has left great dredge-cuts containing water rich in lime. Buck deer, needing lime for horn growth, will travel miles to drink the water.[10]

Whence comes this instinct, this life-cycle? E. L. Grant-Watson, the British naturalist and biologist, postulates an invisible but objective environment that "may well be called a spiritual world." In it exist those unseen values that find physical expression in our realm.

This theory, which is in opposition to positivist science, is within a traditional stream that flows from Pythagoras into Platonism, the Hermetic and Gnostic philosophers, and medieval religious thought. It is the concept that life forms, or souls, preexist as mental patterns or thought forms, then enter and are embodied in the physical world.

Prof. Adam Sedgwick said life forms are "precipitated" into our realm, adding that we don't "say created in these days; it's not the fashion." The late Dr. Gustaf Stromberg, internationally known astronomer whose book *The Soul of the Universe* was introduced by Albert Einstein, called the life-form patterns "autonomous fields" of "emergent energy." His theory was that they came from a realm or dimension of a nonphysical or quasiphysical nature that lies beyond the measurements of science. These pattern molds form all living things as they are filled in with physical matter.[11]

As science advances, the evidence that there is a source of life energy—an invisible background interpenetrating our world of sensuous phenomena in which there are guiding principles—is increasing. Instead of developing entirely out of the vagaries of chance and the whims of natural or sexual selection, life exhibits an exact, precise mathematical structure where mind meets nature. Grant-Watson draws extensively upon the works of the late George Adams who studied plant morphology in the light of projective geometry. He also quotes a letter he received from Carl Jung discussing the remarkable parallel between numeral forms such as the Fibonacci series of fractions that seemingly govern the phyllotaxis of plants and morphology.

That such complex life cycles as those of the butterfly, the moth, and the dragonfly could develop wholly through natural selection or of their own volition is inconceivable. To make all the complex factors intermesh, the plans for the cycles must have been thought out *before* the insects existed in the physical world. But whose mind, or minds, did the planning?

There is God, the Great Creator, of course. St. Thomas Aquinas defined creatures as lucid ideas in the logos, or mind of God. But traditional theology does not necessarily have the only answer. As another British scholar and anthropologist, T. C. Lethbridge, says in his curious, thought-provoking book, *Ghost and Ghoul,* there is such a thing as delegated authority.[12]

It would appear that evolution is not a haphazard process, but is the result of experimenting, creative intelligences. Many of earth's life forms seem to be the product of minds on a not too much higher level than our own. While some are indeed complex, indicating the designing thought of brilliant, artistic, mathematical minds, others are simple.

Lethbridge writes that there are creatures (like certain vicious parasites, leeches, weasels, borers, mosquitoes, black widows, and sweat bees) that "appear as if the characters who thought them into being were not entirely the attractive personalities one would expect to find in a Christian Heaven. Why should they be? It is quite unnecessary to think of the zoological world as being the direct product of an Almighty Mind. . . . If evolution is going on all the time and forever, some of the great thinkers of 2000 years or more ago should be quite a long way up the ladder by now, and perfectly capable of designing a hermit crab or a caddis fly."

An interesting thought!

But whether his designing intelligences once lived on the physical earth or represent an entirely different order of existence, they may be compared to our own selective breeders of plants and animals—creating variations in living things with the satisfaction experienced by artists, writers, and architects. The intellects that designed the duck-billed platypus and the koala bear must have had a charming sense of humor!

When conditions change, when situations or other creatures threaten a species, perhaps the "intelligences" responsible for it may retool, affect the chromosomes, and bring about variations or mutations. From time to time, as organisms become more complex, they may introduce entirely new creatures, distinctive and complete. Who can say?

But that there is an invisible psychic realm influencing physical life seems quite evident. Of this domain the great psychologist William McDougall wrote: ". . . . a great unknown in which great discoveries await the intrepid explorer, a vast region at whose mysteries we can hardly guess, but which we can look forward to with wonder and awe, and toward which we may go on in a spirit of joyful adventure, confident in the knowledge that, though superstition is old, science is still young and has hardly yet learnt to spread her wings and leave the solid earth of sense perception."

8

Cosmic Cycles
and Bio-Clocks

There are biological clocks ticking away within all living
things, timing the manifestations of external rhythms and
cycles. They respond to forces mundane and cosmic that
come and go, rise and fall, flow and ebb.

They are linked to the daily rotation of the earth, to the
sun's position, to the solar or lunar day, or to lunar tides and
phases. Others react to barometric pressures, to the synodical
month, or to the year with its march of the seasons. They determine the times for changes in metabolism, feeding, mating,
egg-laying, and migrating.

The most fundamental bio-clock produces the approximate
twenty-four-hour "circadian" rhythm (meaning "about a
day"), which varies from twenty-two to twenty-five hours.
In some animals scientists have discovered twenty or more
processes with circadian rhythms. Honeybees will return to a
certain flower or feeding station at about the same time each
day. During the mating season most ducks, woodpeckers, and
song birds lay their eggs at twenty-four-hour intervals until
the clutch is completed.

Fruit flies in captivity, as in nature, lay eggs just after dusk.

Adult flies normally emerge from their pupal cases about dawn, but if the eggs are laid and allowed to develop in continuous darkness in the laboratory, the young flies will emerge at any time of the day. However, if the maggot-larvae hatched from the eggs are subjected to even a single light flash during this period of darkness, the flies will emerge from their cases at the same time of day that they were exposed to the light flash. Apparently, in their natural habitat the clocks of the developing flies are set to local sun time while they are still maggots, and signal the flies for emergence at dawn.

Daily rhythms were first observed in plants. It was assumed that sunflowers, for example, were following the sun around the sky. But it is now known that their movements are independent of light and linked to time alone.

Bio-clocks are set to the movements of the moon and the flow and ebb of tides along the sea shores. The grunion, a small Pacific Coast fish, rides the waves onto the beach on nights from April through June just after the tides are at their monthly highest. They quickly dig holes in the sand into which they deposit their eggs and sperm, then replace the sand. This permits the next generation to develop over the period of a month without being washed out by the surf of the usual high tides.

On the nights of the third lunar quarters in October and November the palolo worms of the Southwest Pacific swarm in large numbers and release their reproductive elements into the sea water just as dawn breaks.

The fiddler crab's shell is darkest during the day for protection against enemies and sunlight, and is pale during the night. When removed from the beach to darkness in the laboratory, the crab's shell continues to darken and pale in response to an internal clock. However, the shell will reach its darkest color about fifty minutes later each day due to a second clock inside the crab, for the tides also occur fifty minutes later from day to day.

Again, crabs hide in burrows at high tide, but at low tide

scuttle out to feed on the marshes and the beach exposed by receding waters. In the laboratory they still become most active on the falling tide fifty minutes later each day, at exactly the same time as their fellows on the distant beach.

In 1955 two biologists in Paris trained bees to feed on sugar water every day at 8:15 P.M. One night immediately after a feeding, the hive was sealed and placed aboard an airliner for a flight across the Atlantic. In New York, scientists at the American Museum of Natural History placed the hive in a laboratory. At exactly 3:15 P.M. Eastern Daylight Saving Time—a precise twenty-four hours after having been fed in Paris—the bees poured out of their hive. In this and similar experiments it was proved that despite the distance and differences in local time, the bees' alarm clocks rang right on their twenty-four hour schedule.[1]

Oysters open their shells at high tide. Dr. Frank Brown, Jr., of Northwestern University, took some oysters from New Haven Harbor, Connecticut, and placed them in pans of salt water in a dark room in Evanston, Illinois. The temperature was kept constant, and the water on an even level.

For two weeks the oysters opened their shells in time with the high tides at New Haven. After fourteen days the rhythm ended. Hours passed by. Then a new rhythm began, and the oysters now opened their shells at the moon's zenith and nadir positions with reference to Evanston, or when it would have been high tide in Evanston if that were a coastal city.

The New Haven rhythm was not simply inherited by the oysters. "Obviously," writes Dr. Brown, "some subtle atmospheric fluctuation related to local lunar time is able to substitute for local ocean tides and reset the periods of maximum activity. The same factor must continuously signal the lunar periods."[2]

Biologist John D. Palmer in the March, 1966 issue of *Natural History* states that his experiments with robins reveal that they can reset their biological clocks in periods as short as three days. The birds have an activity rhythm from sunrise to sunset and sleep during the night. If a laboratory is equipped to subject the robins to darkness during the day and light throughout the night, they will adjust to the reversed periods within a few days, awaking at the time they had previously gone to sleep.

However, the presence of light or the changes between light and darkness are not the causes of the activity rhythm. A caged bird can be placed in an isolated chamber in which a dim light intensity and the temperature are constant day after day, and its periods of activity and rest will continue to be almost identical to birds in natural daylight.

Obviously the rhythmic activities of organisms are not merely responses to changes in temperature, light, or the ocean tides. Without the stimulation of these factors, the bio-clocks of the crab have the ability to measure accurately and simultaneously solar-day and lunar-day intervals. The birds react to the solar day. And this is true of other living things, ranging from flowering plants to mammals, that are removed from natural habitat and placed in artificial constant environments. The bio-clocks tick on.

Nor can the living clocks be explained in terms of known principles of physics and chemistry. From a biochemical view, their behavior is unorthodox. Metabolic processes can be greatly speeded up or slowed down by raising or lowering temperatures, but the timing of the clock periods are generally independent of temperature. Even dried seeds, whether kept in a freezer or a hot incubator, display the same annual rhythm in their capacity to germinate. Again, the accuracy of the clocks is not affected by drugs known to alter the rate or character of the metabolic changes.

Daily changes of both light and temperature, however, are responsible for resetting circadian rhythms to local time. These same twenty-four hour cycles, by measuring the changing lengths of night and day, enable creatures to adapt themselves to natural annual cycles.

Man, too, is an animal, and the same subtle clocks are

ticking away inside him. He has a daily rise and fall of body temperature, blood-cell counts, and hormone secretions. There is a monthly menstrual cycle in females. There are rhythms of optimism and depression, variations of moods. Man's responses to any situation are different in the morning from what they are at night, and different in the spring from what they are in the autumn. Pathologists have found rhythms in certain periodic diseases such as abdominalgia, cyclic neutropenia, and arthralgia.

Our health is related to the smooth operation of our biological clocks. Certain toxic drugs aid mice at one time of day, kill them at another. Chick embryos survive more operations at one time of day than another. Future studies will reveal the best time of day for people to take medicine or to undergo operations.[3]

Dr. Britton Chance, an internationally known biologist, may have discovered the basic oscillation to which bio-clocks are set. At the December, 1966 meeting of the American Association for the Advancement of Science in Washington, D. C., he announced his discovery of a 160-second chemical cycle in cells that was keyed to twenty biochemical reactions involving the production of energy. This was the first time a basic mechanism that could explain biological rhythms was known.

And there is more.

All living things have electrical fields. These force fields in organisms change in strength and polarity in response to internal (biologic) and external (cosmologic) events. Voltage-change cycles have been found to correlate with the lunar phases, with peaks appearing when the moon is full and when it is new. Other cycles among the force field bio-rhythms bring daily voltages to a peak in December and to a low stable valley in midsummer. This could be correlated with the sun, which is closest to the earth in mid-December and farthest away in June.

In addition to the lunar and seasonal rhythms, there are other cycles, diurnal and semimonthly, and fluctuations seemingly connected with changes in the earth's magnetic field. Most of the changes in the earth's field are the result of forces from outer space—cosmic and gamma rays, sunspot radiation and other electromagnetic waves that bombard our planet and our bodies.

Studies at Yale University disclosed that the patterns of voltage changes in trees parallel those of human subjects. Occasionally one chart appears to be the mirror image of the other.

All living organisms exist in the pulsating sea of energies serving as receivers, transformers, and projectors. There is a universal electric field affecting all life, while in turn all life exerts its own influence upon the field. Thus each human being, animal, and plant is related to all other life, to the earth's magnetic field, and through it to the changes in the electrical fields of the moon and sun.

All of us who live are a part of the universal whole, fellow creatures in the cosmos, responding to the ceaseless ebb and flow of the universe, And there are other voices from out of the deep that speak in languages still unknown to man.

Is that why a dog or cat will sometimes display a remarkable sense of time? Mrs. I. M. Dunning, of Cambridge, England, told of an Alsatian named Jock who knew when Sunday came around. That was the day his master would take him for a walk. Only on Sunday afternoons after dinner would he carry his master's cane to the door of the house, drop it, then bark impatiently.

One Sunday the family had a visitor, a shy young man who could not summon up courage to say goodbye. Jock began to worry about his walk. He paced the room restlessly and finally trotted into the entrance hall. Seconds later he came back, ambled over to the shy guest, and to the family's embarrassment presented him with his hat!

Novelist Frances Parkinson Keyes tells us about Zip, a medium-sized pit-bull terrier who belonged to the city treasurer of Baton Rouge, Louisiana. Zip had the run of City

Hall, the back alleys of the business district, and the fun of riding on the hood of his master's car. Then came trouble. There were too many dogs. Irate citizens complained. So the city fathers passed an ordinance restraining dogs and hired a dog-catcher to round up stray canines.

Almost the first act of the dog-catcher was to pick up Zip, knowing that this would embarrass the mayor and the city treasurer. After a miserable night in the pound, Zip was rescued by his master and to prevent further trouble he was taken to a friend's farm some miles out in the country. The farmer chained Zip but fed him well and made him comfortable. The dog accepted his confinement in good spirits until Saturday came. Then he violently sought freedom, pulling at his chain and trying to chew it in two, barking and howling. Again from Sunday to Friday, Zip adjusted to restraint, but Saturday was a day of loud lamentations and desperate struggle.

The city treasurer and the farmer held a conference. They decided that Zip knew when Saturday came, that he remembered his master spent Saturday afternoons driving about, and that he may also have realized that on Sunday he was free to roam old haunts because the dog-catcher wasn't working. So the following Saturday Zip was released. At noon he disappeared and he was still missing Sunday night. Early Monday morning he appeared on the porch barking a greeting.

Zip had proved his responsibility and was given his freedom. He drove cattle and pigs, served as a watchdog and performed other odd jobs all week. But on Saturdays he left for the city till early Monday morning.

"The farmer conferred with the city treasurer," wrote Mrs. Keyes, "and found that Zip had reckoned well, arriving at his master's house around three o'clock on Saturday afternoon, and leaving on Monday morning before daylight. This routine continued unbroken for years, and Zip became a familiar sight as he pounded along the country road in the course of his weekly trip. He never lost his way and he never made a mistake."[4]

Gypsy, a black and white cat, belonged to Madeline Hicks of Washington, D. C. In 1953 he attained local fame because he was not only a living clock, but adjusted his morning alarms to standard or daylight saving time. At least he could do so if his mistress told him of the change, which implies a telepathic rapport.

Miss Hicks discovered that every workday morning Gypsy would jump on her pillow at the right time for her to get up—6:45. To prove that this was not merely because he was hungry, she experimented by changing or even omitting his feeding time. But Gypsy meant 6:45 and stuck to it.

She had already learned that she could quiet his uneasiness when she got out her suitcases for a trip by telling him that he would be safe and she'd be back soon. So as daylight time drew near, she ventured upon a more complicated communication. "Gypsy," she said, "tomorrow the time changes. Wake me one hour later than you did today!"

But she didn't really believe he could understand this. So when he nudged her next day she rolled over sleepily. He can't possibly know, she thought to herself. I've got another hour!

But Gypsy gave her a cuff and walked up and down her body. When she persisted in snoozing, he played his final trump. He jumped to the bedside table and started knocking things off onto the floor. Just in time, Miss Hicks snatched up the clock—and found it was 6:45 by the new reckoning!

Each spring and fall Gypsy never failed, except once when Miss Hicks forgot to tell him the time was changing. Even Gypsy couldn't read a clock dial.[5]

Another alarm clock cat served in 1942 in the Idaho Falls, Idaho, home of the man who was governor at that time, B. W. Clark. It was the governor's wartime obligation to see that the high school students arrived in the potato fields daily, but after a few mornings the alarm clock broke. However, the family cat was equal to the crisis. Promptly at seven each day she scratched on the bedroom window and miaowed loudly, thus doing her bit for the war effort and her master.[6]

Another similarly time-conscious cat seems to have had gambling blood in his veins. Dr. Gustav Eckstein, physiologist at the University of Cincinnati, investigated this cat, and first told about it in his book, *Everyday Miracle*.[7]

Willy was a canny feline, dedicated to a comfortable cat-life. But he had one truly extraordinary habit or recreation from which he never varied. Any night but Monday, he might stroll off and not return for supper till almost any hour. But on Monday he wanted his bowlful promptly at 7:30, and fifteen minutes later would pad purposefully down the walk. At the traffic light he waited—if not for the lights, at least for the sense of protection that moving human feet afforded him.

Once across, he walked several blocks to a hospital, where he leaped to a certain windowsill for his evening's diversion. There he would spend the next two hours watching with quiet fascination the activities of a group of ladies playing bingo in the nurses' dining room,

Dr. Eckstein followed Willy on three successive Monday nights. "That cat knows Monday," he wrote. "That cat knows 7:45. I thought it might be food, but there was no food. Or a congregation of cats, but there were no cats. He was there at that exact time to hear and see women playing bingo." When the game ended around 9:45 he returned home.

Willy's time sense served him in still another way. He condescended to grace the home of two ladies who, unlike himself, had to work for a living. Each morning they left the house together promptly at 8:10. Willy, of course, liked to be indoors for breakfast before they left, so he could bed down for his day's snooze. So after his night on the town—Mondays excepted—it was his habit to make tracks for home at the right moment.

If he had plenty of time to make it before the house was locked for the day, he ambled along musing at life and alert for catnip. But if his wanderings had taken him far afield and it was perhaps nine minutes after 8:00, Willy blue-streaked it along the pavements toward home and catbasket. Willy was no slouch.

"All of us know people who are able to wake exactly when they wish to, within a fraction of a minute," Dr. Eckstein concluded. "Mechanically speaking, the brain sets an indicator somewhere in its fabric of cells eight hours ahead—28,800 seconds—and knows when it has arrived at that point. Willy's brain can do that, too."

There are pets that make seasonal changes. "Room Eight," a cat that died in 1968, was one. He adopted the pupils in room No. 8 at the Elysian Heights Elementary School in Los Angeles, and for years was present every school day. On weekends, holidays, and during summer vacations he disappeared, and no one knew if he had a second home or simply roamed.

And there was the Christmas dog.

In 1930 Herbert Neff, of Knoxville, Tennessee, bought a German shepherd puppy and named the little fellow Gyp—prophetically, it proved—for he turned Gypsy and wandered off after the second baby arrived at the Neffs.

Months passed, then on Christmas Eve there was a familiar whine at the door. Gyp was back. He sat under the Christmas tree enjoying the festivities and, next day, some turkey. Then he was gone again. Thereafter year after year Gyp visited the Neffs at Christmas. No one knew where he was during the rest of the year, or how he knew the day of days was approaching. But somehow he did know, and for ten straight years he never failed to appear, or to depart within twenty-four hours, swollen with turkey and dressing.

After this had happened several years in a row the newspapers began playing it up and hundreds of people across the country took an interest in Gyp. Each Christmas Eve friends and total strangers rang the Neff phone and kept on ringing it. "How's Gyp? Is he home yet?" The dog was a local celebrity, and there were plenty of sleuths on hand who tried to find where he disappeared on the twenty-sixth.

But until 1941 they didn't solve the mystery. In that year a reporter on the *News-Sentinel* tracked him down. The dog had been living with an elderly man, J. R. Jones, only a little over a mile from the Neffs. Mr. Jones had no idea that his was the "Christmas Dog" for Gyp's annual absence during that brief period had not been noticed. Because he loved the dog and depended on him for companionship the Neffs let him keep Gyp.

In 1942 the phone callers asking about Gyp were disappointed. He hadn't arrived. "Why don't you go to see Mr. Jones?" some of them suggested. But Mr. Neff didn't want to do that. He wanted Gyp to come on his own.

That year Gyp didn't follow the pattern. He was getting old and the Neffs thought maybe his scratch on the door had been too feeble to hear. At any rate he showed up late Christmas night at the waterworks in Knoxville, where Mr. Neff was superintendent. The night guards let him in and provided a warm bed, and next day he got his turkey. He was so feeble that Mr. Neff didn't want to let him go till he'd had a good rest. Gyp could stay safely inside the fenced grounds for another day, he thought.

But Gyp didn't agree. He scratched his way under the fence and took off for his adopted master, old Mr. Jones. As the months of 1943 passed, the old dog became increasingly feeble. Autumn followed summer, and in November Jones' grandson, a soldier on leave from his military base, spent Thanksgiving with his grandfather. The Sunday after the holiday Gyp followed the grandson as he walked to the nearby railroad station.

Gyp never came back. Mr. Jones waited, and then mourned his loss. The Neffs, along with other dog lovers throughout the country, still kept hoping that Christmas would bring him home for turkey. But alas, Gyp and his mysterious built-in calendar had vanished forever into no man's land.[8]

There are bio-clocks, innate compasses, and cosmic cycles in the homing instinct and migration of animals. There are also enigmas. Scientists who have succeeded in transporting men to the moon still cannot explain all the mysteries involved in migration and precise destinations.

Solar time determines bird migration. As the days grow shorter the birds become restless and finally depart to follow the sun into lands where daylight hours are the longest. Their routes are aerial rivers that they have traveled since the great glaciers of the ice age melted millenia ago. Year after year, generation after generation, vast flocks and solitary winged migrators have used these ancient skyways. Helpless in the grip of relentless instinct, many birds die during these grueling journeys; others arrive at their destination exhausted and emaciated with wing muscles reduced to taut, thin bands.

"The power which forces the bird to migrate is not produced by the bird itself," wrote Carl Jung, "but derives from its ancestors."

The distances flown are awe-inspiring. Sandpipers, yellow-legs, bobolinks, barn swallows, warblers, and others fly between North and South America. The tiny ruby-throated humming bird wings nonstop five hundred miles across the Gulf of Mexico.

From Labrador and Newfoundland the golden plover of eastern Canada makes the longest continuous bird flight known to naturalists. It flies two thousand four hundred miles over the Atlantic Ocean to the coast of South America. After wintering in Argentina, it returns by an entirely different route, traveling across the Gulf of Mexico to Louisiana and Texas and up the Mississippi valley, reaching its northern nesting place in June.

But it's the Arctic tern that holds the distance record. This amazing bird makes annual excursions between the Arctic and Antarctic regions—a round trip of from twenty-two thousand to twenty-five thousand miles, or equal to the circumference of the earth. It arrives in the Far North about June 15 and leaves August 25, spending fourteen weeks at the nesting site and only twenty weeks for the round trip—an average of around 160 miles in a straight line per day. This estimate does not include the many detours in search of food.

Migratory bio-clocks are precisely set. In the Northern Hemisphere the time when birds arrive and when they depart is exactly the same number of weeks before and after the solstice. The number varies with different species. A golden oriole arrives six weeks before and departs six weeks after the summer solstice. For a bluethroat the period is fourteen weeks. But the pivotal point is always the solstice.

It is this remarkable timing that has brought fame to the swallows of Mission San Juan Capistrano, California, in legend, literature, song, and on national television. The main flock usually arrives on St. Joseph's Day, March 19, from Central America. And the residents of Medina, Ohio, insist that a flock of about seventy turkey buzzards has been arriving at nearby Hinckley Ridge on March 15 since 1810. The Cleveland Metropolitan Park District protects the roosting birds from disturbances by sightseers.

There is still another mystery in the rigid regularity of migratory timing. On a single evening in late November during the Southern Hemisphere spring, tens of millions of shearwaters arrive in roaring clouds on islands off Australia, within a period of fifteen minutes to half an hour. Yet these birds have spent the northern summer all over the North Pacific Ocean at points as far away as Japan, the Bering Straits and British Columbia.[9]

Many species of sea birds assemble at special places year after year to lay their eggs and rear their young. Naturalist Ivan T. Sanderson once witnessed a gathering of tropical boobies on a tiny island in the Caribbean off the tip of Cape Gracias à Dios, Honduras. Winging in from all points of the compass, they came in numerous thousands with raucous cries, landing amid clouds of feathers and fighting one another for space on the ground. All arrived within a two-day period.

"What signal had brought all these multitudes from the far reaches of the Caribbean, and perhaps from the Atlantic beyond, to this paltry, over-crowded little island?" asks Sanderson. "By what sense did they pick up the signal or with what mechanism did they act upon it? It is now the predominant opinion among those who have studied this phenomenon that the stimulus comes from inside the animals themselves and is connected with the seasonal nesting and egg-laying urge. But how they judge their individual distances from the nesting island so accurately that they all arrive there virtually at the same time, though they may start from ten, 100 or even 1000 miles away, is still completely inexplicable to us."[10]

How birds navigate is a mystery, but there are a number of theories. Writing in the October, 1966 *Scientific American* Drs. John T. Emlen and Richard L. Penney tell of their extensive studies of Adélie penguins in Antarctica. These flightless birds travel hundreds of miles over virtually featureless land and water, migrating between their rookeries on the continental coast and the outer fringe of pack ice.

Following their trails for distances up to one thousand two hundred miles, the scientists found that the penguins became confused and moved erratically on days with overcast, but traveled straight courses under clear skies. The birds were using the sun some 93 million miles away as a compass. To do this, however, they had to compensate for the sun's constant movement across the sky. Apparently this could only be done by innate bio-clocks that adjusted direction as the day progressed. Moreover these clocks had to reset themselves, when the birds were taken and released at new locations or degrees of longitude, and at different seasons.

Obviously sun navigation is a complex, enigmatic procedure, and some biologists have suggested that the term bio-computer should be substituted for bio-clock. Efforts to determine the precise nature of time-compensation compasses are currently being made at the Institute for Research into Animal Behavior at the Bronx Zoo in New York.

A number of other animals and insects are guided by sunlight. Recent researchers on honeybees, horseshoe crabs, and ants have revealed that they orient themselves by what is called the polarity of light. Waves of light from the sun travel directly outward in one direction at any given point, but as the earth revolves during the day the angle of this direction changes. These creatures do not have to see the sun to determine the degree of polarity or angle of its light. All they require is a patch of light.

Do song birds navigate by the sun like penguins? Apparently some of them do so at certain times, but research into migrational mechanisms is complicated by the evident fact that birds use other techniques at other times. As Dr. Jean Dorst of the National Museum of Natural History at Paris writes in *The Migrations of Birds:* "It is certain that birds do not use one particular sense, but that orientation involves many different phenomena that are difficult to distinguish."[11]

The late Dr. Gustav Kramer, a German ornithologist, in several experiments including the use of artificial lights, found that captive starlings orient themselves by means of the sun. But many birds fly by night. E. G. P. Sauer of the University of Freiburg, experimenting with caged warblers, discovered that during the migrating season under a starry sky they remained oriented to the migratory direction even when their perches were rotated.

Dr. Sauer next placed his warblers in a planetarium, and again they took up the correct position for a flight to their winter quarters in Africa. And when the dome was rotated so that the stars were in a false position, they made the corresponding mistake.

The whitethroat warbler flies from Germany southeastward across the Balkans, then swings due south over the Nile valley to its winter home in central Africa. Dr. Sauer's special pet, Johnny, didn't know this, for he had been born and spent his life in a cage. When the days grew short and the migrating season came, the doctor placed Johnny in a planetarium showing the German sky. The bird took up the flight position heading southeast. Hours passed, then the dome was rotated to correspond to the flight route, and Johnny gradually changed his position until, when he would have been in the region of the Nile beneath an Egyptian sky, he set his course due south.

"When fall comes," writes Dr. Sauer, "the little garden warbler, weighing barely three-quarters of an ounce, sets off one night on an unbelievable journey. Without being taught, all alone, never in the collective security of a flock, it unerringly wings its solitary way southward to its distant goal in Africa, guided by the map of the stars."[12]

How did Johnny know the way to his distant home? What apparatus in his tiny brain related him in such a complex manner to the lights in the sky, to suns light years away?

Sun or stellar navigation with innate compasses and clocks enable birds to travel in definite directions, but there is a deeper mystery. Neither bird nor man nor any other animal is able to find the way home from a strange place with the aid of a compass alone. Bicoordinate navigation requires in addition the equivalent of a map with which man or animal can determine his precise destination in relation to his present position.

Careful studies have shown that each spring 75 percent of the robins in the United States return to within a five-mile radius of their northern home of the previous year. This precision is almost the same as our Intercontinental Ballistic Missiles, but there are other birds that return year after year to the same trees after two thousand-mile cruises. How does the Alaskan curlew and the western Canadian golden plover fly thousands of miles over a trackless sea and hit Hawaii on the nose? How did a homing pigeon in a record-breaking flight in 1931 wing its way from Arras, France, to its home in Saigon, Vietnam—a distance of seven thousand two hundred miles?

Other migrating animals share this wondrous mystery.

Green turtles navigate accurately over fourteen hundred miles of open ocean, swimming from the coast of Brazil to tiny Ascension Island to lay their eggs. Bucking strong winds and crosscurrents, they hold their course to a target only five miles wide.[13]

Monarch butterflies, with only a single migratory flight in their short lives, gather in untold thousands each year on the same group of pine trees in Pacific Grove, California, on Monterey Bay. Canadian scientists tagged twenty thousand butterflies and 125 were found and returned to Canadian museums. It was discovered that these tiny creatures had flown distances of up to fifteen hundred miles.[14]

Eels migrate at maturity from the rivers and streams of America out into the Atlantic and onward to a great deep south of Bermuda. There they breed and die. The little ones divide into two groups. Those hatched in cold currents go east and reach European shores in about three years; those hatched in warm currents return to the American coast and swim up the rivers until they reach the places from which their parents came. Studies by Dr. Denys W. Tucker, of the British Natural History Museum, indicate that European eels are the progeny of American eels and do not return to the Bermuda deep to breed and die.

As for the bicoordinate navigation of birds and other animals, there are several theories but all have their weaknesses. Whatever the answer, it must allow for the fact that homing pigeons have been taken to distant points while chloroformed or inside covered cages mounted on revolving discs and released on dark nights, but have found their way home promptly. Stripped of their feathers by storms, or with clipped wings, they have even walked home.

The most popular theory is that birds are guided in some manner by an ability to sense the earth's magnetic field. Professor Henry Yeagley, of Pennsylvania State University, reports he has attached magnets to homing pigeons and they have become confused and lost even on familiar routes. He believes two factors are involved: first, the earth's magnetic force, which increases from the equator to the poles, but is the same at any latitude; and second, the coriolis effect or minute shove to the west caused by the spin of the earth.

Learning that the combined pull of the two forces was the same at Kearney, Nebraska, as at the university, the professor says he released his pigeons at a point in Nebraska and they flew to Kearney instead of to their home loft. A number of other scientists, including most recently Drs. Arthur Ogel and James Smith at Florida State University, have reported that magnets have no effect on pigeons.[15]

At a meeting of the American Association for the Advancement of Science at Montreal, Canada, in 1964, Dr. Lester Tarkington of the IBM Systems Research Institute presented his theory. He suggests that pectines in the birds' eyes enable them to sense differences in the gradient of earth's magnetic field. The structure and orientation of the pecten membrane make it an ideal miniature instrument for detecting an induced micro-voltage. If so, when a bird circles after being released in a strange location, it is searching for geomagnetic forces that will generate a pattern of pecten currents that matches a set produced in flight near home. After finding this pattern, the bird flies along the geomagnetic gradient, altering direction where necessary to keep the ratio of currents constant.

Since nearly all birds and some fish have pectines in their eyes, this seems to be a logical theory. But it does not explain how other migratory animals find their way to certain places— like the turtles of the Ascension Island and the butterflies of Pacific Grove—and all the other wonders that in this Space Age are still a mystery to man.[16]

9

Without Compass or Map

Mr. Wilson Rittenhouse, a rural mail carrier of Milford, New Jersey, had a problem. In his prized vegetable garden a turtle was feeding on his tomatoes. He had no wish to share the products of his labor and decided that deportation would be the answer. While on his mail route the following day, he deposited the turtle along the roadside a mile and a half from his home.

Two weeks later the turtle was back, again feasting on tomatoes. Rittenhouse marked the shell and took the animal a mile and a half in another direction. Another two weeks and the gourmet returned the second time. In desperation Rittenhouse placed the turtle in a box, drove across the Delaware River bridge into Pennsylvania, and continued on for five miles—a total distance of about ten miles. That's quite a distance for a turtle, but at the rate of travel he had first exhibited he should have been back in the garden in around fourteen weeks.

Four years passed. One day Mrs. Rittenhouse went into the garden, gave a cry of surprise, and called to her husband. Their marked turtle was home, once more gorging himself on tomatoes.[1]

The directional or homing instinct is by no means limited to migrating creatures, but extends throughout most of the animal kingdom. Young turtles, newly hatched on land, crawl straight to the water. Even the limpet, a snail-like creature without eyes, ears, or other sense organs except tentacles, can find its way back if moved from its home spot.

In *Science,* published by the American Association for the Advancement of Science, biologists Kenneth S. Rawson and Peter H. Hartline of Swarthmore College relate their experiments with mice. By inserting tiny transistor radios under the skin of the animals, they have found that the mice can navigate directly back home from unfamiliar territory with the surety of pigeons.

Pet toads hop home. Teddy, a big one, lived in a garden in Wakefield, Massachusetts. His owner, F. H. Sidney, decided to experiment and Teddy the toad became the "goat." Sidney fastened a tiny identification tag to Teddy's leg, placed him in a box, and took him on a night train to a station about eight miles away. At 10:30 P.M. he released the toad. Shortly after 6 P.M. the next evening, a dusty and weary Teddy came hopping into the garden as Sidney was watering his plants. A rough journey for poor Teddy merely to satisfy human curiosity.

As the sleepers and lovers of an earlier, unhurried age knew, horses can find their way back. Charlie lived on a farm on the English-Welsh border. In the autumn of 1958 he was sold to Mrs. Anne Tomkin, of Dunmow, England. Three months later in midwinter, Charlie became homesick and sniffed the air for a Welsh breeze. As nearly as his course could be plotted, he made it at about twenty miles a day, swimming eight rivers, crossing five major highways and two railway lines to reach his old home.[2]

The story of Pierre's horse appeared on December 1, 1953, in *Le Parisien Librere,* a newspaper with the second largest circulation in France. Pierre Thomas lived in the village of Ymeray and made his living by traveling to carnivals and rural fairs with a mobile rifle range or shooting gallery. He became somewhat of an institution in the Eure-et-Loire Department of France. The heavy wagon was pulled by a horse that loved Pierre, and Pierre loved his faithful horse. But the passage of time is relentless and a man must somehow survive.

The horse grew old and Pierre saw sadly that pulling the heavy range was becoming too great a strain on the beast. He could not afford to put him out to pasture, pay for his keep and for a new horse besides. So reluctantly he sold him to a friend who owned a smaller carnival attraction.

This grieved him, of course, and it was a problem, too, for the old horse knew his route as well as Pierre did and pulled the wagon from one village fair to the next without guidance. No young horse could really supplant him. But one does what is necessary and makes the best of it.

Pierre sold his horse in October. At the end of November, while Pierre was away at a fair, the old horse came back to Ymeray. His stable was closed, but he kicked on the door until neighbors heard him and came to feed and care for him. He must have come a long, long way, over who knows what kind of country. He was covered with dust and bespattered and caked with mud. All four of his shoes were gone, his hooves were cut and very tender.

We don't know what happened to Pierre's horse after this, but we feel that such devotion and endurance were rewarded by a better fate than disposal to a glue factory.

Heavily populated areas and urban traffic are no barriers to homing ducks. Sophia, who belonged to Mr. and Mrs. J. W. Meehan of Los Angeles, California, came to them as a duckling. As she grew older and larger the couple decided she would be happier with some companions in Echo Park Lake. But about a year later she, too, came home. She had to travel some nine miles through midcity congestion to make it.[3]

A similar experience with a duck named George has been reported by John Turnbull, Associate Dean of the College of Liberal Arts at the University of Minnesota in Minneapolis. George lived with the Turnbulls from Easter, 1944, to September. Then the family decided that he would be happier with others of his kind in Como Lake Park, St. Paul. More than a month later he reappeared in the Turnbulls' backyard, tired and dirty after waddling a mile and a half through crowded city streets.[4]

Even hogs can be homers. The *Canadian Journal of Agriculture* once reported the case of a pig that swam a mile across a lake to rejoin its mother. It is commonly believed that if hogs try to swim they will bleed to death from cutting their own throats with the sharp points of their cloven hooves. This is likely only if they are very fat. Lean hogs can swim well. In the days of sailing vessels they were carried on shipboard to serve as emergency compasses. If the ship was lost or in danger, the hog was thrown into the sea. Instinctively it would head for the nearest land.[5]

Jim Kjelgaard, the nature writer, tells of an Indian guide who, with a hunter, was overtaken by a sudden blizzard in the Canadian wilderness. The heavy snowfall and wind reduced visibility to almost zero. There were no landmarks. The Indian turned around three times, then started off through the storm. An hour later the two men were back in their cabin.

Kjelgaard says that many white people who have spent their lives in isolated areas have developed this ability. Once he followed a trapper through a trackless Wisconsin swamp, and they emerged from the swamp within twenty feet of the place where he had said three hours before that he was going to come out. He had no compass, and the sun was obscured by clouds.[6]

A few blind persons are blessed with this sense of orientation. Ernest Elmo Calkins, the deaf author of the autobiography, *Louder, Please!,* offers some examples in an article in the December, 1934 *Atlantic Monthly*. One man, going home for Christmas from the Perkins Institution for the Blind, left the train "in the wee small hours in a snowstorm that had gathered several inches. Alone, he walked to his home, six miles out into the country."

And there was the totally blind fisherman who would row out alone into the waters in the morning and row back to the exact starting point in the evening. This compensation for the sightless is rare, however. Even the late Helen Keller, despite her brilliant mind, was comparatively helpless even in familiar surroundings, and used cords to guide her steps around the grounds of her own home.

Bud, a collie, found his way from Albuquerque, New Mexico, to Fort Scott, Kansas—almost eight hundred miles. The dog had been shipped by rail to Albuquerque in a crate. He returned home eight months later by foot.

From the Indiana-Illinois border to Colorado Springs is about a thousand miles—a long, weary way for any four-paw (or human being either) to trudge home. For Stubby's little mistress, who was crippled and dumb from birth, the day her dog came home was the happiest in her young life.

Thirteen-year-old Della Shaw and Stubby, a mongrel, lived with Della's grandparents, Mr. and Mrs. Harry McKinzie, in Colorado Springs, Colorado. In 1948 McKinzie remained home while his wife and granddaughter, accompanied by Stubby, went to Indianapolis to visit relatives. They stayed four months, then set out for home in a truck containing some furniture. Somewhere between Indianapolis and Decatur, Illinois, Stubby jumped or fell out of the truck.

Such grief is hard for anyone to bear, but for a handicapped child who poured out most of her affection upon a devoted pet, the blow was especially cruel. Della could not speak, but her mute tongue did not make her grief any easier for her grandparents to watch. McKinzie went to the newspaper and to friends to ask for publicity for Della and Stubby. But it did not bring results.

A year and a half went by until a day in late March of 1950, when McKinzie happened to walk by a house where they had lived before the Indiana trip. There was Stubby on the sidewalk, just sitting, staring vacantly into space. His footpads were swollen and bleeding, his body bloated from hunger. Dirty and dazed, he hardly seemed to recognize McKinzie when he called to him.

But when the grandfather took the dog home to Della, love broke through exhaustion, and the dog and his young mistress told each other without words just how they felt about it.

"We know she's happy at last," the grandfather said to reporters. "We can tell by the look she's got on her face. And once Stubby gets all the food and sleep he needs he'll be his old self again."[7]

Schultz, a German shepherd war dog, hoofed it some two thousand miles from Wakarusa, Indiana, to Seattle, Washington, to be with his master. Pfc. Richard B. Anthony said he had shipped the dog to his mother in Wakarusa because Schultz didn't get along with Blackie, the mascot dog at the U.S. Marine Base near Seattle where he was stationed. Anthony had originally bought Schultz from the pound.

Officers at the Marine Corps Recruiting Office identified Schultz and said he had been born into the corps in 1942. He had served with the Marines in China during World War II, and wore an identification tag bearing his picture, serial number and his earlier name of "Sgt. Hardy of the 3rd Marines." Schultz's toenails were worn down when he arrived in Seattle, but otherwise he was in good shape.[8]

Cats, too, are homers. Dogs are supposed to attach themselves to humans, and cats to places. But while some security-seeking cats will give their home prime consideration and accept changing families with unconcern, there are others that possess a doglike devotion to the humans they own. All cat lovers know there is a great variance in cat personalities.

To every dog his master is a Napoleon, hence the popularity of dogs. Cats are independent, unpredictable. Their past has had its grim period. They are still associated with Satan, witches, and medieval torture. Yet in ancient Egypt the cat was sacred, and men were put to death for even accidentally killing one. When a cat died its owner went into mourning and shaved his eyebrows as the pet's body was mummified and ritually entombed.

Through all the changing attitudes of the centuries, the cat, perhaps more than any other animal, has remained supremely and consciously itself. Refusing to ingratiate itself, sometimes aloof, supercilious, and comfort-seeking, it nevertheless loves its human companions. Thus at times certain cats—perhaps more in tune with the ancient cat-god, Bast—care enough to set forth upon formidable adventures and hardships, traveling incredible distances to search for those they love.

Such a cat was Cookie who owned and was owned by Florence Sunderlin. She was shipped 550 miles from Chicago to Wilber, Nebraska, by railway express. Six months later she was back home in Chicago.

And there was Tommy, a feline of dubious heritage, who came back to his Seattle, Washingon, home from Palo Alto, California, a distance of 850 miles. Owner B. F. Sanders said his tom had disappeared while he was visiting in California a year and a half earlier.[9]

The Stacy W. Woods family moved from Gage, Oklahoma, to Anderson, California, taking with them their yellow cat, Sugar. In June, 1951, the family decided to return to Gage, and left the cat behind with a friend. Sugar stayed with the friend about two weeks, then vanished.

Fourteen months later, in August, 1952, Mr. and Mrs. Woods were milking in their barn at Gage when a bedraggled ball of fluff leaped through an open window onto Mrs. Woods' shoulder. It rubbed against her neck ecstatically, joyously purring. Could it be Sugar?

Mr. Woods couldn't believe a cat could hike or hitchhike about fourteen hundred miles. Then he recalled that Sugar had a peculiarly deformed hipbone from a broken right rear leg in kittenhood. He ran his hand over the cat's flank and felt the deformity. It was Sugar![10]

Collies seem to be unusually sensitive to the homing instinct and its mysterious guidance, perhaps because they originated in the Scotch Highlands, a land of mist whose people often have "the sight." There, centuries ago, the dogs were named after the black-faced "colley" sheep they protected.

The most famous collie of his day and one of the most remarkable dogs of all time, was Bobbie, who made his way alone and afoot from Indiana to Oregon. His only goal was to rejoin his master and on his epic journey full of painful hardships he steadfastly resisted the temptation of comfortable new homes.

A large dog, tawny and white in color, Bobbie was easily identified—he had been born with a bobbed tail. His father had been half English sheepdog, a tailless breed used for centuries to pasture flocks alone and drive off the wolves of an earlier Britain. In addition he had distinctive markings—scars resulting from injuries and three missing teeth.

These distinctions enabled Colonel E. Hofer, president of the Oregon Humane Society, to launch an investigation and give wide publicity to Bobbie's amazing feat. Hundreds of letters were received by the society from persons who had seen or befriended the dog on his long trip west. The reports were analyzed and checked; questionable ones were eliminated. From these accounts, additional inquiries to local humane societies, and personal interviews, Charles Alexander was able to tell the tale of Bobbie's long journey in his book, *Bobbie: A Great Collie of Oregon*.[11]

Frank Brazier, owner of a restaurant in Silverton, Oregon, was the dog's master. On August 6, 1923, Mr. and Mrs. Brazier waved farewell to their friends and drove out of Silverton to begin the long, hot trip to Indiana to visit relatives. In those days of hand-cranked cars, unpredictable tires, rough roads, and springs that bounced like the flickering figures of an old nickelodeon movie, crossing the continent was a formidable undertaking. But to Bobbie, who rode in the back seat on top of the luggage, it was high adventure.

Finally they reached Wolcott, Indiana, where they would stay the night with relatives, to leave the next morning for their final goal, Bluffton, a hundred miles farther east. Mr. Brazier left his wife at the house and drove to a garage for a carburetor adjustment. Bobbie went along, riding on the running board as he often did on short trips. As the car stopped in front of the garage, the dog leaped to the sidewalk, slipped on the pavement and fell against an eighty-pound bull terrier.

Brazier drove on into the garage, confident that Bobbie could handle his challenger, but he didn't know that the bull was a canine gang leader. As a chorus of barking rose in volume, he walked to the garage doors and caught a glimpse of Bobbie disappearing around the corner with the huge terrier and a rabble of snarling companions in hot pursuit. He gave chase but by the time he reached the corner all the dogs had vanished.

When the work on his car had been completed, Brazier drove all around the town. There was no sign of the collie and his tormentors. Dusk came. Despite his weariness from the trip, he couldn't sleep. All through the night he drove slowly over the town's streets and along the country roads, sounding the horn for Bobbie. The big dog would always come bounding into the car at the signal. But not this time.

Next day the weekly paper held up its press time to insert an ad offering a reward for the dog. The Braziers waited. Finally they drove on to Bluffton, hoping Bobbie would be turned in to their relatives in Wolcott. But when they returned days later, they were saddened to learn that nobody had found a big collie thousands of miles from his home. Heartbroken, all they could do was start westward for Oregon.

Bobbie was lost. The pack had chased him too far out into the country for him to know, after so much tumult, where they had started from. Apparently he remembered that it had been a garage, and from now on he stalked garages, sniffing every car, then going on. He was hungry, desperate, and quarrelsome from fright. Free of the harassing pack, he was eager to return to his master—but where was he?

There was no scent—only the open sky, fields, and strange roads stretching in all directions. He had nothing to help him but a certain instinct for good people. After days of starvation and running, always running, he would sniff out some home where dog lovers lived. And there he would pause, sometimes only overnight, sleep off his exhaustion, then go on courageously.

Traveling in the wrong direction, Bobbie came at last not to Wolcott, but to Wolcottville, a village in northeastern Indiana. Here he stayed for a week as a welcome guest in the home of a hardware clerk, resting, recovering his strength. When he left, he again went in the wrong direction, a hundred miles to the south, where he swam across the White River near Indiapolis and joined a group of friendly tramps in their hobo jungle camp. One of the tramps he was to recognize at the end of a journey that took them both west.

After two days of dining on mulligan stew and crackers, he headed northwest. He swam across the Wabash River (after being thrown off a toll bridge by a watchman) and later the Tippecanoe River. Here a friendly woman living in a vacation cottage took him in. He accepted food and water, but he wouldn't stay. Utterly confused, he must have traveled in a circle in this northwestern Indiana region, because five days later he was back at the river cottage.

"You're lost," the woman told him. "You can't find your master. Why don't you stay with me? I'll love you. What's your name? Laddie—Shep—Jack—Bobbie?"

Bobbie raised his head and gave a short bark.

"Now I know your name," the woman continued. "Why not stay with me? I'll treat you like a king!"

The collie thanked her with his eyes, rested his weary head on her lap and spent the night in a bed she made for him. But when morning came, he trotted out the door and along the path by the river bank.

"Bobbie!" the woman shouted. "Come back!"

The dog stopped and looked back. In his eyes she read wistfulness, but she sensed the purpose, the determination, that drove him. Bobbie continued up the path. She didn't call again.

Now something happened. Deep within him came a stirring, an awakening of sleeping instinct. Perhaps it was a legacy from his sheepdog father, a long-dormant talent that had guided his remote ancestors through the forests and glens of ancient Briton. Or perhaps it was an affinity created by love between dog and master. But somehow Bobbie knew that he must go west, that home would lie at the end of the westbound trail.

Putting behind him past hesitations, he crossed northern Illinois and entered Iowa. In the town of Vinton he had a crushing disappointment. The horn of a parked car sounded exactly like the one on his master's automobile. He leaped inside among startled passengers to find they were strangers.

But they were kind strangers. The driver of the car, F. E. Patton, secretary of the Vinton Gas Company, took Bobbie to his home, fed him, and kept him overnight. After breakfast the man knelt in front of the dog, placed his hands on his head, and told him he was welcome. Bobbie licked Patton's hand in appreciation, went to the door and whined, and then he was gone.

Thanksgiving Day found the collie in Des Moines, cold and thin and hungry. Again his ability to locate dog lovers led him to a friendly family and a temporary home for several weeks. Once he disappeared for days. When he returned, the handsome collar given to him by his master had been replaced by a flimsy leather strap from which a bit of rope was dangling. Someone had tried to keep him prisoner and he had escaped. Just before he left Des Moines he narrowly escaped capture by a dogcatcher.

Westward across Iowa and Nebraska, and Bobbie was on the Great Plains, under the big sky and with the horizon so far, far ahead. There was a light snow on the ground and a cold wind ruffled his fur. At no time did he retrace the route by which he had come east, nor trail his master's return trip home, which led south into Mexico. Most of the time Bobbie lived on rabbits and squirrels that he caught or that had been recently killed along the highways.

When he reached the Missouri River bridge, a group of guards chased him back. One fired a shot at him. The collie didn't understand why they would not let him on the bridge, but he knew that he had to cross that river. He broke away from a guard who had seized him, leaped over the rail and into the water among floating cakes of ice. He fought his way through the turgid flood to the Nebraska shore, where he crawled out of the water shivering and exhausted.

Bobbie was next reported in Denver, where he appeared at the Carrie Abbee home, hungry, his feet sore and his muscles stiff. Here he stayed until his strength and health returned. And this was good! For ahead of him was the most dangerous, agonizing part of his long journey—the ice-armored Rockies and snow-banked valleys in the dead of winter.

Bobbie's exact course and his adventures between Denver and the Columbia River in Oregon are unknown. It took him two months to cross the vast, desolate, blizzard-plagued stretch. He burrowed under the snow to escape freezing and killed his own meat.

There can be little doubt that he went north from Denver, thus missing the high Colorado Rockies where he probably would have perished. Reaching Wyoming he would have turned northeast and crossed this great wilderness—a vast, forlorn country for a lost, heartsick dog. In southern Idaho with its numerous icy rivers to conquer, Bobbie probably passed south of the Lost River Range and the Sawtooth Mountains, then again northwest along Interstate Highway 80 North.

Earlier in the midwest and back on the Great Plains, he had been a strong dog, trotting tirelessly after his periods of rest. Now he was gaunt and exhausted, his feet bruised and throbbing with pain. In eastern Oregon the frigid Blue Mountains were to the west, but Bobbie's strange homing instinct led him north to the Columbia River.

A family in the Dalles (Dalles County) reported that they had fed Bobbie or a collie that certainly looked like him. And probably it was Bobbie since he came into Portland from the north. The only point at which the dog could have crossed the Cascade Mountains in a thousand miles north and south would have been along the gorge of the Columbia River.

It was February. As the weary collie plodded into Portland the earth was frozen and a bitter wind whipped the light snow. His feet were bleeding, his body emaciated under matted fur. At East Portland he found the last of the friends who were to help him, a white-haired Irish widow, Mary Elizabeth Smith. She cried over the poor suffering dog, coaxed him into her kitchen beside the wood range, where he collapsed after a pan of water, too tired to eat the food she offered. For many hours he lay in a stupor.

As he slept Mrs. Smith worked over him. She soaked his feet in disinfectant. The pads of his toes were worn away, oozing blood, with the bones exposed in places. His legs were swollen into thick, shapeless columns. She cried over his mangled paws, and finally she got the idea of coating them thick with warm paraffin wax. Anything else he could have licked off.

She left him sleeping by the stove as she visited a neighbor, telling about the poor waif she had taken in. When she came back he woke and took more water, but he ate very little. He seemed beyond hunger.

"After a bit he came to where I was sitting," Mrs. Smith said later. "He tried to raise one forefoot, then the other to my lap. But he was just too weak and it must have hurt his sore muscles. He was trying to thank me, I guess. Then he laid his head on my lap and I petted him. Finally he got up and stood by the door, his nose against the crack."

Mrs. Smith opened the door and watched in pity as he limped down the frozen path, through the open gate, and turned south. A chill wind was blowing in from the west. Dusk had fallen. Bobbie disappeared into the growing darkness.

He had seventy more miles to go. Near collapse, it took him two weeks to reach Silverton, but soon he was in the Willamette Valley where the chinook winds were warm and moist. Now he was so tortured by pain, so hungry, so utterly weary, that he couldn't think.

Seemingly he had forgotten the restaurant in Silverton, and his dazed mind returned to puppyhood. He crept through the town, probably past the restaurant above which the Braziers now made their home, out to their old farmhouse, where the fox terrier playmate of Bobbie's own puppyhood had died. But strangers were at the farm now. They found Bobbie lying on the little dog's grave, and although they did not know him, they fed the weak, famished dog, and left water and more food beside him.

Rest, food, and familiar surroundings restored his memory. At dawn he hurried back to Silverton as fast as his pain-racked legs would permit. When he reached the café he had left six months before, he hobbled through the open door and past the tables into the kitchen. Mrs. Brazier and her daughter had time only to give cries of amazement as the collie went past them and up to the stairs to the living quarters. There Frank Brazier had just fallen asleep after working the night shift.

Exhausted though he was, Bobbie made the long leap from the doorway onto the bed, landing in a heap on the sleeping man. With a shock Brazier awakened to find the dog he loved licking his face between great howls of joy. The dog's cries were so loud that people gathered in the street below.

Quickly the news of the homing spread. Bobbie had finally reached home and his master!

Nothing could coax the dog out of the room that day. He ignored food and other members of the family. "He would do nothing but lie on his master," wrote Charles Alexander. "Now and then he broke out crying loudly again. And he was not the only one who wept."

The collie had traveled at least 3,000 miles, in midwinter, across prairies and plains, over rivers and ranges of mountains. Now for three days after his return he lay on his back with his paws in the air because they were too tender to rest on the floor. The nature of his recent diet was evident when he refused all but raw meat for weeks.

Bobbie had been remembered by his benefactors because of a prominent scar over his right eye where a horse had kicked him, hips that didn't quite match after a tractor mishap, and his missing three front teeth, torn out by the roots while digging for a ground squirrel. His original collar and the substituted strap with its dangling bit of rope, acquired in Des Moines, had been additional identifications.

Nor did Bobbie forget those who had helped him. In 1924 he was being taken for a walk near Salem, Oregon, when he and his master came upon two tramps sitting beside a fire. The dog threw himself upon one of the men, licking his hand and crying. The hobo said that in September, 1923, this dog had stayed at his jungle camp enjoying mulligan for several days after swimming the White River near Indianapolis.

Later, in Portland, Oregon, while the collie was being exhibited by a realty board, he broke free and rushed up to a woman, barking and crying in recognition. It was Mrs. Mary Elizabeth Smith, who put her arms around his neck and wept. Bobbie had not forgotten.

Honors poured in upon Bobbie. Medals and gifts came from as far away as Australia. He was given a gold collar, and keys to the cities of Portland, Seattle, and Vancouver. Letters arrived by the hundreds from all over the world.

Bobbie didn't understand nor care for all this attention. He only knew he was home and with Frank Brazier, his master. Amazingly after that incredible ordeal, he lived for twelve more years, and they were happy ones spent with those he loved.

10

ESP: The Gift We Share

In the autumn of 1924 the late inventor, Grindell-Matthews, was given a black kitten about six months old. From the first she was very devoted to him. One night while she was playing on the roof garden outside his Hanover Square home in London, she fell eight feet down onto a paved area. One of her teeth was knocked out and her back seemed to be broken.

The veterinary surgeon said the only thing to do was to put her to sleep. But as Grindell-Matthews held her, she crawled up on his shoulder as if imploring him to keep her with him. She was not in pain since the lower part of her body was paralyzed, so the inventor asked the surgeon to make an X-ray examination.

The plates disclosed a definite fracture of the spine. Although it would take much time and the cat might never walk again, Grindell-Matthews decided to leave the kitten for treatment. Two weeks later when he visited her she was so glad to see him that he took her back home, although it meant he had to feed her every two hours on a special diet for a month.

In time the cat began to play again, dragging her hindquarters over the carpet and occasionally walking a few paces on all four legs. And all the time she displayed a devoted affection, never leaving him while he was at home, and sleeping at the foot of his bed.

About a year after her injury, Grindell-Matthews had to go on business to New York, and the cat was left in care of his housekeeper. He had been in the United States for three weeks when one morning he awakened from a nightmare in a bath of perspiration. In his vivid dream he had seen his cat struggling in the hands of a white-clad man with a goatee beard. The bedroom was reeking with chloroform. As soon as his secretary appeared he had him send a cable to London asking if the cat were well. But no reply was received.

Grindell-Matthews made arrangements to leave as soon as possible and ten days later arrived in London. During those ten days he could not get away from the smell of chloroform, although no one else could detect it.

On his arrival home the housekeeper told him she had had the cat put to sleep because it was starving to death. It had refused to touch food after he left, and the sight of the cat dragging itself feebly about had been too much for her. She had been afraid to reply to his cable.

When the date and hour of the cat's death were checked, they tallied with the time of his nightmare across the Atlantic. Moreover, the veterinarian who performed the task, a stranger to the inventor, had a goatee beard.[1]

Not all telepathic dreams are so clear and direct. In an account given to Renee Haynes, author of *The Hidden Springs*,[2] Osbert W. Hewitt of Headington, England, said that during the late 1930s he had a cat named Mitzi. One evening while visiting friends in London the conversation turned into a heated discussion of the Spanish Civil War that sent him to bed late, weary of war and politics.

Then came a nightmare in which Mitzi appeared crying with pain, with blood flowing from a badly mangled ear. The cat was attired in the uniform of a Spanish Volunteer and sobbing like a person. "Kill me, kill me! I can't stand it!" she wept. Not at all surprised in his nightmare that she could talk, Hewitt tried to comfort her and promised to take her to a doctor. But her continued cries became so violent that he awakened in a cold sweat.

It was 4 A.M. and Hewitt was too shaken to go back to sleep. At breakfast he had just finished telling his friends about his extraordinary dream when the telephone rang.

His housekeeper was calling from Headington to ask if he could return home early, as Mitzi had been badly hurt, apparently by some other animal. Around 4 A.M. she had entered the house through Hewitt's bedroom window and had awakened the household with her cries. They had found her lying on his pillow with her ear nearly torn away, and other injuries. Hewitt returned home, taking a veterinary doctor with him, and Mitzi recovered.

When Freda Aston, of Tulsa, Oklahoma, was a young girl her family had an English mastiff named Fife. The dog was fifteen years old when he was badly mauled in a fight. His wounds were treated and he seemed to be recovering but one morning he could not be found. Since it was summer they feared Fife might be lying parched and helpless somewhere under the hot sun.

Then Miss Aston's mother had a dream. In it she had a vision of Fife standing proudly, his body glossy and muscular as it had been in his prime. He stood on a knoll, happily wagging his stump of a tail. When he looked down at his feet, her eyes followed his. Beneath him on the ground lay the old battle-scarred Fife stretched out in death.

The next morning her mother took Freda by the hand. "Come, we are going to find Fife!" As she told the child about her dream they walked to a place resembling the scene of her vision, a group of hillocks almost a mile from their home. "This looks like the place," her mother said.

"Sure enough, it was," Miss Aston wrote. "There lay the old body that had housed Fife's brave, loyal heart for so many years, just as she had seen it in her dream."[3]

A classic case of dreaming about the death of a pet is that of Sir Rider Haggard, famous British novelist, whose still-popular thrillers, *She* and *King Solomon's Mines,* appeared in Queen Victoria's day. His report and affidavit originally appeared in the *Proceedings* of the (British) Society for Psychical Research, October, 1904.

About 12:30 A.M. on July 10, 1904, Haggard cried out in his sleep, then began gasping and struggling. His wife awakened him, and he related his nightmare, which had begun with a sense of depression, followed by a struggle for life as if he were drowning.

Then the dream became more vivid and he seemed to be trapped inside the body of his dog, a black retriever named Bob: "I saw good old Bob lying on his side among brushwood by water," he said. "My own personality seemed to be arising in some mysterious manner from the body of the dog, who lifted up his head at an unnatural angle against my face. Bob was trying to speak to me, and not being able to make himself understood by sounds, transmitted to my mind in an undefined fashion the knowledge that he was dying." Haggard also told his wife that he had received a detailed picture of a marshy area near a weir.

That afternoon Bob was reported missing. Four days later Sir Rider and his groom found the dog's body about a mile from the house, floating in the Waverly River and lodged against a weir. Wounds on the body disclosed that Bob had been badly injured. The veterinarian said the skull had been fractured and the two front legs broken. He added that the body had been in the water over three days, probably since the night of July 9.

Two railroad section hands then told Haggard they believed the dog had been struck by a train. They took him to the trestle-bridge over the river and showed him the dried blood and part of a dog's collar that they had found on Monday, July 11, when they started their week's work. Later that day they had observed the dog's body floating below the bridge, from which it could easily have drifted on to the weir.

But if Bob had been struck by a train that crossed the bridge at 7 A.M. that Monday, the blood would still have been fresh. There were no trains operating on Sunday, and Midland Railroad officials said no regularly scheduled trains crossed the bridge at around the time of Haggard's dream. However, a special train of empty freight cars had been made up at Harlesdon, which should have reached the main line by midnight. But because its headlight had gone out, the train had been proceeding very cautiously and actually arrived at 2 A.M.

Thus delayed, the train would have crossed the river bridge at about the time of Sir Rider's dream. Without a warning light, it would have struck the dog in the darkness, hurling him into brushwood at the water's edge. From this point he could have fallen into the stream.

Nor are these occurrences limited to birds, dogs, and cats. The Reverend Charlie W. Shedd, D.D., pastor of the Memorial Drive Presbyterian Church in Houston, Texas, reports the case of one of his parishioners. The young woman said she was awakened about two in the morning by a horse neighing—an impossibility in a busy city environment. But riding was her hobby and she and her two horses, pastured about five miles away, "were like being in tune together."

She tried to go back to sleep but wakened again to the same sound. It came back as she sat up—this time loud and clear— and with it the urge to go to the pasture.

"How silly can you get?" she asked herself. "Are you losing your mind? It's two o'clock in the morning!"

But the compulsion was so strong that she got dressed and drove down the freeway. "When I got there, would you believe it? There, in the glow of my flashlight, I found my palomino mare standing in broken wire neighing her lungs out."

The mare stood still while her mistress untangled the barbed wire fencing and set her free with nothing more than some minor scratches.

" 'What do you think happened?' the palomino's owner asked Reverend Shedd. 'I couldn't possibly have heard with my ears through the sounds of the night, the hum of the freeway, the noise of a big city like this!' "[4]

In all of these cases the apparent telepathic or psychic impulse was begun by the animals themselves, not by their masters. Their cries for assistance or of desperation crossed the gulf that usually separates man from the other animals. But impulses can bridge this gulf from people to animals just as readily.

Marcella, a Llewellyn setter, knew when her master died. His widow told the story to Archibald Rutledge, the naturalist. "My husband was away on a routine trip, and Marcella slept on the floor in my bedroom," she said. "I was awakened at midnight by her growling. When I turned on the light, she was at the door, her hair bristling. Her voice was deep and hoarse and strange . . . She acted as if she actually saw something that filled her with dread, yet at the same time she gave the impression that it was something she saw and I did not."

The woman slipped on her dressing gown as the dog first howled mournfully and then ran to the closet, cowering and whimpering. Since Marcella was a hunting dog and usually very brave, her behavior was both startling and frightening. Within half an hour a long-distance telephone call brought the sad news that Marcella's master had been killed in a highway accident. "In some way, I don't know how," the widow concluded, "I believe Marcella saw it all."[5]

Bobby Sox, so named because she was a smoky gray cat with white feet, lived in Madison, Georgia. Mrs. Gladys Carter said her sister Harriet had taken in the abandoned kitten one cold, damp day. Bobby Sox enjoyed squirrel-chasing, but her favorite sport of all was riding on the back of their collie. When the dog would finally shake her off, she would curl up beside him and purr her thanks.

About two years after Bobby Sox was adopted into the family, Harriet became seriously ill and was taken to Emory University Hospital in Atlanta where she died several days later.

The family returned from the hospital the day of her death to find the cat on the porch, crying pitifully. When the door was opened she ran into the living room, hesitated, then gave an anguished wail. Wandering from room to room she stopped at intervals to utter grief-stricken cries. When she came to Harriet's room she walked around the bed several times, then jumped up on the pillow and patted it gently with her paw.

"No one present that night doubted that Bobby Sox knew Harriet never would return," wrote Mrs. Carter. "But how did she know?"[6]

As we will see later, some higher animals do have a comprehension of death, but such concepts must vary in nature and depth. Apparently Bobby Sox was intelligent enough to understand that she had lost her mistress, and her reaction was grief. In the following case the reaction appears to have been one of bewilderment and fright.

Richard H. Lee, of Prescott, Arizona, had a beloved big black tom. One evening while in Phoenix he was killed in a traffic accident. His wife, who had remained at home, learned of the tragedy around midnight. The next morning she found the cat greatly excited. He refused to enter the house and would not permit Mrs. Lee to approach him.

"When I took some food out to him," she wrote in the *Arizona Republic,* "he climbed the stone wall back of the house in a perfect panic." Thereafter the cat stayed in the neighborhood, but he never came close to the house. Occasionally Mrs. Lee would see him on top of the stone wall, watching, but if she entered the yard he would run away.

Jhan and June Robbins, in an article in *This Week*

magazine in 1960, told the story of a canine mascot named Flak who belonged to a six-man bomber crew stationed near Tunis in North Africa, during World War II. Flak remained snobbishly aloof from other airmen at the base, but always he appeared on the field just before his masters' plane returned from its missions. The varied arrival times of the bomber were supposed to be beyond canine comprehension, but somehow Flak always knew.

One noon while his crew was out on a mission, Flak suddenly began howling loudly and sorrowfully. No one could comfort him. And when the bombers returned from their mission, Flak for the first time failed to trot out to the flight line to meet them. He knew that the plane bearing his six masters had been shot down just before noon over Italy, and he had howled his requiem.

Danton Walker, the late Broadway columnist, supplies the sad account of a Great Dane named Rajah, who knew when the girl he adored died. The dog belonged to Mr. and Mrs. Donald S. Rockwell. Rockwell was manager of Columbia Pictures of Panama, Inc., and at that time he and his wife were living in Westchester County. Rockwell's sister, Ruth, had been living with them since her graduation several months before. She was a moody girl whose constant preoccupation with death worried the Rockwells.

On Armistice Day, 1930, Rockwell went to his New York City office to work for a few hours. Ruth also left the house, saying she might not be back in the afternoon. Mrs. Rockwell was left alone. About three o'clock that afternoon she was in the living room when Rajah suddenly ran upstairs, but immediately returned with a pillow in his mouth that he dropped at her feet. Twice more he raced upstairs, first bringing down Ruth's coat and then one of her hats. He then lay down on the floor resting his head on these objects and sobbed as convulsively as a child. Bewildered by the dog's actions, Mrs. Rockwell tried to comfort him but unsuccessfully. Finally she returned the coat and hat to Ruth's room and replaced the pillow on the daybed on which she slept.

Half an hour later the telephone rang. It was the police. They told her Ruth had gone up in a small sightseeing airplane and had leaped overboard to her death above Valley Stream, Long Island, shortly before three o'clock. The suicide received widespread coverage since Ruth Rockwell was the first woman to take her life in this manner.[7]

These are what parapsychologists call "crisis cases"—telepathic communication at times of danger, injury, or death. Because of the circumstances, they are remembered and recorded. On a subconscious level, however, there may be an ESP rapport between men and men, and at times between owners and pets, that is much more frequent.

When K. G. Dee was a boy his father gave him a liver-and-white registered pointer named Duke. Duke liked to be busy so when his young master went to school, he formed the habit of trotting to a nearby store where he made friends with a deliveryman named Fred. Deliveries were made in a horse-drawn panel truck, and it was Duke's delight to ride with Fred on his rounds. Whenever the driver stopped to leave a package, Duke would remain on the front seat and hold the horse's reins in his mouth. Then when school was out in the afternoon, Duke abandoned these interesting duties and hightailed it for home.

He had been doing this about a year when Fred went to see Mr. Dee, Senior. "That dog of yours is so smart he gives me the creeps," he said. "Why, he understands every word I tell him!"

Though flattered, Mr. Dee was a bit surprised and skeptical. But Fred went on to explain that whenever he took a day off he would tell Duke that he wasn't making the run the next day and not to come to the store. And Duke, too, would take that day off. Then when Fred's vacation was to begin, he told Duke about that, too, and more or less as a joke, wound up with, "So don't show up till a week from Monday!"

"And darned if he didn't do just like I told him," Fred told Mr. Dee. "Jim Hughes who took my place says he never showed up in the alley all week. But he was there waiting for me when I loaded up Monday morning!"

Another odd reaction that Duke apparently plucked out of the ethers took place later when the elder Mr. Dee ran against a local butcher for a city office. At that time young Dee had a paper route, with the butcher as one of his customers. Until the campaign, Duke had gone with him into the meat market for a handout, but from then on he refused to enter the premises and stood outside growling when his master took the paper in.

This was all the more surprising since there had been no contact between the butcher and the Dee family, as they did not trade there or know the man except by sight. The butcher won the election—but though he and Mr. Dee met and discussed the dog's odd behavior, Duke himself would never again enter that market for a bone![8]

We cannot know how much pets understand, but "explaining things" to the more intelligent disturbed animals does sometimes calm them. It is not the words, of course, that they understand but in some way they do seem to receive and assimilate our thoughts.

We once had a cat that became uneasy if we began packing for a trip, but she would quiet down when we told her she would be cared for and we would soon return. Another cat belonging to friends was deeply devoted to the man of the house. After he died the cat wandered listlessly for days, crying and ignoring her food.

"Finally," the widow told us, "I took the cat in my arms, looked in her eyes, and told her that Henry was not coming back and that she would have to stop grieving. When I explained that we both would have to adjust to our loss, she calmed down and has been living a normal cat life ever since."

Psychic literature abounds with accounts of ESP between man and pet, both experimental and spontaneous. It is quite possible that telepathic "impulses" or "images" are continually being received by everyone. Because they are so diverse and frequent, they usually go unobserved.

This theory was suggested by the British parapsychologist H. H. Price in an address before the Society for Psychical Research in London. Dr. Price, who is a Fellow of the British Academy and professor of logic at Oxford University, said "the reason most of us appear to receive no telepathic impressions is that we may receive too many, so that no one of them makes any distinct or individual mark upon our minds.

"I will appeal to a frankly materialistic analogy, drawn from the more familiar world of the detective story," he continued. "When a certain object, say the poker, has been handled by a great number of people, it will be useless to look for thumbprints on it: not because there are none, but because there are too many, and they are all blended together into an undifferentiable mess."[9]

There are individuals, however, who are able to identify chains of telepathic perception consciously. Most often this happens between identical twins, devoted husbands and wives, or with other close ties. It usually exists between humans and animals among primitive peoples and children.

Writer Morton Thompson had a brother who "talked" to horses. Lewis Thompson learned of his own strange talent when he was sent to a private school near San Diego, California, that purchased horses from a nearby Indian tribe. At that time the ten-year-old boy could go out on the range with only a rope and ride an unbroken horse bareback to the school corral. Thereafter he lived among horses, ate with them, and dreamed their dreams.

When he was taken to Caliente, Santa Anita, and other tracks, Lewie would look over the horses as they passed by him and name the winners. Some of the horses looked right back at him, craned their necks, or made noises at him. "They tell me and I hear what they say in my head," he would explain simply. "They tell me how they feel, what they think of the jockey, the track, the other horses."

Since he claimed to have only the opinions of the horses as to which would win a race, he was occasionally wrong. Once a horse he named came in second and the angry boy said the jockey pulled the horse! Lewie didn't care about betting. He just wanted to watch the horses and be near them. He said the two-year-olds were too young to know what they were talking about and were unreliable. They all talked big and they all said they would be the winners! Sometimes he couldn't name a winner because "the horses don't know themselves."

Once he told Jock Whitney that a horse Whitney formerly owned would win in a race. The odds were 22 to 1. Whitney laughed and chose another runner. Lewie said Whitney's choice was lame. Whitney looked the horse over, turned to Lewie, and said: "That horse is sounder than you, my boy!" But the horse Whitney chose fell back in the third furlong and came in limping. The 22-to-1 shot won.

When Lewie reached the age of sixteen he lost his ability. Now and then he tried to regain it, but he always failed and finally he gave it up. But he still loved horses and could calm angry, kicking ones by patting them and looking them in the eye. This affinity with his hoofed friends continued until, as Air Cadet Lewis M. Thompson, he was killed during World War II.[10]

Among certain contemporary primitive peoples, some forms of animal magic inherited from earlier eras still exist. Of these, perhaps the strangest is the calling, the summoning, of the porpoises in the Gilbert Islands. But it is magic of a haunting, astonishing, and tragic kind. Here men with a strangely godlike telepathic power summon the sea's most intelligent dwellers to them with brotherly promises, then turn traitor, allowing their guests at a feast to become its main dish.

Few white men have ever been permitted to witness the

calling of the porpoises. One was Sir Arthur Grimble, knighted in 1938, who tells the story in much greater detail in his book, *We Chose the Islands*.[11]

Sir Arthur was in the British Colonial Service during World War I and finally was made Resident Commissioner of all the Gilbert and Ellice Islands. When he retired in 1948 he had become Governor of the Windward Islands. He has given in both England and Canada a popular series of radio broadcasts. A skeptical man, as befits a government servant, he saw something on the beach of Butaritari lagoon that challenged his reason.

According to his own telling, Sir Arthur was a skinny man— pitiably so in the eyes of the islanders—and in discussing his sad state with the chief, old Kitiona, he was told that the only cure was for him to eat porpoise meat. It turned out that Kitiona's kinsmen in Kuma village, seventeen miles away, were the hereditary porpoise callers of the high chiefs of Butaritari and Makin-Meang.

There were very few who were skilled in porpoise calling, who could speak the words of invitation with proper feeling. It was necessary to put oneself into a dream in which the spirit went out of the body and sought the porpoises below the western horizon, to bid them to a dance with feasting at Kuma village. When the telepathic dream went out with the right *mana* the porpoises leaped with joy to the surface of the water and followed. Once the caller had led them to the lagoon, he would run ahead of them to re-enter his body and tell the tribe that the porpoises had come to the feast.

Intrigued, Sir Arthur asked if he could witness the sight, and the chief promised to arrange it. On the day appointed, he called in his canoe for the commissioner. It was a windless day with a white-hot sun. The sails were useless and it required more than six hours of exhausting paddling to arrive in the village. On the beach they were met by the hereditary porpoise caller. From now on, he said, the word "porpoise" must not be used. They must be called only "our friends from the west." Otherwise they might not come.

He showed Sir Arthur a little hut of coconut leaves beside his house. He would now enter the hut, to leave his body in the dream, while his guests waited in the main house. The villagers were very silently preparing for a feast, making wreaths and polishing ceremonial shell ornaments. But the hot hours passed and nothing happened.

Then suddenly from the dream-hut came a weird howl. They jumped up to see the "caller" burst through the leaves of the hut to sprawl on his face in the sand. Gobs of saliva hung on his chin and he clawed the air, whining like a puppy. Then came a staccato chant: "Arise! Arise! They come! Let us go down to greet our friends from the west!"

The villagers echoed this with a roar and dashed for the beach. Everyone wore wreaths as they waded out through the shallows toward the reef. There they waited. At last another cry arose, and a man stood pointing out into the glittering sea beyond the reef. Here came the porpoises!

"The king of the west comes to meet me," murmured the caller and a few yards away Sir Arthur saw a great shape, dark in the brilliant green water. Others followed, a long line of them, coming closer to the islanders, who bent close above them, crooning an invitation.

Unbelievingly Sir Arthur saw the great sea mammals follow them ashore, and permit the natives to heave them over the shallows onto the beach.

"They showed no least sign of alarm," he said. "It was as if their single wish was to get to the beach. . . . There they settled down, those beautiful, dignified shapes, utterly at peace, while all hell broke loose around them."

The shrieking islanders tore off their wreaths and flung them upon the dying porpoises "in a sudden dreadful fury of boastfulness and derision. My mind still shrinks at that last scene— the raving humans and the beasts who were so triumphantly at rest." He left them here, knowing that when the tide receded the natives would return and butcher them.

That night there was a great feast, and a chief's portion of the meat was brought to Sir Arthur to cure his meagerness of body, but he could not eat it.

"I never did get fat in the islands," he concluded.

11

The Magnet of the Heart

When the Eugene Moses family moved from Buffalo, New York, to Michigan City, Indiana, in June, 1952, they gave their collie to a neighbor. Six-month-old Clancy had never left the vicinity of his Buffalo home. It was not the place that Clancy loved, but his family. About a week after his loved ones had moved west, Clancy left Buffalo to follow a strange and wondrous trail.

Six months later there came a scratching on the door of the Moses residence. There was Clancy, lean and footsore but unmistakably Clancy. A veterinarian said it was evident from his worn toe nails that he had walked a great distance in a short time. When Clancy saw the familiar throw rug in the living room that had been his bed, he curled up and went to sleep.[1]

In Evansville, Indiana, there arrived another traveling dog named Skipper. Some of his travels were by ship and rail with his mistress, but the last journey was by the sore-paw route on his own.

Mrs. Georgina Hill acquired Skipper, a wire-haired terrier, in Germany in 1949. She brought him back with her, and later when she moved to Duluth, Minnesota, he went along. But she had to give him away, because she simply didn't have room for him in the new house.

She later moved to Evansville, a place where Skipper had never been. He stayed on in Duluth and then was given away a second time, to an Air Force family on their way to Texas. Apparently he wasn't happy with them.

In September of 1953, while Mrs. Hill was working as the food service director in Evansville College's Union Building, who should trot into the kitchen but Skipper! "And he isn't taking any more chances of losing me," Mrs. Hill told reporters. "I can't get more than six feet away from him."

Among the many similar cases investigated by Dr. Joseph Banks Rhine when he had charge of the Duke University Parapsychology Laboratory, was that of Tony, a black cocker spaniel. When his owners, the L. F. Doolens, moved from Aurora, Illinois, to Lansing, Michigan, they gave Tony to friends in Aurora. He stayed less than a day.

Seven weeks later, while walking down a street near his new home, Mr. Doolen was pounced upon by a barking, bedraggled black dog. Not believing his own eyes, he bent down, patted the animal and fumbled for the collar. Yes, it was Tony. He was wearing the odd cut-down collar bearing the right-angled slot that Doolen had cut with his own knife.[2]

Another case from the laboratory files tells the story of King, a Belgian shepherd owned by Clifford and Wayne Burke. King had lived with the Burke family in Sandpoint, Idaho, for about three years when he disappeared. Several weeks later the family moved to Richmond, California, and the brothers gave up all hope of ever seeing their dog again.

One morning almost exactly a year after they left Idaho, the family found a weary King stretched out on the front porch. He leaped up, barking joyously, wagging his "pendulum of the heart." He had reached the end of his twelve-hundred-mile journey.

Identification is of prime importance in these astonishing reunions. "There never has been any doubt in our minds," wrote Mrs. Burke. "We know King was our dog. If you had seen him come to Clifford and lay his head on his knee like a tired traveler, you, too, would never have doubted. He always, when I petted him, stood on his hind feet and put his front paws on my shoulders. And tired as he was the day we found him, that was one of the first things he did."

King's identification was also confirmed by a scar on one of his paws, his dislike of hissing noises, and his habit of sneaking onto a special place on the sofa. Mrs. Burke and one of her sons took him out for a ride the day after his return. King sat on the rear seat and every once in awhile raised himself up, put his paws on the son's shoulders and licked his cheek.

"Love called to Lassie and Lassie answered by walking 2000 weary miles from Owensboro, Kentucky, to Los Angeles," said Tom Cargo in his story in the Los Angeles *Herald Express,* in March, 1960.

Lassie was a mongrel, and a male in spite of his name. When his owners, Mr. and Mrs. Allen W. Neal and their three children, moved from their small Kentucky farm they left Lassie behind. They hated to do this, but the car was overloaded and Lassie got fussy on long trips.

So Mr. Neal, a cement mason, left the dog with his brother, planning to have him shipped out to California later. The kids cried and Lassie was miserable. Three times he ran away from the brother and went to the old farm, hunting his folks. The last time he was seen in Owensboro was in October, 1959. After that it was assumed he was dead or hopelessly lost.

The Allen Neals settled at 13272 Sunburst Street, Pacoima, California. On March 10 of the following year Mr. Neal took his wife to a doctor in downtown Pacoima. While he waited he saw a little brown mongrel limping painfully toward him. It looked just like Lassie. Mr. Neal whistled. With a feeble yelp the dog leaped for him.

"I couldn't believe it!" Mr. Neal said. "When I put him in the car he jumped from the back seat to the front just like he always did. When my wife came out and saw him we almost cried. Taking him home to the kids was a happy feeling for all of us."

As for identification, he had the identical body markings, had an unusual appetite for cinnamon toast crusts, and performed immediately all of Lassie's bag of tricks.

Cats also provide us with sore-paw stories. TV and radio reporter Walter McGraw tells of a cat that made not one but five trips from upstate New York to New York City. A family of New Yorkers had made it a pet at their summer home, and at the end of the season Daisy was pregnant. A city apartment is no place for a feline maternity ward, so the family found a new home for Daisy, then closed their cottage for the winter and returned to the big city.

Daisy appeared one month later—carrying a kitten in her mouth—at the strange apartment thirty miles from her new home. A few days after her arrival, she disappeared for a week only to reappear bearing a second kitten. This continued for a total of five weeks and five kittens.

"True," writes McGraw, "she might have made the last four-and-a-half round trips by memory, or by following smells and marks, but how, other than clairvoyantly, could a cat, walking on the ground, in a strange city of 8 million people, find the home of a family who had gone there via fast, modern, off-the-ground (except for tires) transportation?"[3]

Vivian Allgood, a registered nurse, had a mute black cat who answered to the name of Li-Ping. In April, 1955, Miss Allgood moved from Sandusky, Ohio, to Orlando, Florida, leaving her cat behind with her sister in his accustomed territory. But the cat pined for his mistress inconsolably, and at the end of two weeks he vanished.

Months later the nurse was sitting one afternoon on a neighbor's porch when a bedraggled black cat appeared on the sidewalk. "Why, that looks like Li-Ping!" she cried. At once the cat ran up to her, making the strange rasping cry that had been the only sound he could utter from kittenhood. His coat was ragged, with great patches of fur gone.

For a week the cat with the Chinese name and sagacious heart slept for hours, and between snoozes consumed quarts of milk and pounds of liver. Soon the missing fur grew in and his coat was clean and bright once more. And never again did Li-Ping have to travel weary miles to find his mistress.

One of Dr. Rhine's cases concerns Clementine, a cat that traveled approximately fifteen hundred miles from Dunkirk, New York, to Denver, Colorado, to find her owners, Mr. and Mrs. Robert Lundmark. When the Lundmarks moved from Dunkirk in 1949, they left Clementine behind on the farm because she was about to become a mother. She had her kittens, but when she had fulfilled her duty and they were weaned, she took off.

How she crossed rivers, mountains, and prairies and what frightening experiences and hardships she endured will forever be mysteries. Somehow she made it. A little over three months after she was last seen in Dunkirk, the Lundmarks heard her scratching at their front door in Denver, mewing imperiously. She came in, rubbed affectionately against her owners, but was afraid—probably from sad experience—of strangers in the room. Her coat was rough and matted, her paws cracked and worn, and her bushy tail had dwindled to a rag. She was so exhausted she slept for three days.

How could any cat possess such incredible devotion to its owners? Surely the newcomer must have been a cat that resembled Clementine. The Lundmarks, however, had no doubts after an examination of their pet. Clementine had a rare anomaly—seven toes on her front feet. There was also a scar on her left shoulder from a burn suffered back on the farm, and two oddly shaped white spots on her tummy. The vet confirmed the fact that she had had kittens.[4]

The long-distance record for a cat is held by Tom, who pussyfooted it at least twenty-five hundred miles across the continent from St. Petersburg, Florida, to San Gabriel, California. The hike took him two years and six weeks, certainly an act of tremendous devotion and determination. Mr. and Mrs. Charles B. Smith had given Tom to Robert Hanson, who purchased their home in 1949. They moved to California and two weeks after their departure, Hanson wrote that Tom had run away.

Early in August, 1951, Mrs. Smith heard a cat wailing in the yard one afternoon and asked her husband to chase it away. Instead of running, the cat leaped into Smith's arms and began to purr. Smith blinked, did a double take, then shouted, "Hey, Betty, come out here! It's our old Tom!"

Mrs. Smith was doubtful. A well-fed, sleek cat had been left with Hanson, but this one was skinny and worn and so weary that he had collapsed on the kitchen floor. His fur, parched by the sun, came out in handfuls, and his paws were covered with scabs. Then she thought of a sure test. Tom had been raised on baby food and had developed an unusual fondness for Pablum. She put a saucer of it on the floor and exhausted though he was, the battered cat dived into it up to his whiskers.

"No doubt about it," said Mrs. Smith, "that was our Tom and we were certainly glad to see him." And Tom was happy too when he dropped into a well-deserved sleep beside his empty dish.[5]

In contrast to "homing cases" in which lost nonmigratory animals find their way back to familiar homes, these are known to parapsychologists as "trailing cases." These pets appear at new homes they have never known in parts of the country they have never even visited. It is not to a point on the earth's surface that they are guided, but to a human owner. Their navigation is not celestial or magnetic, but they follow a directional beam of love, a magnet of the heart.

Untold numbers of dogs and cats are lost forever daily. Why is it that most lost pets wander about helplessly, while a few can return to their owners over hundreds of miles across a strange land? The answer must lie in an ESP rapport, a special and rare psychic resonance on a subconscious level that overcomes the barriers of space, time, and species.

Furthermore, pets have found their way to masters over sea as well as land. For the dramatic story of Hector we are indebted to Captain Kenneth Dodson, U. S. N., who checked all accounts and interviewed the officers of the two ships involved in the dog's strange and extraordinary feat. The details will be found in the captain's book *Hector, The Stowaway Dog.*[6]

The S. S. *Hanley* was being loaded with timber and grain at the old Government Docks in Vancouver, B. C., on April 20, 1922, when Second Officer Harold Kildall saw a large black-and-white smooth-haired terrier trotting up the gangplank. Once on deck, the dog stood perfectly still, looking and listening, then he sniffed at the fresh-sawed planks and the sacked grain. He then ran ashore and boarded the next vessel.

Kildall watched as the terrier boarded four other ships loading along the dock. Each time he sniffed around with an odd purposefulness, inspecting the decks and cargoes. The dog's persistence interested the officer, but he became busy with preparations for sailing and forgot the matter. Several hours later the *Hanley* began her voyage to Yokohama, Japan.

The following morning when Kildall came down from the bridge, there was the terrier lying on a coco mat outside the captain's cabin. Unnoticed, he had come aboard again. Kildall, the captain, the other officers, and crewmen tried to make friends with the dog. But the handsome terrier was no hail-fellow companion. He allowed his head to be patted, but showed no return of affection and remained aloof in unapproachable dignity.

During the eighteen-day voyage the dog stood the midnight

to 4:00 A.M. and noon to 4:00 P.M. watches on the bridge with Kildall. All of his actions revealed that he was no stranger to a ship. His usual nonchalance ended, however, when the coast of Honshu came abeam of the freighter. Now he began pacing the deck nervously.

The *Hanley* dropped anchor near the Customs Jetty in Yokohama harbor and began unloading her cargo of timber. The nearest vessel was about three hundred yards distant. It was the S. S. *Simaloer,* also unloading a cargo of timber. Kildall noticed that the dog's attention was centered on the Dutch freighter and that he was sniffing the air, prancing back and forth in rising excitement. Then two men from the *Simaloer* boarded a sampan that headed for a landing on a course that carried the craft close to the *Hanley's* stern.

The dog watched, whining softly; then as the sampan came closer, he began to leap and bark in wild excitement. This attracted the attention of one of the sampan's passengers, who, after a close look at the dog, began shouting and waving his arms. As the craft came alongside the *Hanley's* accommodation ladder, the terrier leaped into the water and the shouting man hauled him aboard and hugged him as the dog licked his face joyfully. Dog and master were together again!

The dog's name was Hector, and his master was Willem H. Mante, second officer aboard the *Simaloer.* Mante had the same duties and watches to stand as Kildall had on the *Hanley.* Back in Vancouver the *Simaloer* had changed its berth for bunkering while Hector was off on a shore leave before the long voyage. Although a sympathetic captain had delayed sailing time while Mante frantically searched the waterfront, the dog could not be found.

Willem Mante, who entered into a long correspondence with Captain Dodson, wrote, "I've had several dogs after Hector, as I'm a dog lover, but none of them could ever take his place. As long as I live, I'll never forget the faith and friendship of that one-man, one-ship dog, Hector."

In his book Captain Dodson asks: "What mysterious instinct could have governed Hector's methodical search for the one ship out of many which would carry him across an ocean to rejoin his beloved master? Did the character of the *Hanley*'s cargo and perhaps other signs tell him that the *Hanley* was bound for the same destination as his own ship? Did he then attach himself to the officer whose duties were like his master's? Any answers would be the guesswork of men who know only what happened."

But no such possible clues as the nature of a cargo plus the long arm of coincidence suffice to explain the mystery of how a cocker spaniel named Joker found his master. During World War II, Army Captain Stanley C. Raye had to leave Joker in his Pittsburg, California home for overseas duty on a Pacific Island. Joker was lonely and miserable. He moped around for two weeks, then disappeared.

Two army doctors reported that the dog turned up at Oakland, about thirty miles away, where he stowed aboard an Army transport. Since no one claimed him he was about to be destroyed when an Army major adopted him. The ship made several ports of call, but when it stopped at a certain South Pacific island, Joker leaped ashore and found his master. The dog's joy was so great that no one could dispute the reunion, and the major relinquished his claim.

This astounding dog somehow knew his master had taken a ship—although he had never been aboard one—and managed to find another vessel that would anchor at the same island where his master was stationed! Although that island was only one of several ports of call, seemingly he knew it was the right one and left the ship.

Joker never again left his master until his death. He died early in 1958 at Great Falls, Montana, at the advanced age of fourteen-and-a-half years, a wise old cocker spaniel who never disclosed his secret.[7]

There are a number of cases in which pets find their way to

hospitalized masters. Eldon Roark, in his book *Just a Mutt,* tells about a little girl, Verla Mae Williams, of Memphis, Tennessee, who was separated from her little fox terrier, Tippy, when she was taken to Cheerfield Farm, a tuberculosis sanatorium near Memphis and twelve miles from her home. After she left, Tippy was restless and unhappy for a week, then disappeared. The next day, word came that Tippy was with his young mistress at the institution, a place where he had never been before.

When young John Anderson Perkins left his Dorchester, Massachusetts home to undergo abdominal surgery, he left behind his ten-month-old mongrel, Waggles. For three days Waggles was miserable. On the fourth day a succession of dogs answering his description tried to slip in through all the many doors of Boston's Children's Hospital. On the last of these attempts at entry, Waggles was caught by John's grandmother, Mrs. Virginia Kroge, and sent home in disgrace via taxicab to be locked up. Children's Hospital is some distance from Dorchester, and there are over twenty-five hospitals in Greater Boston. But Waggles knew the one that housed his nine-year-old pal.[8]

Nor are dogs the only pets who make hospital visitations. Dr. Rhine has reported the case of young Hugh Perkins, the son of Sheriff F. C. Perkins at Somerville, West Virginia. Hugh was taken to a hospital at Philippi, one hundred miles away over the mountains, in 1939. One snowy night soon after his arrival he saw a pigeon fluttering outside the window and asked the nurse to let the bird in.

"Look at its leg quick!" he said excitedly. "I'll bet it's my bird—number 167!" The nurse read the band: AU 39 C&W 167.

And in another Children's Hospital—this time in Los Angeles—five-year-old Johnny Lewis lay dying of leukemia. Johnny had a parakeet he dearly loved, and begged his parents to bring the bird to his room. Hospital regulations, however, prohibited pets. But the parakeet got the message over some mysterious broadcast band and a few days later flew in the window of Johnny's room. This was too much for officialdom —he was allowed to keep the bird.[9]

In 1960 Bessie Boyd Frazer, a reporter for the Medford, Oregon *Mail Tribune,* told the sad story of Spot, a short-haired pointer, who was moved from the country to Yreka, California. His owners kept him tied up now in their backyard, with a rope so short that he couldn't always reach his water pan or his food. Also they would go off and leave him tied for days at a time.

When this happened Toni, a girl who lived next door, would give Spot food and water. She would pet him and tell him how sorry she was that his unkind owners caused him so much suffering. She did this for a period of months before his owners moved away, taking the hapless dog along.

Meanwhile Toni had acquired a part interest in a mining claim in the Humbug district, and each weekend she went out to the mine. One night she heard something moving about under the cabin. When morning came she investigated, and there was Spot, thin and cowering and miserable. When she pulled the dog out from under the cabin he collapsed; his mouth was peppered with painful porcupine quills. She removed them with pliers and tried to give him water. But Spot could only lick her hand and give a feeble whimper as he died at her feet.

Bessie Frazer wrote: "He had found a dog's best friend, but how and where he came from she will never know."

The unity of all life includes even vegetation. Cleve Backster is a specialist with more than twenty years of experience in the applications of psychogalvanic reflexes in behavioral studies. One day in 1966 he watered an office plant, then thought he would experiment to see how long it took water to rise from the roots to its leaves. He attached psychogalvanic reflex electrodes to a top leaf. Between the electrodes was a small electrical current, and resistance to this current was recorded by a pen resting on a continuous moving graph.

When this is used on human subjects the resistance goes down and the pen moves up on the graph if there is an emotional reaction. Backster expected the water to reduce resistance since it is a good electrical conductor. But to his surprise the resistance went up and the tracing on the graph indicated a reaction pattern typical of a human subject experiencing an emotional stimulation of short duration. Could it be possible, he wondered, that plants feel emotions?

Continuing his experiments Backster placed a leaf of the plant in a cup of hot coffee. There was no response. Then he considered something more of a threat to the plant. *I'll go get a match and burn the leaf,* he thought. Instantly the pen on the graph shot upward. Was it possible that the plant had actually read his mind?

Since that day Backster has made awe-inspiring discoveries with fantastic implications. He found that plants react to the emotional crises of other life forms. When the lives of brine shrimp were ended in boiling water or when fertilized chicken eggs were broken, his philodendron plants—kept in other rooms—reacted bioelectrically. As we write, these experiments are being duplicated at several universities, and they may well become the first repeatable-at-will laboratory demonstrations of ESP.

Plants may have memories, also. In a dramatic experiment one of six men was chosen by lot to be a "murderer." Each man went alone into a room containing two plants, and the one secretly chosen to be the "killer" destroyed one of the plants by pulling it from its pot and tearing it to pieces. Backster then went into the room, attached his apparatus to the remaining plant, and had the men return to the room one by one. When the "murderer" came in, the needle on the chart jumped, revealing an emotional reaction!

Reactions or perception capability continue even when the

leaf is detached from the parent plant, trimmed to electrode size, or shredded and redistributed between the electrode surfaces. This, Backster believes, indicates that the source of the perception is the cell, and that every living cell has a primary perception with some sort of rudimentary consciousness. When millions of cells are combined in the body of the plant, the united consciousness of the cells becomes very sensitive and perceptive.

Is this why some persons have a "green thumb" and others a "black thumb"? Does it explain the power of prayer upon plant growth; of why a plant that receives special attention and loving care will grow higher or bear more blossoms than its fellows?

A scientific report of Backster's experiments was published in the *International Journal of Parapsychology,* Vol. X, No. 4. Popular accounts have appeared in *National Wildlife,* Feb.-March, 1969; *Argosy,* June, 1969, and other periodicals.

This implication of a collective mind, a vast communication network, means that life is a sharing and that no living thing is truly alone—a wondrous affinity that recognizes no divisions between the human, animal, and vegetable realms.

12

The Wizards and the Geniuses

There are smart dogs—alert, sensitive, entertaining. From time to time they bark their way into the news and appear on television programs. When asked the sum of four and three, they bark seven times. Such dogs can be taught to start and stop barking in response to their master's signals.

Moreover signals can be given subconsciously. The dog may have learned to relate his barking to his master's unintentional, habitual change in facial expression, or to the movement of his hands or eyes. A clever dog, told to add three and three, may notice that his master is tense until he barks six times. Then his master relaxes and the dog stops barking.

The true test for genius in an animal is his performance when the master or owners are absent. Chris, the Mathematical Mongrel (who was part beagle) passed this test. Owned by Mr. and Mrs. George Woods, of Warwick, Rhode Island, he became a local celebrity, appearing at clubs and on television. He communicated with taps of his paw instead of barks.

Mr. Woods, who was chief chemist for the Apponaug Finishing Company, said Chris was five years old when he began to display his abilities, but the dog told him (paw-wise) that he could have performed at two if he had been asked. At first he did simple things—like counting backward from twenty-five. Then he began to subtract, multiply, and divide, finally graduating to working out the square and cube roots of numbers. He gave his answers by tapping his paw on the arm of his interrogator.

Chris was tested by a number of scientists and professors. Dr. J. B. Rhine came from Duke University to make a special study. Dr. Henry F. Nugent, professor of psychology at the Rhode Island College of Education, conducted hundreds of tests only to admit he was "enthusiastic but baffled." James E. Reilly, an executive of Rhode Island's S.P.C.A., said he was convinced Chris had somehow touched an intelligence level the average man had not reached.

Once two of Du Pont's engineers asked the dog a question of computer complexity. Usually Chris answered almost immediately, but this time it took him four minutes. The amused engineers made their own calculations. Ten minutes later they came up with the same answer the dog had given in four!

When Chris was asked how he knew so much, he tapped out *s-m-a-r-t d-o-g,* indicating the proper letters as the alphabet was recited. And for those who asked how he did it, he quipped, *w-i-t-h m-y p-a-w.*

When Chris branched out into fortune-telling he informed the local police, correctly, that a raise in salary was coming their way. He announced coming changes in the weather, and once predicted the winners of the daily double at Narragansett Park paying $82.40.

In 1959 when he was nine years old, a heart ailment forced Chris's retirement from public performances. Mr. Woods put to him a question we ourselves would be reluctant to ask a friend: "When are you going to die?"

But Chris seemingly took it in stride. "He put his paw on my arm and tapped out 1962," Mr. Woods told newsmen.

"Then he tapped out the month, June, and the day, the tenth."

Chris missed out on his last prediction by twenty-four hours. He died June 9, 1962.[1]

The classical cases of animal genius have resulted from the work and training of European experimenters, particularly in Germany where the dogs of Mannheim astonished scholars. One day shortly before World War I, Frau Paula Moekel, annoyed by her young daughter's mistakes in arithmetic, exclaimed, "Even Rolf could do sums like these without making mistakes!"

At once the dog, a Bedlington terrier, came over and touched her arm. When Frau Moekel laughingly said, "Rolf, what's the total of two and two?" he tapped her arm four times. Later she said to him, "If you could only say yes and no we could talk to each other. So if you wish to say yes give me two pats. If you want to say no give three pats."

Rolf caught on at once. When she said, "Rolf, do you wish to be spanked?" he gave three strong pats!

While in time it was discovered that Rolf could add numbers under one hundred, it was his conversational ability that left his visitors shaken and bewildered. Frau Moekel and the dog evolved a code of the most used letters, with those most frequently used requiring the least number of pats. Rolf's spelling was phonetic and his sentences short, but communication was still laborious since some letters took as many as twenty pats.

When Prof. William Mackenzie, of Genoa, examined Rolf he asked him the meaning of autumn. "Time for apples," was the reply. And when M. Edmond Duchatel, the French psychologist, visited Rolf, he brought along his secretary, a prim lady well along in years. When she was invited to question the dog she asked, "Rolf, is there anything you would like me to do for you?"

There must have been a mischievous gleam in Rolf's eyes as he tapped out his reply: "Wag your tail!"

Rolf even understood pictures. When the well-known zoologist Prof. H. E. Ziegler of Stuttgart wrote Rolf up in a scientific journal, he told of giving the dog the pictures of a flower, a mouse, and an elephant to identify. Rolf spelled out the mouse and the flower but disappointed them by rapping out *K-m-a K-r-a-l B-e-r-t-o* for the elephant.

It was several days until his mistress recalled that shortly before this she had shown the dog the picture of Kama, the stupid elephant owned by Herr Krall, and his blind horse, Berto.

In appreciation of this feat, Herr Krall sent Rolf a picture book; the text said that the animals in the illustration were unwilling to learn.

This is the "letter of thanks" that Rolf tapped out in reply:

Dear:
   The book amused Lol very much. Daisy must see it. [Lol was Rolf's pet name for himself and Daisy was the cat.] Animals gladly learn. Bookmaker lies. The Christchild comes. Mother fetches it. Horses shall have trees. Many kisses.
                                                      Your Lol.

By this, Rolf was telling Herr Krall that though he was pleased at getting a present, he was indignant at the lie that animals did not want to learn! Christmas was coming, and he wanted Krall to get a tree for his horses. Rolf loved Christmas trees very much.

Lola, Rolf's daughter, was more of a philosopher, in some ways surpassing her sire's genius. After two years of patient training by Henny Kindermann, she could add, subtract, divide, and multiply; also tell the time of day, the day of the week, and the month. She recognized and used properly such abstract terms as "love," "fear," and "hate." These abilities were confirmed by a number of scientists who observed the dog with awe.

Like other dog wizards, Lola spelled words phonetically, although she could calculate mathematically to the fraction. When asked the sum of one-seventh plus five-eighths, within seconds she answered, "forty-three fifty-sixths." Frau Kindermann offers this example of a typical performance in her book *Lola: The Thought and Speech of Animals.*

"In our presence Lola solved a number of sums . . . Lola then told us the time (4:16 P.M.) and after this she did some spelling. When shown the picture of a flower, she rapped *b-l-u-m* (*blume*), and to the drawing of a cat she responded with *t-i-r* (*tier,* or animal); when finally to a question of what was the name of the Mannheim Dog, she replied *M-e-i-n f-a-d-r* (*vater,* or father)—we all expected her to say *R-o-l-f.*"

Lola was taught to tap out a shorthand-spelling with her paw and became a surprising conversationalist. Some examples of her replies and comments follow:

"Would you like to be a human being?"

"No—because of work!"

"Do you want more from me? [her owner]"

"Yes, constancy in your love."

Lola was a typical dog in her enjoyment of walks. If rain kept her indoors she would remark reprovingly, "Mistake to go out so little!"

As the wartime food grew poorer and scarcer, she peevishly tapped out, "The food has been getting worse lately. I get too little nourishment from it!"

She had a keen sense of fun and made many jokes. But Lola's conversation did not deal entirely with the physical. She discussed life, death, and the future of the soul. Once too she ran away into the woods and could not be found for nearly a day. When Frau Kindermann asked where she had been, she replied, "I went to marry a dog."

This proved true, for she produced nine puppies after this excursion. Some weeks before their birth she even foretold their number.[2]

Kurwenal, a dachshund philosopher, was the greatest of the dogs trained by the German noblewoman, Baroness von Frey-Loringhaven, who devoted much of her life to proving that animals have minds and souls like men. His story is told in the *American Kennel Gazette* of March 1, 1938. Instead of paw taps, the baroness taught the dog to speak in a bark-alphabet with each letter assigned a certain number of barks, and timing in between them.

General von Hoff of Stuttgart wrote a pamphlet on the dachshund, asserting the truth of the dog's strange gifts on his "honor as a general." Later Prof. Dr. Siegmund-Schultze of Berlin came to Weimar to test the dog. He brought with him a package of biscuits and asked Kurwenal their trade name.

"Knapsack!" the dachshund barked out. Then he went on without stopping, "A knapsack is a bag carried on the back."

Even when the baroness was many miles away the dog carried on long impromptu talks with his investigators, and he could calculate faster than most of his questioners. At times Kurwenal grew sad at the atmosphere of incredulity and skepticism that he was forced to endure. Once after Professor Plate of Jena had badgered him tiresomely, Kurwenal plaintively barked out, "If only he would stop trying to trick me!"

In a single year over five hundred distinguished European scientists investigated the dog, among them the noted Prof. Max Muller. One afternoon Dr. Muller was discussing the slaughter of animals for food with the baroness, who was a vegetarian. He turned to Kurwenal and asked, "Kurwenal, what do you think about it?"

Promptly the dog barked this reply, "The Christian religion forbids killing."

In his report Dr. Muller wrote, "This dachshund, in the intellectual sense, is more in the sphere of humans than of animals . . . The dog shows us what a wrong attitude we have toward the educated dogs, how much the animals understand us, and how very little, as a rule, we understand them."

Shortly before he died in 1937 Kurwenal was asked what he thought of death. "I am not afraid of it," he replied. And when asked if dogs have souls, his answer was that they have, "and they are like the souls of men."

There was also an American dog whose performance challenged accepted theories of animal behavior—Jim, the Wonder Dog, of Sedalia, Missouri. A black-and-white Llewellyn setter owned by Sam Van Arsdale, Jim was a mind reader and a prophet. So incredible were the dog's faculties that one national magazine, *Reader's Scope,* refused to publish an article about Jim until they had a statement that the account was true from Dr. A. J. Durant, chairman of the Department of Veterinary Science of the University of Missouri.

The dog's brilliance was discovered by chance. One autumn day when Jim was three-and-a-half years old, he and his master were walking through the woods. Just to be talking, Van Arsdale said, "See that elm tree, Jim?" And Jim trotted over to the elm and placed a paw against its trunk. Unbelievingly his master tried him with a hickory, an oak, a walnut, and a decayed stump. Jim touched them all in turn in the same manner. In the following months Van Arsdale discovered that his pet's identification ability went far beyond trees.

In 1933 when Jim was eight, he was brought to the University of Missouri for tests under the direction of Dr. Durant and Dr. Sherman Dickinson of the School of Education. As a crowd of students and faculty members watched on the campus behind the administration building, Jim, who was not aware that dogs were color blind, picked out the girl in the blue dress, the man with a moustache, a certain license plate number, and identified various makes of automobiles. But even more bewildering was the fact that the instructions were given in French, German, and Italian as well as English.

It was Jim's prowess as a prophet that left his owner and friends numb with bewilderment. Affidavits of witnesses are on record, stating that the Wonder Dog predicted Kentucky Derby winners for seven consecutive years. The names of the participating horses were written on separate pieces of paper and spread in front of Jim, who proceeded to place his paw on the winner.

Other predictions included the sex of five babies before their birth; Roosevelt's victory over Landon in 1936; and the triumph of the Yankees in the World Series that same year. Van Arsdale, a wealthy, nonwagering hotel owner, ignored all offers from gamblers and stopped the Kentucky Derby tests when he learned the results were being leaked to the betting fraternity.

Jim died peacefully in 1937 at the age of twelve years, taking his secrets with him.[3]

Animal genius may arise spontaneously as it apparently did with Jim. Sally Carrighar, in her book *Wild Heritage,* tells of a Capuchin monkey from Peru that developed its own system of painting, drew geometric patterns, and turned to its art when mentally exhausted by mechanical problems given it by scientists.

Or, if the potential exists and the situation is ideal, genius may be developed by training. The famed "Talking Horses of Elberfeld" are a striking example of this approach.

What Prof. Edouard Claparède, a noted Swiss psychologist, termed "the most sensational event which has ever appeared in the field of animal psychology—perhaps, indeed, in the whole realm of psychology" began around the turn of the century.

Incredible tales had reached the universities of Europe. Hans, a horse owned and trained by Wilhelm von Osten, a retired mathematics teacher of Elberfeld, Germany, could perform four basic mathematical operations; could spell words and compose sentences; could read the face of a timepiece. Thousands of spectators came and were never charged a pfennig for observing the feats of the Russian stallion. Commissions and committees arrived and departed in violent disagreement.

Von Osten died in 1909 and left Hans to his friend, Karl Krall, a prosperous jeweler, who immediately added to the school two Arabian stallions named Muhamed and Zarif; a blind horse called Berto, and a Shetland pony, Hanschen. Using more efficient training methods, Krall had his astonishing equines not only adding, subtracting, dividing, and multiplying after a few weeks, but extracting square and cube roots at the end of four months. They gave their answers by stamping with their hoofs; for example, to give the number thirty-four they struck three times with the left (a value of ten) and four times with the right hoof (unit value).

At the end of six months Krall had also taught his charges to spell—phonetically as usual—and to respond to questions in both German and French. As in the case of Jim, the Wonder Dog, this suggests that it was not the meaning of words that was communicated to the horses, but the thought itself. An account of the methods of training will be found in *Modern Psychical Phenomena,* by Hereward Carrington.[4]

By chance one day Krall noticed that the horses were rapping outside the daily lesson and exhibitions, and he recorded the raps, finding to his surprise that they represented attempts at spelling, similar to the first efforts of children. With additional training, one of the most remarkable characteristics of these horses came about—spontaneous conversation.

One morning when Krall came into the stable, Muhamed tapped out, "Albert [the groom] has beaten Hanschen." And another time he tattled on the pony, saying "Hanschen has bitten Kama." Kama was a young elephant more interested in eating than learning, and was soon returned to a zoo. In his place another horse named Amasis was added to the school.

Once when asked why he was slow in answering, Muhamed replied "I am tired! My leg hurts!" On another occasion when hungry he said, "John, give me some oats." Zarif one day was idle during a lesson, and Krall asked Muhamed, "Why is not Zarif nice and good?" Muhamed said, "Because he is lazy!"

Muhamed, the most brilliant of the stable, was touching in his eagerness to learn to communicate with his voice instead of his hoofs. But all too soon he realized that his guttural mouthings were pitifully inadequate. Suddenly he stopped trying, and with his hoofs he tapped out, "I have not a good voice."

"What must you do to speak?" asked Herr Krall.

"Open my mouth."

"Then why don't you open yours?"

"Because I can't!"

Maurice Maeterlinck, a Nobel Prize winner in literature, wrote of his visit to the stable: "Krall adores his pupils, and in this atmosphere of affection has in a manner of speaking humanized them. There are no longer those sudden movements of panic which reveal the ancestral dread of man . . . He talks to them long and tenderly, as a father might talk to his children, and we have the strange feeling that they listen to all he says and understand it. If they appear not to grasp an explanation or demonstration, he will begin it all over again, analyze it, paraphrase it ten times in succession, with the patience of a mother."[5]

These amazing stallions vanished in the flame and carnage of World War I as draft animals, while the little pony, Hanschen, was eaten during the famine.

The feats of the Elberfeld horses strike at the heart of the current behavioristic, mechanistic concept of animal psychology. If our book proves anything, it is that this concept is woefully inadequate. Even the skeptical scientists of the day did not go to Elberfeld to conduct personal studies. Like the astronomers of Galileo's day who refused even to look through his telescope, they could not endure having their dogma shaken to the roots.

The Elberfeld horses had no monopoly on equine mathematical genius. Black Bear, a talented little Shetland pony of Briarcliff, New York, could also extract square and cube roots of numbers, and proved it during an exhibition at Columbia University. When only a few weeks old, Black Bear was abandoned after his mother was sold. Thomas Barrett rescued the pony and several years later began training him after he noticed the pony could recognize numbers.

Black Bear made his New York debut on December 5, 1927, under the sponsorship of the American Society for Psychical Research. Among his feats were telling the time indicated on a watch; solving several problems of making change by picking up the correct coins from a table and dropping them into the hand of an observer; locating spectators in the audience who had been described to him; and giving the area of a rectangle drawn on a blackboard with the lengths of the long and short sides indicated by numbers. He indicated objects, directions, yes, and no by motions of his head; and spelled sentences or chose numbers by nipping up lettered or numbered leather tabs hung on the bars of a stanchion rack.

The Pulitzer Prize winning novelist of that era, Zona Gale, was fascinated by Black Bear's apparent clairvoyance. He told her she was from New York City, adding that he liked to go there himself and e-a-t.

"Black Bear," she asked, "were you ever in another body?" He nodded his head. "Whose body?"

"King Solomon!" he answered.

"When did King Solomon live?"

"B.C. Long time ago."

"What was the date of the Declaration of Independence?"

"July 4, 1775." This was Black Bear's only recorded error.[6]

According to a report in the April, 1931 issue of *Psychic Research* magazine, Black Bear displayed his clairvoyance by describing correctly playing cards of which he saw only the backs. He either answered correctly or refused to reply at all.

One of the pony's visitors was a Mrs. Fletcher, a stranger

to both Black Bear and his owner. She asked, "Black Bear, there is an anniversary coming soon. Can you tell me what it is?"

"Birthday," the pony replied.

"Can you tell me when it will be?"

"Friday."

"What date will that be?" was her next question, and Black Bear at once spelled out *August third.*

Black Bear died in 1932, about the time that a "talking horse" in Richmond, Virginia, was attaining far more fame than the little pony ever received. Although Lady Wonder could solve simple problems in arithmetic (such as ½ x 18 or ¼ x 32), she was primarily a mind reader and a prophet. And there seems to be little doubt that she was for a time a telepathic recipient.

Mrs. Claudia Fonda bought Lady in 1925. Her first hint that Lady was different came when she noticed that the horse came running not when she called her, but when she thought of calling her. In the beginning Mrs. Fonda taught her to count and spell with blocks that she could push around. Later they developed a "typewriter" on which the letters were spread out in front of the mare, facing the audience, not Lady Wonder. The horse operated this device by lowering her muzzle onto levers that flipped up letters or numbers giving the answers to questions put to her.

In December, 1928, parapsychologists Drs. J. B. Rhine, Louisa Rhine, and William McDougall, came to the somewhat shabby stable on Richmond's Ruffin Road and conducted several hundred tests. For example, Dr. Rhine wrote on paper the words Mesopotamia, Hindustan, and Carolina and, keeping the words out of sight, said, "What are the words I have written, Lady?" The horse immediately "nose-spelled" them without an error. When Dr. McDougall asked the horse to give the name of his colleague, she spelled out "Rhine," and when he asked, "Where can I borrow money?" she answered "Bank!"

Some months later Dr. Rhine returned for further tests. Lady was alert and lively whereas she had previously appeared somewhat lethargic. But gone was her ability to perform some of her astonishing earlier feats which included giving answers without Mrs. Fonda present. Seemingly the horse had lost her telepathic gift and was now responding to conscious or more likely unconscious signals from her owner.

In her heyday, and apparently on rare occasions later, Lady could answer unspoken questions and questions asked in foreign languages. A friend of ours was present when Lady answered a question given in Chinese, indicating that as in other animal subjects the response was to a thought, not words. This friend, Mrs. Mary Hyde, of Alexandria, Virginia, wrote on the pad, "What is the name of our dog?"

Lady seemed uncertain, so Mrs. Hyde asked aloud, "Lady, what do I call my dog when I go to the door?" The horse muzzled the letters *G-i-n-g*, and Mrs. Hyde expected her to add *e-r*, but instead Lady chose *y*. "I do call the dog Gingy at the door, but I was thinking Ginger," Mrs. Hyde said.

S. Ralph Harlow, a minister and retired professor of religion at Smith College, went to see Lady Wonder. On his business card he wrote the figure 8, keeping it concealed from Mrs. Fonda and all spectators. "Lady," he asked, "will you add two to the number I have written?" Her answer was 10. Then he wrote 20, and again she nosed up the correct numbers. She told Harlow that his little granddaughter was living in Athens, Greece, and after two false starts accurately named the child as Linda.

Lady told a startled and shaken Associated Press reporter, Paul Duke, his name, birthplace, and the amount of his salary to the correct cent. In his feature story of December 9, 1956, Duke told of the man who asked the mare if his wife was true to him. "Lady snorted and twitched, and then replied, 'Are you?' "

As a prophet, Lady predicted the winners of heavyweight

championship bouts, the entry of the United States and Russia into World War II; and the nomination, election, and third term of President Franklin D. Roosevelt. She missed, however, when she said Thomas Dewey would be elected President in 1948. When she was asked what had happened, she replied: "Funny, he too sure!"

Lady was asked to solve the fate of a number of missing children. Her answers pose some fascinating problems, for she was frequently correct, or gave a clue that was later reinterpreted as probably correct.

During a bitter cold January in 1951, little Danny Mason was lost in Quincy, Massachusetts. No trace of the four-year-old could be found. The police searched everywhere but failed to turn up a clue. Naturally the parents were in torment. Friends of theirs visited Lady Wonder, who spelled out on her typewriter the words, *Pittsfield Water Wheel.*

Detectives investigated several water wheels in the Pittsfield area but found nothing. Then District Attorney Edmund R. Dewing said, "We got to mulling over the message and we thought it might have been twisted—that the horse meant to say Pit Field Wilde Water." They dragged the Field-Wilde quarry and found Danny's body.

Two other children disappeared in the winter of 1952-53, in Napierville, Illinois. One of the mothers, Mrs. Geraldine Rosentiel, went to see Lady Wonder. Lady told her that her son would be found in the river. The river had been dragged several times and a large sum had been spent pumping out two quarries. But several months later the children's bodies were found in the river.

One morning Mrs. Fonda entered the stable to find the partition kicked down and Lady Wonder lying barely conscious on the floor. She had suffered a heart attack and a few days later—on March 19, 1957—she died. On the following morning a group of about thirty persons gathered at her burial in Michael's Road Pet Cemetery in Henrico County. In a simple ceremony the poem, "An Arab's Farewell to His Horse," was read. Life for Mrs. Fonda would never be the same again.

How can horses extract cube and square roots of numbers? Quite likely the answer is that they accomplish their feats in the same automatic, instinctive manner as "idiot savants" and mentally retarded lightning calculators. They are not independent thinkers, but receivers. With no preliminary thought, they know the answers instantly.

There's Willy, an inmate at the Pacific State Hospital in Pomona, California. Willy plays checkers, two or three games daily, and he takes on all contestants. He makes his moves clumsily, like a robot, chattering constantly about other matters. In nine years he has never lost a game, usually winning in twenty to twenty-five moves. Willy has an IQ of sixty. He can't comprehend simple arithmetic.[7]

At a meeting of the American Psychiatric Association at Los Angeles in May, 1966, Dr. William Horwitz and associates submitted a paper dealing with twenty-six-year-old twins known as George and Charles. They are patients at the New York Psychiatric Institute. They can tell you instantly and correctly on what day of the week any particular date fell, or will fall, in any year or century over a seven-thousand-year span. "This is much more than memorizing calendars covering a couple of centuries in the past and present," says Dr. Horwitz. "There are no calendars for such a huge span of time."

Yet, if you tell the twins that a box of jelly beans costs thirty-five cents and they have a dollar, they cannot tell you what their change will be. They cannot do the simplest multiplication or division problem. Asked how they can do their marvelous calculations, they can only reply, "It's just in my head."

George can remember in detail the weather for any day during the past five years. Both twins can recall the exact date when any event happened at the hospital, even such minor occurrences as when a certain nurse had a cold. And they can tell you when many famous Americans were born and died, but they cannot recall who Napoleon was.[8]

Willis Dysart had practically no conventional schooling, yet his lightning calculations during the Presidential election in 1940 enabled a Minnesota newspaper to scoop its competitor on the returns. When given the time of a person's birth, Dysart was able to state immediately the number of days, hours, minutes, even seconds that person had lived! He could multiply instantly any seven-figure number by any six-figure number. A contractor once asked him how many bricks would be needed to built a house after he had been given the dimensions, the size of the windows and doors, and the number of bricks per square foot. Dysart without hesitation named the total. When the building was completed, the contractor had half a brick left over.[9]

The Elberfeld horses made no further progress after six months of schooling. Often they could not answer such simple questions as telling the number of persons present. Their intelligence appeared to be on the level of a six- to eight-year-old child.

The motor automatism of their replies to mathematical problems was indicated by the fact that Muhamed could tap out the cube root of 216 as rapidly as he could add four and ten. Again, the horses sometimes spelled words in reverse order, suggesting mirror writing, a characteristic of automatic scripts.[10]

It may be said that the conscious mind is only the surface of a deep mental well. This well is the subconscious mind that can think independently, but can it make rapid complex calculations? Our animal geniuses, however, present evidence of being telepathic recipients. This may be more than mere thought transmission between a man and his horse, since the animals have solved problems in advance of the human investigators.

In 1955 Dr. William Mackenzie—the "Grand Old Man

of Italian Science" of Genoa University—was asked if he remembered his lengthy testing of the Elberfeld horses. "Could I ever forget!" was his reply. Since the horses solved complicated problems instantaneously there could have been no telepathy, for the answers were not known. He suggested the possibility of such a group psychic association as seemingly exists between the subconscious minds of sitters in table-turning circles. He called the horses "living four-legged tables" and compared their mathematical wizardry with clairvoyance.

While awareness of telepathic messages may be an occasional occurrence here, it again seems quite likely that all thought images are projected into a universal mind—a "Mind-at-Large," as Aldous Huxley termed it. As in physics, there may also be a "field theory" in psychology.

Within this mental medium each species may have its Jungian archetype, its ancestral wisdom pool, its reservoir of instinctive knowledge. From this source comes the architectural skill of the termite, the engineering ability of the spider, the "deep-knowing" of all animals, including man himself.

Thus there are two forms of intelligence: one, particular to the individual, a consciousness reacting to stimuli from the known senses; the other, superior to the individual intelligence, linked to a source outside of the organism's biological range by an extrasensory perception that relates it with other organisms.

Actually the brain may not be a creative organ, but one of limitation. It may be designed for collecting information on our immediate environment, limiting our consciousness to what we need to live on the earth level. Like a resistance transformer, it may be blocking the full voltage of a current deep within us. Is this why ESP is more apparent when we are sick, asleep, or under a drug?

Sometimes the current jumps the transformer or a fuse is blown. Then we may have lightning calculators both human

and animal, idiot savants, inspiration, psychic healing, psy-
chometry, clairvoyance, and other *psi* phenomena. In fact, as
Sir James Jeans says in *The Mysterious Universe:* "Mind no
longer appears as an accidental intruder into the realm of
matter; we are beginning to suspect that it is the creator and
governor of matter."[11]

•

13

The Prophets and the Seers

Early one afternoon William H. Montgomery decided to go fishing for flounder off the New England coast. The boat was prepared and, when he was ready to cast off, he whistled for Redsy, his setter. Never since puppyhood had the dog failed to respond to such an invitation, but now he just crouched on the wharf, barking furiously. Again and again with coaxes and commands, Montgomery tried to get his pet aboard, but the dog only barked more.

Feeling "strangely uneasy," Montgomery related, he called off the trip. Out over the bay he could see perhaps fifty other boats heading for the flounder banks. It was a fine, cloudless day with scarcely a breeze. But surely Redsy had a reason behind "pouring his very dog's soul into his protest."

Some of those boats that went out that afternoon never returned. Forty-five minutes later the wind rose to a scream as a catastrophic storm unexpectedly moved in from the sea. Successive tidal waves, thirty to forty feet in height, struck from the coast and hammered boats, houses, and cottages into kindling wood. Over six hundred lost their lives. "What Redsy had saved me from," wrote Montgomery, "when he trusted his subtle canine senses and insisted I should, too, was the great hurricane of 1938."[1]

In the files of Dr. J. B. Rhine's Institute of Parapsychology, Durham, North Carolina, is the account of a woman who formerly lived near Lawrence, Kansas. Her cat had a litter of three kittens under the kitchen, and one morning she noticed that only two kittens were there. The mother was gone all day. The next day there was one kitten under the kitchen; the third day, none. And on the fourth day, a cyclone destroyed the house and barn and some of the livestock, including the family dog which was crushed under the house.

The cyclone wrecked two other farmhouses along the road, but just missed a third house four miles away. Weeks after the woman's family was reinstated at home, the cat returned, her three kittens trailing behind her. She had started removing her kittens from the cyclone's path in time to move one a day on an eight-mile round trip. Then she had kept them at the first house, which she seemingly knew would be undamaged, until they were able to walk so far.

It is not only the so-called higher animals whose sharp senses detect some of Nature's strange early-warning signals. This perception extends throughout the animal kingdom. Shrimps crawl onto dry land before a storm, and jellyfish head for deep water. Naturalist Ivan T. Sanderson once watched thousands of fiddler crabs march inland from the coast of Honduras well ahead of a hurricane. The march, several miles long, began twenty-four hours in advance of the storm. The coastal low-lands were flooded, but the crabs knew exactly how far they had to travel to avoid the dangerous effects of the tidal wave.

Sanderson also tells us about the European swift, a re-markable bird, which—except during nesting seasons—lives entirely in the air, nourished on flying insects that they catch on the wing. They migrate to northern Europe from South Africa in the spring to nest, and remain in Europe throughout the summer.

Finnish ornithologists have found that when a summer

cyclone from the North Atlantic is approaching, the birds leave well in advance and fly hundreds of miles to either the north or south. Moreover, their helpless young, which have to be left behind, immediately go into temporary hibernation, a state they never enter when their parents are around even if left alone for long periods.

"How do these birds know several days in advance that a cyclonic storm is coming, and how do they then know exactly the only two possible directions in which to fly in order to escape the fury of the storm and the starvation in which it would result?" asks Sanderson. "While it is obvious that the swifts must have some built-in device that is sensitive to oncoming cyclones, we still don't know what part of the body houses this mechanism or how it produces one type of reaction in the adult birds and quite a different one among the nestlings."[2]

"Avalanche dogs" is another name for the famed St. Bernards in the Swiss Alps because of their uncanny ability to anticipate snowslides. Horses, too, seem to sense the weather changes that cause avalanches. One horse, which had for many years done regular service through the Scaletta Pass, was a docile, obedient animal, but would refuse to move forward if he foresaw an avalanche. Once while pulling a sled of travelers, he stopped near the top of the pass. The travelers forced the compliant coachman to use the whip and the horse pushed forward, trying by speed to escape the danger. Moments later the avalanche fell, and barely missed burying the travelers.

When the Bezymyanny Volcano erupted in the Soviet Union during the winter of 1955-56, not a single bear was killed. Russian scientists said all the bears had left hibernation and gone to safer lairs before the volcano's activity was noted on their instruments.[3]

Prior to the eruption of Martinique's Mt. Pelee in 1902, cattle became so uneasy that they could hardly be managed, dogs howled continually, snakes left the vicinity of the volcano, and birds stopped singing and flew away from the trees on the mountainside.[4]

It is well known that animals have a presentiment before seismic disturbances. Prior to the severe Alaskan earthquake in 1964, animals in zoos as far south as Seattle became excited. It has been observed that, as long as ten hours before shocks in Peru and Chile, seabirds that fish by diving close inshore will fly many miles out to sea. After the quakes they return to eat the fish that have been killed.

Waterfowl and other birds apparently sensed the coming of the 1963 earthquake in southeastern Montana and left before the first shocks. Dr. Edgar W. Spencer, of Washington and Lee University, said after an on-the-scene study that the birds disappeared from the major quake area several hours before the first shock was felt.[5]

A woman said her spitz dog saved her life in the Tashkent, Soviet Union earthquake of 1966 by dragging her outdoors and away from the house a few minutes before the ground began to shake. Ants picked up their pupae and made a mass migration out of their ant hills about an hour before the first shock, according to a Tashkent schoolteacher. At the local zoo antelopes and mountain goats refused to go into their indoor pens for months before the quakes, and tigers and other big cats later began to sleep in the open.[6]

The disastrous earthquake that destroyed 80 percent of Skopje, Yugoslavia, came on July 26, 1963. Early in the morning of that day a tremendous uproar among the animals in the zoo awakened keepers. Elephants, wildly trumpeting, charged the bars of cages; tigers and lions paced their enclosures and roared in fright. Two bloodhounds at police headquarters howled and leaped at the windows trying to escape, and officers on patrol noticed the absence of birds.[7]

What is involved in the preceding cases is probably not extrasensory perception, but what Ivan Sanderson and other naturalists call supersensory perception. Such acute awareness may detect approaching hurricanes by water-level fluctuations or drops in barometric pressure. Slight sounds or a rise in temperatures may herald avalanches. Volcanic eruptions and earthquakes may be preceded by greater tensions in the earth's magnetic field. Animals may respond to minor trembling and small foreshocks.

Human beings are likewise affected. Up to 80 percent of mental patients appear to be upset by geomagnetic disturbances, and sometimes in advance of detectable aberrations. Man, too, appears to have built-in warning mechanisms for natural catastrophes, but unlike some animals, is too insensitive to note them.

The Soviet report previously mentioned states that the medical service in Ashkhabad, near the Iranian border, announced a dramatic upsurge in heart complaints in 1948, but cardiograms showed the patients healthy. Within the subsequent two months catastrophic quakes ripped the region. This suggested to Soviet scientists that some persons with very minor heart irregularities might perceive small variations in geophysical factors, such as static and magnetic fields, caused by the buildup toward an earth tremor.

Some causes of foreknowledge may not be so subtle. Brian Vesey-Fitzgerald, writing in the British *News of the World,* tells of a friend's cat that liked to sleep on or beside the television set. One day the cat jumped off the set, stared at it intently, and ran to the door to be let out. Thereafter whenever the set was operating the cat left the room. Several weeks later the main tube exploded, scattering fragments of glass about the room. We have noticed that electric bulbs sometimes announce their demise with a hum, and a defective tube could do the same for a sound-sensitive cat.

Could a dog, however, notice the slight cracking sounds of a tree about to collapse? In 1956 Ted and Dorothy Friend told the story of a woman with the delightful name of Welcome Lewis in their column in the San Francisco *Call-Bulletin.* She had brought her boxer with her on a visit from Los Angeles, and took him to Lafayette Park for exercise.

"When I parked my car and tried to get out, he refused to budge," Miss Lewis said. "He barked and made a great fuss, and I couldn't move him an inch. In disgust I returned to my hotel and there he came out of the car meek as a lamb. The next day I passed Lafayette Park and noticed that a huge tree had fallen on a car in the precise place I had parked. I learned, too, that the tree had fallen only a few minutes after I had driven away and another car had driven in."

A friend of ours, Mrs. Gertrude Springer, of Delton, Michigan, found that a neighbor, affectionately called Aunt Rilla by the community, had a prophetic dog, too. Aunt Rilla, injured in an accident, had considerable difficulty in getting about, and after she was settled in a chair it was hard for her to rise. One day when Gertrude visited her she found the telephone ripped off the wall and broken plaster around it.

"Did you know we were hit by lightning?" Aunt Rilla asked. "I could have been killed if it weren't for this mutt we took in." Affectionately she rubbed the ears of an ungainly-looking mongrel who put his head in her lap.

"He's a young dog to be so smart," she went on. "He knows I can't get about easy so he waits till I'm on my feet before he asks to go out. And he'll stay outside at the back door till he hears me moving around before he barks to come in, too. You'd think he was human, he's so understanding and considerate."

Gertrude laughed. "That sounds more like superhuman to me! Did he grab you when the lightning hit?"

Aunt Rilla shook her head. "He knew ahead of time! I was sitting there reading in that rocker right by the telephone, when he began to growl and bark and carry on so to get out, I thought he was going crazy. I heaved myself out of that chair in a hurry, and he still made such a fuss running to the door that I hobbled after him as fast as I could. I had my hand on the door when the bolt ripped through the phone, burned out the wires, and tore up the plaster. How in Heaven's name did that dog know lightning was going to strike right beside my chair?"

Coincidence?

During the Depression years of the 1930s Mrs. Maude S. Translin of Palo Alto, California, worked at Stanford University. Her home was on the edge of the city near railroad tracks. Since there was a hobo jungle in a creekbed nearby, she was nervous at having to be alone every night until very late, and was delighted when a friendly policeman gave her a watchdog. Spotty was an extraordinarily intelligent animal, an odd mixture of shepherd, hound, and German police. He understood perfectly that he was needed every night to guard his mistress, but that during the day he was free to ride around with her son, who managed a movie theater.

One hot afternoon she drove home from the university about five. To her surprise she found Spotty waiting for her on the back porch. It was the only time since they had owned him that he had ever come home before dark. He followed her in and planted himself between the dining room and kitchen where he could see both entrances.

Mrs. Translin opened the windows and doors to cool off the house and went into her bedroom to change. Before she was dressed a loud rap came on the front door. Since there was no screen, the house was wide open. Too late she realized how reckless that was in that isolated area. Not knowing what else to do she called out, "I'll be right there," and a rough male voice growled agreement. Then as she was pulling on a robe she heard Spotty's toenails clicking across the floor and a hoarse yell, "Will this dog bite?"

"Indeed he will! Just stand still," she called, and ran to the door in front of Spotty. He was rumbling in his throat, teeth bared and hackles up when she caught his collar.

Her knees began to shake when she saw the man standing

there. He was a husky, mean-looking bruiser with a bitter sneer on his face, down-and-out and full of resentment.

"I'm hungry and I want a meal," he snarled.

Mrs. Translin looked back at him steadily. "I can't let go of the dog but if you will shut the door and wait, I'll bring you something out in the yard."

When this was accomplished and the man left, she sank down trembling with her arms around Spotty. How had the animal known he was needed? He had come several miles through the intense heat long before her son would drive him home in comfort. And, why on that one day only, out of the three years they lived there?[8]

During World War II many stories appeared in the English newspapers of cats who were equally heroic. As rats are said to leave a doomed ship, so the cats, too, seemed to know when a bomb would hit a house. Some pet owners even wrote letters stating that so long as their pet cat remained peaceful they were not afraid during the air raids, but when puss grew wild and wanted out, they made for the bomb shelter at once. A special award, the Dickin Medal, engraved with a motto, "We Also Serve," was struck for these pets.

How can a cat know where a bomb will fall? How can dogs foresee lightning bolts, explosions, and the coming of a possibly dangerous stranger? Does precognition mean that events are foreordained, that living things are the helpless victims of predestination?

This may seem to be true because our conscious minds are limited to a linear time concept. But subconsciously we can perceive a greater aspect of causes and effects in a larger range of time. Time has latitude as well as longitude, is relative to movement, and there are various rates in the flow of time in different environments. Beings and things, organic and inorganic, are in motion, creating the events that are about to take place. The conscious mind cannot comprehend the future event that a series of apparently unrelated activities and movements will bring into existence, but seemingly, on rare occasions, the subconscious mind from a vaster level of perception and contact with the universal mind can do so.

The world's thinkers have pondered this great mystery and presented illuminating theories. Thus we have Albert Einstein's space-time, John Dunne's serialism, Dr. Gilbert Lewis's two-way time flow, and Carl Jung's synchronicity in which two events cross the barriers of space and time to produce what seems to be an incredible coincidence. We have multiple, recurring, and uni-dimensional time.

But it would appear that predestination is only a fractional truth. The event about to take place has in effect already occurred, because with or without the use of our free wills, the decisions and factors—internal and external—that will cause the event are in unalterable motion. When subconsciously the important causes are discerned and the effect foreseen, we have a prophetic dream, vision, or premonition.

Premonitions of death may be more frequent than is usually believed. There was a wise and gentle tomcat who lived through the German occupation of World War II at Versailles, France, in the antique shop of M. and Mme. Thibault. He was the one bright love in their troubled lives. They called him "Pussy," and taught him to hold out a paw and shake hands with everyone. Since Pussy's outgoing heart did not distinguish between friend and foe, he would approach a German soldier freely. Outraged by this, some stalwart patriots accused the Thibaults of keeping a "collaborationist cat," but fortunately neither the cat nor his owners was punished.

When Pussy grew older he came down with a serious attack of dysentery. In spite of all the vet could do, the condition became chronic. Finally, nothing remained to be done for him. Pussy was as dear to his owners as a child, but it was impossible to cope with his distressing condition, and he himself was so wretched that his life was now completely joyless. The grief-stricken Thibaults called the vet to come for him and put him to sleep.

To add to their sorrow, Pussy *knew*. Perhaps his own loving nature made him more sensitive to others. He and the vet had always been the best of pals, but this time when he arrived Pussy looked at him coldly.

Dragging his poor tormented body out of his basket he walked straight to monsieur and madame and with sorrowful dignity held out his small paw to each of them in turn. Then he faced about, his back to them all, crept into his basket, and buried his head in his paws as the vet carried him out.[9]

Mrs. M. H. Cummins, of Worcester, Massachusetts, tells the following story:

"Our smooth-haired fox terrier, Dagon, lived to be nearly 15 years old. During the last six months of his life, going upstairs was quite a problem for him, as he had to stop on almost every step to catch his breath.

"But one hot night in July I heard him come upstairs, shortly after midnight, just as briskly as he had ever done. He came to my side of the bed, and I stroked his head for a moment, whereupon he went around to my husband for the same attention. Then he pattered away to our boy's room.

"Somehow I felt uneasy about him and I got up. I saw Dagon just touch the cheek of the sleeping lad, then hurry to my sister's room. A minute later, he trotted quickly downstairs.

"For some time I was puzzled and uneasy. Finally I decided to investigate. He was lying at the foot of the stairs in his characteristic attitude: forepaws crossed, head resting a little sideways on them. He was dead.

"He had come upstairs to say goodbye."[10]

In a letter to the late Alan Devoe, Anna Nielson wrote that a stray cat that had reverted to the wild came to the door of her house one chilly day. She would not enter the house or accept milk but began to walk away, mewing, often stopping and looking back. Miss Nielson followed her and was led to the hayloft of the barn where deep in the hay four tiny blind kittens were concealed. This struck her as strange since cats usually go to great lengths to hide the location of their kittens.

The next morning Miss Nielson returned to the barn and found the kittens, frantic with hunger, trying to nurse. But their mother lay still in death. "Then I understood," Miss Nielson wrote. "Nature had told the mother that death was coming; and with her last strength she had made sure that someone would care for her little ones."[11]

The traditional belief that rats will desert a doomed ship may be supported by the curious experience of actor Raymond Massey and his wife. Mrs. Massey told the late Broadway columnist, Danton Walker, that during the 1940s they purchased a town house in Manhattan's East 80's. Across the street was an unoccupied old brownstone mansion that several months later was taken by a socially prominent woman and her family. This woman told Mrs. Massey that she could not get rid of the army of mice that also inhabited the dwelling.

Glancing out the window some days later, Mrs. Massey noticed to her astonishment a mass exodus of mice pouring from the basement of the brownstone. They came out in groups, running along the gutter as if confused and panicky. When some of them scurried across the street to the Massey residence, she called the exterminator. A few days afterward the woman across the street committed suicide.

With some difficulty and the help of several cats, the Masseys finally routed out the mice. Again the brownstone was vacant for a time, then was sold to a wealthy playboy. And just before his death made front-page news, Mrs. Massey again saw the mice move out in a mass migration, and again had to summon the exterminator to keep them from taking permanent residence in her own house.

The next owner of the house across the street was a prominent businessman. While watering plants in a window box one morning, Mrs. Massey saw the mice horde come forth again. "I went cold all over," she told Danton Walker. A few days later the businessman cracked up over the Hudson River while flying his own plane and drowned before rescuers could reach him.[12]

There is little doubt that dogs can sense death. Their death howl before the passing of a member of the household is a frequent and well-attested phenomenon. This may be due to an olfactory perception; perhaps dogs are able to detect some very slight odor that starts in the human body hours before death.

Thomas Hardy, the English poet and novelist, had a wire-haired terrier named Wessex as his close companion for thirteen years. The dog had a great liking for one of his master's friends, William Watkins. One spring evening Watkins called at the Hardy home and the dog as usual rushed into the hall with excited barks. Suddenly Wessex cringed and gave a long piteous whine, but when Mrs. Hardy investigated, nothing seemed amiss.

The dog joined his master and Watkins in the study and from time to time he went up to their visitor and touched his coat solicitously with his paw, which he always withdrew with a sharp cry of distress. Watkins, when he left after about an hour, was seemingly feeling fine and in good spirits.

Early the next morning the telephone rang. Usually Wessex barked loudly when this occurred, but this time he lay silent with his nose between his paws. The message was from Watkins' son, who said that his father had died quite suddenly about an hour after returning from the Hardy home.[13]

The late MacKenzie King, Prime Minister of Canada for twenty-two years, was very fond of his dog, Pat. The night before Pat died, the Prime Minister's watch fell off his bedside table for no apparent reason. He found it lying on the floor in the morning with the hands stopped at 4:20. "I am not psychic," MacKenzie King said, "But I knew then, as if a voice were speaking to me, that Pat would die before another twenty-four hours went by."

That night, with a last effort, Pat crawled out of his basket, climbed up on his master's bed, and died. The time was exactly 4:20.[14]

Perhaps a master can influence a living pet from beyond this life, especially in time of war when death seems close and the barriers thin. Seemingly this happened at the beginning of the century, to Capt. Carey I. Crockett, grandnephew of Davey Crockett of Alamo fame. A captain in the Philippine Constabulary, Carey Crockett was a tough, hard fighter like his forebear. His body bore many knife and bullet scars and he had killed seventeen men in close combat. He was certainly not a man given to visions.

At this time Captain Crockett was in the thick of the fighting against the native Visayans in the Philippines. He was in charge of the garrison in the town of San Ramon, on the east coast of the island of Samoa. In the interior, Lieutenant Stanley Hayt of the Philippine Scouts garrisoned the town of Dolores.

In December, 1904, Lieutenant Hayt and his whole force except for a sergeant were massacred. Hayt's constant pal had been his little fox terrier, which had been seen throughout the attack but disappeared after his death.

Many weeks later in February, 1905, Captain Crockett went with a task force on a scouting trip into the interior, leaving sixty-five men behind at the stockade at San Ramon. On their way back they camped for the night in the jungle. He was roused from sleep by the sergeant on guard, reporting that "something white" had been racing up and down in front of the sentries for some twenty minutes. Buckling on his revolver Captain Crockett stepped out into a slashing rain.

The jungle stank of death. He followed the sergeant to the racing white form and stopped in astonishment. It was the little terrier that had belonged to Lieutenant Hayt! He bent down to pet it, marveling that the little creature could have lived through three months unprotected in a venomous jungle, never seen by either their own men or a Filipino.

As he stroked the dog, his body grew rigid. In a way he was never able to explain, he got an urgent warning. "Go back to the stockade! The Visayans are going to attack San Ramon! Go back!"

They were a day's march away, a steep descent down a snaking mountain trail. All day the exhausted men had been plodding and the rain was a wall of hissing pellets. Yet Captain Crockett never hesitated. He knew "orders" even when he heard them with his inner mind. Breaking camp immediately, they fought their way through a cruel night of thunder, lightning, and lashing trees. At 5 A.M. they reached the stockade at San Ramon. Fifteen minutes later the attack came. One hundred Visayans were killed and of these sixty-five were picked off at the top of the fourteen-foot stockade.

If he had not heeded that mysterious message and returned with his task force of sixty men, the only slightly larger number of soldiers he had left behind would have been massacred like Lieutenant Hayt's garrison in December.

Crockett adopted the lieutenant's little dog, which lived for years thereafter but never again was a focal point for messages from beyond. Did Lieutenant Hayt send his small terrier from wherever it huddled in the jungle swamp, to warn of the attack? Captain Crockett always thought so.[15]

14

Tales of the Trail's End

There are many reports of the almost simultaneous deaths of owners and pets. Some could be coincidence. But, as we shall see, in circumstances of despair, certain animals, like men, can by an act of will deliberately die.

At Jarrow-on-Tyne, Durham, England, there was a bird lover named William Milburn. From time to time he kept wild birds in his home, but during his twilight years only one was left—a song-thrush that refused to fly away. She burst into melodious song whenever Milburn appeared, and would perch on his shoulders or atop his head as he walked about the house.

When Milburn was stricken with influenza, the thrush sang very little. He died early one morning, and that day and the three days that the coffin was in the house the bird did not sing at all.

When the day of the funeral arrived, the thrush was still silent. But as the pallbearers raised the casket to take it from the house, the bird began to sing more beautifully than ever before. Loud and clear came the notes of her requiem as the procession moved away. When the hearse left for the church and cemetery, the thrush again became silent. She never sang again, for the following morning she, too, was dead.[1]

When Thomas A. Beasely, aged sixty-seven, of Peoria, Illinois, suffered a sudden heart attack, he collapsed on the floor in his bedroom and died shortly thereafter. Several hours later his pet collie, Lady, who had been his inseparable companion for six years, scratched on the door of his room. Admitted by a member of the family, she crossed to the spot where her master had lain after his collapse and sniffed around uneasily. Suddenly she gave an odd cry and fell on her side, dead.[2]

During World War II when the Seabees followed the triumphant U. S. Marines in the Gilbert Islands, the engineers found a little white mongrel puppy left behind by the Japanese. The crew of an LCT claimed her as a mascot, fed her canned milk through an eyedropper, and successfully brought her to adulthood. They named her Puddles, and she became one of the most thoroughly babied dogs that lonely men ever adopted.

The time came when that particular LCT had served its time, and orders arrived that the craft was to be junked and sent to the bottom. Puddles now became a problem. She would not permit herself to be adopted by another crew, and regulations prohibited her from being taken to the States. Placed aboard another craft she whimpered continually and refused to eat. So the new crew let her go back to watch the condemned craft as it was stripped of equipment. Forlornly she sat on the beach while the men carried off spare parts, lockers—and her dog house.

When the LCT was towed out to be sunk, Puddles was still watching. She knew her home was going. Doubtless she somehow sensed that the crew she loved would be separated. It was the end of her happy time under a tropic sun.

After the craft had slid beneath the waves, the men came back to the beach. Puddles was still there, but she was no longer watching the disintegration of her little world. She was dead.[3]

Nor are such deliberate deaths limited to birds and dogs. In 1952 an Australian stockman, Colin Bell, committed suicide. His favorite horse, an eight-year-old chestnut named Toby, apparently sensed tragedy and became increasingly nervous. When Bell's relatives and friends gathered at the Bell homestead near Brisbane to hold memorial services. Toby went berserk. Repeatedly he dashed headlong into a post in uncontrollable frenzy until he fractured his skull and died.[4]

Charles B. Hefelfinger loved life—all life. His pockets always bulged with candy for the children of the old Webster school in Bethlehem, Pa., where he was janitor. Here, too, a flock of pigeons descended for cracked corn. Some he called by name as they perched on him, pecking at his buttons or pulling out loose threads. Even on stormy Sundays he went to feed his birds.

When Charlie retired they followed him to his home. They came at the same time, then disappeared. In that daily hour they belonged to him alone. When he was almost eighty, illness sent him to bed. Neighbors noticed then that his birds were sitting tightly along the ridgepole of his house. They sat quietly, heads under their wings, waiting.

When Charlie's spirit was freed, in response to some strange signal the pigeons took flight. They knew that Charlie would never feed them again. They never came back.

There were also wild geese who "knew." The Gambill Wild Goose Reservation, near Paris, Texas, was named for its founder, John Gambill. According to Joe F. Combs, feature writer for the Beaumont, Texas, *Enterprise,* Gambill once nursed a wounded honker back to health on his farm. Next autumn the gander returned bringing twelve geese which became tame as chickens.

The following year they came back a hundred strong. When Gambill gave his farm to the state, more than three thousand geese wintered there in safety. During the winter of 1961-62,

Gambill died in a Paris, Texas, hospital. And as he died, to the bewilderment of doctors, nurses and nearby residents, hundreds of geese flew over from the reservation, then circled round and round the building, calling with plaintive cries, honking their requiem.

Certain birds of portent and animals of destiny are identified with some old European families. They may appear just prior to a death or at the time of a death. Some of them are living animals, others seem to be apparitions.

The "Dun Cow of Warwick" in England is definitely an apparition. Its hoofs are silent and leave no trace on the grass. It comes to warn the Earl of Warwick before a member of the family dies. A similar omen for the Warders of Arundel is the appearance of two white owls on the roof of the manor house.

According to legend, "white birds" of unidentified species have appeared for centuries on the Salisbury Plain whenever the Bishop of Salisbury is dying. They are exceptionally large and fly like the albatross, with unmoving wings of dazzling brilliance.

In 1885 the birds were seen by Miss Anne Moberley above the palace grounds just before the death of her father, the bishop. Again, in 1911, Miss Edith Olivier, who had never heard the legend, was returning from taking the Wilton choir boys on their annual picnic. Toward dusk as they were riding in a wagonette, she saw two great white birds sailing over the meadows in the direction of Salisbury three miles distant. She pointed them out to the boys. Neither Miss Olivier nor her youthful charges had ever seen such birds before, and they were the top subject for conversation during the rest of the trip. On arrival in Wilton they learned that the bishop, who had apparently been in good health, had died suddenly earlier in the day.

At Longleat, the great estate of the Marquis of Bath, the omen is the disappearance of a bird. When the master of the house is about to die, it is claimed that one of the swans living on the artificial lakes around the house takes flight never to return.

The present Lord Bath says that during World War I, when his elder brother the Marquis was fighting in France, his mother saw a swan fly away. This happened one morning in 1916 while she was standing by a window. She saw five swans flying slowly toward her, then they circled the huge mansion, coming quite close. Suddenly one bird left the formation and disappeared, while the others returned to the water. The children tried to comfort her but their mother was depressed all day. Next morning the official telegram announcing the death of her son was brought to her.[5]

In a dispatch from Paris dated October 18, 1958, Paul Ghali, a reporter for the Chicago Daily News Service, tells of the experience of a friend of his, "a well-known diplomat." Visiting the diplomat in his home in Place Rue St. Florentin, next to the United Nations regional organization offices, was his cousin, a Hungarian woman refugee from the 1956 revolt.

At breakfast one morning she appeared distressed.

"What's wrong, Aunt Ergie?" asked the diplomat.

"I heard that owl last night."

"Nonsense, what owl?"

"No nonsense, just like back home. In Hungary an owl comes and hoots at the bedroom windows each time a member or a very close friend of the family dies."

The diplomat laughed. "Even if it weren't rank superstition," he said, "it couldn't happen here. How could an owl get anywhere near your window? We are in the middle of the city. There are no trees to attract any kind of bird. Besides, I can't think of any relatives, here or back in Hungary, whose time is up."

But next day at breakfast the diplomat himself looked tired. "Aunt Ergie, you were right. I heard the owl myself last night. What sinister hoots in the dark! It must have been perched on the roof of the American Talleyrand Hotel. A nuisance, to be sure, but I don't believe in your death omens."

"We'll see," Aunt Ergie said quietly.

At lunch time the telephone rang. It brought news that the wife of the diplomat's first cousin had been killed in an automobile accident fifty miles outside Paris.

Abbott Butler of the great Benedictine Abbey of Downside in England was one of the outstanding scholars and historians of his day. Shortly before World War I while he was visiting in Ireland, one of the Roman Catholic peers of the realm, named Gormanstown, died. The abbott went to the funeral. The Gormanstown title is the second oldest of all the viscount-cies of the British Isles, going back to A.D. 1478. The manor is on the border of County Meath not far from Dublin.

A coachman met the abbott at the railway station. During the drive the man was silent. As the carriage passed through the grounds of the estate, the abbott noticed groups of two and three dogs under various trees in the park, and in an attempt to be friendly he remarked, "I see the family is very fond of dogs." The coachman frowned and made no reply.

Later, in the drawing room as they waited for dinner to be announced, the abbott turned to his hostess and said once more, "I've noticed you have a lot of dogs about the place."

The woman visibly stiffened with embarrassment, offered no comment, and abruptly began a conversation with another guest. And it was this guest who drew the abbott aside after dinner.

"I must explain to you why your remark about the dogs disturbed our hostess so much," he said. "I thought everyone knew, although it's seldom mentioned, especially at a time like this."

"What do you mean?" asked the puzzled abbott.

"This is a very ancient family," the guest continued. "Whenever a head of the house dies, beginning several hours before the death and until the body is in the ground, all the foxes in the neighborhood come to the estate and surround the house. I assure you that until the peer is buried there won't be a fox outside the demesne for miles around! Why this happens, no one knows, but it is embarrassing to the family."

When Abbott Butler went to his room for the night, he drew back the curtain and saw clusters of the animals under the trees in the moonlight. Later, after the funeral, the abbott made further inquiries, and the appearance of the mourning foxes of Gormanstown was confirmed by all who knew the family or the district.

Gerald Heard, the well-known British-American writer, offers additional information resulting from his own inquiries.[6] A relative of his employed near Dublin became acquainted with the Earl of Fingall, the premier Catholic peer of Ireland and a man of scrupulous honesty. Earlier the earl had been master of the hounds with one of the most famous fox-hunting packs in all Europe, the Meath Hunt.

"A strange thing happened while I was Master of the Meath," Lord Fingall told Heard. "The Lord Gormanstown of that day died and my huntsman told me that as long as the body was above ground there would be no use in drawing a covert. Naturally no hunt was scheduled during this mourning period, but I considered the belief countryside superstition.

"As a Catholic dignitary it was obligatory for me to attend the funeral, and it was proper for a funeral guest to enter the small domestic chapel alongside the house and pray by the coffin. When I walked to the chapel door it was dusk, and there on the steps sat two dogfoxes. To my astonishment they showed no fear of me, but drew aside a few paces to allow me to enter. Naturally I could ask no questions, but this experience ended my skepticism."

Several years later Heard's employer in London, Sir Horace Plunkett, employed as one of his secretaries a male member of the Gormanstown family. With Sir Horace's permission, Heard interviewed the man and his questions were answered with mild embarrassment. Yes, it was true that at each death of a head of the house, the foxes came into the manor grounds and stayed there prowling about the house until the burial. This was never, of course, publicized. No family member knew when or why it began, but only that it was a happening of great age and without explanation.

While the Gormanstown fox-funeral may be a freak survival from a time long ago, the psychic power of totemism still exists.

Earlier in this book we told of anthropologist Geoffrey Gorer who found astonishing psychic kinships between West African tribes and certain wild animals. And we told of scholar Ronald Rose who found totems were vehicles for information that was apparently acquired telepathically by Australian aborigines. The appearance of the animal or bird announces an accident, the illness or the death of another member of the same totem clan. Such appearances are usually apparitions, but sometimes the abnormal behavior of an actual animal induces the telepathic message.

Totemic beliefs could cause the recipient of a simple telepathic message from another person to believe the totem animal brought the warning. But the appearance of actual animals at times, however, indicates an external controlling intelligence. If so, what and where is it?

Here we must return to the "spirit of the colony" or "soul of the hive" concept. Thoughts can create. From many minds and associations between beings, there may have developed on higher, psychic levels, independent mentalities, separate entities that are symbolic of the represented animal or totem. Again, for each species of higher life there may exist a kind of god-form.

Consider the experience of Paul M. Vest, of Santa Monica, California, who seemingly has some clairvoyant ability. He had a Chihuahua named Gringo who became seriously ill. The dog was taken to a pet hospital where the diagnosis was an acute stomach and intestinal infection. During the next few days Gringo's condition worsened despite the use of antibiotics and other medication. Internal hemorrhaging developed, and the veterinarian said nothing more could be done to save the pet.

Mr. Vest brought his dog back home. Gringo hadn't been able to eat, was too weak to stand, and could in fact scarcely lift his head. That night Vest was holding the dog on his lap. A feeling of intense compassion enveloped him. He thought, "Isn't there somewhere a power, a force that will help this suffering, dying little dog?" It was not a prayer, said Vest, but a vivid concept empowered by deep feeling. As it was only a question in his mind, he expected no answer.

"But almost immediately," he said, "a strange thing began to happen. First, Gringo's ears pricked up as though he had heard someone speak. Then slowly he lifted his wobbly head and his eyes fixed on something out of my line of vision to my left. An uncanny but not unpleasant feeling passed over me as I sensed the presence of something or someone in the room. I turned quickly and saw the strange figure Gringo's eyes seemed focused upon.

"As incredible as it may seem, the figure resembled a small man with a rather doglike head, yet it was more like a man than a dog. It did not stand fully upright, but inclined at a slight angle. Although I saw the figure for only a few seconds it definitely was there, a solid, three-dimensional object. When I no longer could see the figure, it was apparent that Gringo still could, and from his intent, listening expression it was obvious that the dog was hearing sounds inaudible to me."

Beneath Vest's fingers Gringo's tiny body was tense and trembling. Moments later the dog looked up at his master. The glazed appearance had left his eyes. Shakily he got to his feet and wagged his tail. He drank some warm milk. That night he slept soundly and the following morning ate a good breakfast. All fever, retching, and bleeding were gone.

"Gringo is alive and healthy today," Vest wrote, "but I know that without the intervention of some being from perhaps another dimension, Gringo would not be here now."[7]

If pets can visit their dying owners, even occasionally join them in death, it is not surprising that some attend funerals. These acts cause us to wonder anew at the great depth of empathy that can grow between some masters and pets. And in the minds of animals, does the concept, the understanding of death differ from that of man?

In the English magazine *Tomorrow* (Autumn, 1963) a correspondent told the story of his grandfather and a cat named Bill. The pair shared their activities by day and their bed by night. Then the grandfather was seriously hurt in a railway accident. For a week he fought for life in a hospital about four miles from the village where he had spent his life and where Bill now roamed listlessly.

He died in the hospital and his body was taken from there to the church, also several miles away, so that the funeral cortage at no time approached the home. After the service the coffin was carried out into the churchyard for burial. As the committal rites were concluded, one of the uncles looked up and in astonishment grasped his sister's arm. There was Bill coming across the field in a direct line from the grandfather's home. The cat moved with dignity to the open grave and stood for a moment looking down at the coffin. Then, having paid his respects, he turned around and headed for home.

Can cattle, too, feel grief?

Mrs. Grace N. Isaacs, in her article "Magic Zoology in the British West Indies" (*Tomorrow* magazine, Summer, 1953) tells a strange story. A man named Henry owned a large cattle ranch near Trelawney. He seemed to have a personal affection for his animals and was unwilling to leave them in the care of an overseer. He died quite suddenly. The coffin was placed on a wagon for the journey to the church and cemetery. The distance from the house to the gate of the estate was great, and a large group of mourners had gathered.

As the procession slowly moved along, the mourners were startled when the moaning and bellowing of cattle broke the silence. The herd of animals came up from the surrounding pastures and stood in long lines behind the fence on both sides of the drive. They pawed the ground, flourished their tails, and tossed their heads as they lamented in tones so different from their usual gentle lowing.

"Telling the bees" of the death of their keeper aloud, or by draping the hive in black crepe, is an ancient custom. But more extraordinary are authenticated stories of bees who attended the funerals!

In April, 1961, the Associated Press reported that when Sam Rogers, cobbler and postman of the Shropshire village of Myddle in England, died, his children walked around his fourteen hives and told his bees.

On Sunday, relatives gathered at the grave. Moments later his son breathlessly summoned the rector, Rev. Ayling. From Sam's hives over a mile away the bees came by thousands. Ignoring the flowering trees they concentrated entirely on the funeral wreaths. Half an hour later they returned to the hives.

Said the minister: "I have no explanation to offer. Of course, I try to rationalize such events, but if I didn't, I would say that those bees came to say goodbye to Sam."

The annals of psychic research contain numerous other accounts of puzzling phenomena at times of death—even the stopping of clocks. In the following tale roosters were stopped, and we suggest that if donkeys and cattle can come to a funeral, it may be possible to silence chickens.

Granny Elizabeth Muncy was a strong-willed, independent mountain woman past eighty years old who lived alone in a small farmhouse near Inez, Kentucky. She made pets of her chickens, stroking them in her lap, talking to them, giving each one a name. In February, 1944, she was on her death bed and in the care of her daughter Lydia, who lived nearby. At that time she had about a dozen roosters who fought among themselves and noisily dominated the henhouse.

The morning before Granny Muncy died the roosters were

so noisy that the old lady couldn't sleep. "I don't want any noise like that when I die," she told Lydia. "I want to go quiet."

The next morning not a rooster crowed. Her grandson, Henry T. Stepp, of Detroit, Michigan, said it was weird, uncanny. Granny expired at ten o'clock that morning, and the birds remained silent until the following day.[9]

There are the magnets of loving hearts that have guided lost dogs and cats to the new homes of their owners, but what strange compass or directional beam pilots pets to the graves of those they have loved?

One of Albert Payson Terhune's stories about his Sunnybank collies deals with an odd angle. Few animals remember their young for years after they are weaned, but his Sunnybank Jean was an exception. Jock, one of her pups, remained her puppy still, long after he was a grown dog. She took the best morsel from her own dish to him, brought him ripe bones, and even when he grew bigger than she, daily washed him from his head to the tip of his plumey tail with her loving tongue. Wherever Jock went, Jean trailed after him in worshipful devotion.

But Jock got distemper and had to be isolated. In those days before antibiotics the disease was almost invariably fatal, and although Jock struggled to survive as hard as Terhune did to save him, they lost the dog. During the quarantine Jean had been kept far away with the other collies, where she moped and refused to eat.

They buried Jock far out in a field, a quarter of a mile away. But next morning when Jean was released, she began pacing the grounds methodically, sniffing for her "puppy" and giving the occasional sharp bark that had always brought him running in the past.

Finally she entered the field where Jock was buried. Immediately she raced back for Terhune, tail wagging, and caught hold of his coat. Pulling and coaxing she led him to the mound that was Jock's grave. Then she lay down, her tail still wagging. She seemed to think that Jock was close and that here if anywhere he would come back to her.

Daily until her death years later, regardless of the weather, Jean would visit Jock's grave. Sometimes she stayed stretched across it for hours at a time.

"Her waiting had no grief in it," said Terhune. "It was full of gay hope."[10]

At St. Kilda, near Melbourne lived Mr. and Mrs. Robert King, their little girl, and Mrs. King's elderly father, who had a black-and-white cat named Felix. When the old gentleman died at ninety, Felix could not be comforted. He barely ate, and roamed the house and yard, searching and crying. The family found the cat's grief hard to bear in addition to their own, and to distract the pet they took him for a ride. On the outskirts of Melbourne they stopped at a traffic light.

And then something happened. Somehow Felix knew. He got to his feet, his coat bristling, stood trembling for a few seconds, then sprang out of the car's open window to the street. Dodging through the traffic, he was soon out of sight. The family went home to wait for him but he never came back.

Ten days later Mrs. King and her daughter went to the cemetery with some flowers. There pacing back and forth on the grave was Felix. As they approached, the cat became frantic with joy. He ran up to the little girl and began boxing with her just as he formerly did with the grandfather. Not only did this odd little game identify him, but he had the scar above one eye inflicted by an air-gun pellet, and the kink in a once-broken tail. Yet the cemetery was ten miles from their home, and at least five miles from the place where the cat had jumped out of the car.

Twice before, they were ready to leave and got Felix as far as the cemetery gate, but each time he leaped out of the automobile at that point. Mrs. King then arranged for the custodian to feed and care for the cat.

After John Hetherington interviewed the family he drove out to the cemetery. There was Felix, still pacing like a sentry, occasionally resting. Later Hetherington wrote: "This story haunts me. Perhaps it's because there are in it features that lie beyond the frontiers of human understanding."[12]

15

Some Steps Beyond

We have had stories of pets—frivolous, wise, roguish, and
often touching; tales gathered from many sources. All were
vouched for as true and many have authentication. Some of
our incidents have been sad, many inspire wonder, and others
are so enigmatic that we can only guess at the mysteries they
conceal.

"Life is a foreign language; all men mispronounce it," said
Christopher Morley. And without question we also misunder-
stand it. But what is truth?

In Greek mythology Proteus was one of the ancient gods of
the everchanging sea. His duty was to guard Poseidon's herd
of seals. Each noon he emerged from the waves and rested on
a rock with the seals about him. He was known as the Shape-
Shifter. He knew the future, and the right moment to ask
him for the truth was when he rested thus in the clear light of
high noon.

So here on earth, Truth too is a shape-shifter, and we must
gaze on it as upon the Gorgon's head, unterrified, to pierce
its veiled forms—enduring its shifting aspects in order to be

"initiated into the secret for all sorts and conditions of life."
No human mind is profound enough to find THE truth—but
on this level where Truth is a shape-shifter, only A truth.

From the truths and half-truths of these stories, each must
find his own truth, to his own satisfaction. Our purpose is only
to open the doors of wonder and turn you loose.

Earlier we presented evidence that the minds of men and
animals are rooted in a common soil—the great collective unconscious, the earth-mind that merges the thought images of all
species. As between humans, so telepathic communication can
exist between masters and pets, especially at crisis periods of
illness, danger, accident, or death. And from this reservoir of
wisdom may come the instinct that leads life along ageless
trails, and the inspiration that creates genius.

This is a medium that ignores the apparent limitations of
space and time, born of love, that offers resonance between
hearts, and guides the lost pet over weary miles to a new home
he never knew. Can we believe that these astonishing sensi-
tivities of the animal mind and spirit are transitory, and in the
end, meaningless? Do the factors that can foresee events and
the affection that makes a good Samaritan die with the dust of
the physical body?

We can hardly expect to find certainties in this nebulous
realm. Perhaps it is not so important what we believe as that
we believe something—and keep testing our beliefs. But upon
one conviction we stand—that man cannot assign a surviving
soul to himself, and deny it to his animal brothers; that both
man and animal are creatures of instinct and reason with the
difference one of degree and not of kind; and that if consciousness does survive, it is a quality of life itself and not of *homo
sapiens*.

Not only great poets like Tennyson have been convinced

> "That nothing walks with aimless feet,
> That not one life shall be destroyed

Or cast as rubbish to the void
When God hath made the pile complete."

Standing with us on this conviction are theologians like
Martin Luther, John Keble, and John Wesley; authors like
Alexander Pope and Charles Kingsley; naturalists like Louis
Agassiz; and many, many brilliant minds. Referring to a life
to come, John Wesley wrote: "The whole brute creation will
then, undoubtedly, be restored, not only to the vigor, strength
and swiftness which they had at their creation, but to a far
higher degree of each than they ever enjoyed . . . as a re-
compense for what they once suffered . . . they shall enjoy
happiness suited to their tastes, without alloy, without inter-
ruption and without end."

The reports that follow are controversial. We do not reject
a phenomenon because of its popular explanation, and these
incidents can be interpreted in more ways than one. But regardless of the correct answers, when physical life ceases to exist
it seems to leave behind a psychic residue that can affect human
minds.

Gypsy was a springer spaniel with curly brown and white
fur. She was a dog who was in love with the sound of her own
voice, and "sang" at the drop of a hint. A whistling boy in the
street, the radio of a passing car, or anyone in the household
singing at work would set Gypsy off into her act. She belonged
to Mrs. Ethel Bailey, of La Mesa, California.

"She loved best of all," her mistress said, "to sit on the piano
bench beside me and pour forth a soulful dirge—a reversion
to her dim, canine past when her ancestors sat at the mouths of
caves to cry at the moon or weep to the stars."

In October, 1936, Gypsy ran under the wheels of a car
and was killed. Her cruel death saddened the family. Mrs.
Bailey couldn't bear to touch the piano for several days. When
she did, it was to try out a new melody. As her hands picked
out the unfamiliar notes she was not thinking of Gypsy at all.

But almost at once she heard a low whining. It seemed to come from the porch, and was followed by a howl. She opened the front door but saw nothing. Just then a cousin who was visiting her came in from the side yard with an armful of garden flowers. She had never known Gypsy and the dog's death had not been mentioned to her.

As she put the flowers into a vase she inquired, "Ethel, what dog was howling along with you as you played?"[1]

The late Dr. Nandor Fodor, the noted psychoanalyst whose contributions to parapsychology have been exceptionally valuable, told of the experience of Mrs. Henry Wipperman, of Howard Beach, Long Island, New York, in his book *Between Two Worlds*. She had two dogs, Skippy and Teddy. Skippy died from asthma and was buried in the yard. That evening, Mrs. Wipperman said, Skippy's distinctive, familiar wheeze could be heard in the house. Not only was it heard by Mrs. Wipperman and her mother, but the other dog Teddy raised his ears, and began looking all around for his playmate.

Seven years later Teddy was dying. "I broke down crying and patted his head," Mrs. Wipperman said. "He let out a long sigh. The next day he was dead and we buried him. That evening I heard the special pant he developed when he became sick. I was embarrassed to mention it, but when I heard it again I asked mother, 'Did you hear him?' She said yes, she had heard him, but did not want to tell me lest it upset me."

Dr. Fodor points out that hallucination is not the answer in this case. Not only was Skippy's wheeze heard independently by both women, but by Teddy. This manifestation may be of limited time. "The life substance or the personality that makes up a devoted animal may persist for awhile," the doctor writes. "Whether it endures, that is the great question which concerns human beings and animals alike."

It is evident that very few dogs and cats can manifest in this manner, just as few are capable of finding their way back home over a thousand miles. Factors other than loving and being loved must be responsible. To varying degrees pets may be "psychic sensitives."

Fingal was a remarkable cat whose story was told in the English magazine *Prediction*. He had exceptionally developed senses of responsibility, sympathy, and affection for the other pets in the family. One was a turtle who repeatedly fell helplessly on its back while clambering about his outdoor rockery. When this happened Fingal would run in great agitation to members of the family, insisting on their coming promptly to the rescue.

One day Fingal remained outside by the rockery so stubbornly that his food was taken out to him. When he continued his vigil on the following day, the family realized something was wrong with the turtle. A veterinarian put it to sleep when he found it could not recover, so they buried the turtle in the garden while Fingal was kept indoors. But as soon as the cat was let out he ran to the spot where the turtle was buried and stayed sadly close for several days.

When one of the pet rabbits was sick, Fingal knew and stood like a small guardian by the cage until it recovered. Seemingly he sensed, too, when a human being was fatally ill, but in this case he remained at a distance, even though it was one in whose lap he had loved to sit. This happened so often that the family came to dread it as an omen. "Fingal is psychic," they admitted to each other.

Then Fingal himself developed a fatal illness and the vet was called to put him to sleep. Once more he knew, and the farewell look he gave his mistress was full of love and devotion. "I understand," it seemed to say. "It will be all right."

"Fingal had been as regular in his comings and goings as an elderly bachelor," his mistress, Celia Dale, said. "He liked to go out in the evening, stay an hour, and return punctually at nine o'clock. Then he would tap loudly on the French window to be let in."

Shortly after his death the tapping commenced again, and

would be so insistent that they would open the window. Then it would cease. Several times, too, they were sure they heard purrs from his favorite yellow cushion.

Then one afternoon a friend brought over her Siamese cat. When the Siamese approached this particular chair with its yellow cushion, he arched his back in fright. Then his eyes lowered slowly, seeming to follow another small being that moved to the window. When that was opened the Siamese settled quietly down on the cushion as if it had been vacated for his use.

Not only sound but touch was experienced by Francis Anderson, of Canoga Park, California, when his dog came to say farewell. In 1944 he had adopted a homeless stray, a mixture of chow and husky. Ted became a devoted pal, tagging at his heels in the one-man devotion of the chow. In the summer of 1955 Anderson was invited for a week's fishing trip by a friend who owned a small boat. Taking Ted along was too full of problems so the dog remained at home.

In the middle of their sixth night out in the boat Anderson was awakened by Ted licking the side of his face. He could feel the weight of the dog's body against him. Forgetting that he was aboard a fishing boat he put out a hand to pat Ted, felt him move slightly away, and distinctly heard a low whine. Then he came wide awake. With his flashlight he searched the boat but there were only his sleeping friend and himself aboard.

It was 1:10 A.M. The rest of the night he couldn't sleep, haunted by the feeling that something was wrong with Ted. When they docked next day, he phoned his wife and asked about the dog.

She hesitated, then said the dog was dead. "I heard him wailing in your bedroom last night and went in to quiet him. He was lying on your bed with tears running from his eyes. Then he let out another whine and just seemed to stiffen."

"What time was it? Do you remember?"

"It was around 1:00 A.M. or a little after," his wife said.[2]

Psychic manifestations by animals after death seem to be limited, with few exceptions, to dogs, cats, and horses. Take the ghost horse that Angus McDougall, the North Carolina sculptor, and his brother Ken heard when they were aged sixteen and thirteen. Present at the time was their famous father, Dr. William McDougall, professor of psychology at Harvard for many years, and head of that department at Duke University when he died in 1938.

The family had taken a picnic supper to a deserted New England farmhouse, where they could enjoy a majestic view of the White Mountains. A Miss Baird, whose aged father owned the farm, drove them in her Model T Ford until the long-unused trail became so rough and heavy with brush that they finished on foot.

At the top, in the midst of an overgrown pasture, stood the ruins of an abandoned two-room house. With the red western sunset shining between its shrunken timbers, it was a gaunt and desolate wreck. The adults gathered on the cliff a short distance away to admire the view and prepare the meal, while Angus and Ken ran back to explore the ancient house.

Its shingle roof was still intact but the single door hung inwards from a broken hinge. Inside was only an earth floor and a rough stair leading to a windowless attic room. Ken climbed the stair while Angus stepped outside and walked to the back.

"There several lank elderberry bushes had grown up over the roof forming a sort of tunnel or passage against the wall," Angus said. "I stepped inside this passage, and at once heard a horse snorting and kicking inside the house. I thought it might be Ken playing a trick on me, but a moment later he appeared round the corner and stood beside me under the bushes, and we could both hear it.

"We put our ears to the wall and listened, but that was hardly necessary. The snorting and kicking were desperate and loud. We dashed around to the front and went in. But the house was as silent and empty as before. Ken began looking for a cellar with a live horse in it, but there was only the solid earthen floor and the two rooms, one above the other. We stood staring at one another in utter bewilderment. Ken turned very white in the face, and no doubt I did, too. Without speaking we walked slowly back to rejoin the picnic party by the cliff.

"When we got there Miss Baird was in the middle of telling the sad history of the place. Many years before, her father's tenants, a young couple with two children, pulled out one autumn and headed west in their wagon. They took their tools and a few bits of furniture with them. They left behind on the land an old white horse, too weak to start out on such a long journey. Evidently it took shelter in the empty house during a winter storm, the door swung shut, and it was trapped inside.

"When Mr. Baird came out to inspect his property early the following spring, he entered the house and found the carcass. He buried it under the earthen floor inside the house. Outside, the snows were not yet melted and the ground was frozen. No one had lived there since that time. In all the intervening years there were very few people even near the place. Obviously it was visited only by the animals of the woods, the birds, the winds, and the changing seasons."

The boys told the others about their strange experience. Dr. McDougall, who had given many years to psychic research, did not say much since it was obvious his sons had been frightened. But he did say that since their joint experience had been spontaneous and simultaneous it was of much greater significance than any single-handed account could have been.

"For the record," Angus McDougall concludes, "I want to make it clear that the impressions we received were not at all faint or ghostly, although the setting was strange enough. They were loud, urgent, and unmistakably real. But they were, after all, only a succession of sounds. We saw nothing unusual. There remains the perhaps significant point that Miss Baird was sitting at a little distance away while we went exploring.

Was her knowledge, awareness, and thought communicated to us in terms of a telepathically audible reconstruction of a long-past event? And, if so, what type of experience was this?"[3]

Phantom dogs have appeared on photographs, and while some of these pictures may be questionable, there are others that seem genuine. If ghosts are not wholly subjective images but have any degree of objectivity, then there is no reason why they cannot be photographed under the proper conditions.

An account that appears authentic appears in a handbook on the care of dogs, *That Dog of Yours,* by Anne Elizabeth Blochin, published in 1941 by Macmillan Company of Canada, Ltd. A pet cemetery called "Happy Woodland" was located on property owned by the Blochins. Several hundred people gathered on the day the cemetery's central monument was unveiled. One of the visitors photographed a flower-banked grave marker during the ceremony. The visitor was only interested in the gravestone and saw no dogs, living or dead.

Mrs. Blochin wrote: "On developing the negative, the photographer was amazed to see, clearly defined in the picture, the figure of a dog lying at the foot of the grave. She sent it to us with the query: 'Is this the spirit of your Happy Woodland?' It was the undeniable likeness of a dog, although there were no living dogs in the cemetery at the time.

"When the photograph was shown to the owners of the grave, they immediately recognized it as that of their pet, a beloved small mongrel . . . He had been buried there some months before. That this might not be thought the power of mere suggestion, they submitted several photographs of the dog in life, which show a resemblance so striking as to be remarkable."

Most ghost dogs are seen as apparitions. In the same book Mrs. Blochin tells of her personal experience with a phantom canine. The family had a dog named Solo that escaped from the kennel late one afternoon. About an hour later they were having dinner when the early evening train, which passed near

the house, roared by. An instant later, Mrs. Blochin saw
Solo run past the dining-room window.

"There's Solo!" she cried in relief. "He's home again!"

But night came and Solo did not return to his kennel. Next
morning when he still did not appear for breakfast, she set
off through the woods with one of the other dogs to look for
him. They had not gone far when Solo trotted out from
behind a tree, frisking up to his dog friend. Both animals
wagged their tails and romped together before Mrs. Blochin
turned back for home.

When she looked around to call the dogs, Solo had disappeared again. Back at the house she was greeted by her
husband, who told her that Solo's body had just been found
on the railroad tracks. No train had passed since the one of
the night before. On both occasions when she saw Solo, outside the dining-room window and in the woods, the dog had
been so close that there was no chance of mistaken identification. And on the second occasion her other dog had joined in
the recognition.

The distinguished English author, Mrs. A. M. W. Stirling,
tells of another ghost dog that was observed and touched by an
acquaintance of hers. The account appears in her book *Ghosts
Vivisected*.[4]

Miss Anne Grazebrook, the narrator, while visiting her sister, Mrs. Bond Cabell of Cromer Hall, Norfolk, felt sorry for
a dog named Bounce—a stray of mixed breed who had been
given asylum on the estate. Bounce received very little attention
and petting since he was an ugly, common-looking animal in
harsh contrast to the beautiful pedigreed dogs belonging to
the family. Miss Grazebrook noticed that Bounce seemed
cowed by inferiority and was especially kind to him. He soon
developed a devoted affection for her.

Sometime later, while she was staying with friends in Aber-
deen, she was awakened about five in the morning by the
barking of a dog in her bedroom. "I sat up in bed," she said,

"and to my surprise I saw Bounce. I put out my hand and felt him. He had his collar on and he was warm and solid to the touch. In utter astonishment I exclaimed 'Bounce, how did you get here?' and a human voice replied, 'I was shot yesterday—I have come to say goodbye!' Then the dog was gone. How he came, how he went, whence came the voice, I could not say. I was left in a state of complete bewilderment."

Several weeks later Miss Grazebrook received a letter from her sister's governess. It stated that as the family was going away and it was impossible to find a home for a mongrel like Bounce, it was thought kinder to have him shot. This had occurred on August 24 about noon, and the dog had appeared in the bedroom around five o'clock in the morning of the following day.

"I can only add," Miss Grazebrook concludes, "that at the time when I saw the dog, it did not occur to me even remotely that he was dead. His bark was loud enough to rouse me from a heavy sleep; he did not look distressed, merely excited as a dog might be at the sight of an old friend, and I can only repeat that when I patted him he was apparently alive and tangible beneath my hand."

Both in this case and in the earlier one where Francis Anderson's dog appeared on the fishing boat, the answer may lie in visual, auditory, and tactile hallucinations. Such crisis hallucinations often "come true" and seem to dramatize a telepathic message. In these two cases the principals were asleep and thus sensitive to the reception of ESP impulses or images. And it is in the hypnagogic or half-wake state that the mind is most receptive to hallucinations.

With whatever means Bounce crossed the great abyss, it is touching that this lonely but affectionate dog, shot because of his ancestry and lack of beauty, should at death express gratitude for the only love that had ever been shown him.

Dream imagery from the vast collective unconscious may account for the following vision of another Englishwoman. The

story was told by Violet Bromley-Wilson in the London publication, *The Field,* in 1945.

Under the title "Strange Vision," the author wrote:

"My mother was dying and I went to be with her and took
my maid with me, who had never been to the house before.
My mother died at 2 A.M.

"Later on in the day my maid asked me not to think her
crazy but she would like to speak of what had happened to
her that night. She said: 'I was wide awake in bed when I
found myself outside her Ladyship's door, and watching three
little dogs who kept jumping at the handle like dogs do who
are waiting to go out for a walk.'

"Knowing what strange happenings *had* occurred before
in my old home over dogs, I said: 'What colour were they?'
And she said that they could not have been my mother's, as in
my day, when I was living at home, she kept white terriers.
Still my maid persisted and then said: 'I found I was back in
bed again.'

"Two days after, I was turning out some drawers in my
mother's sitting room downstairs which had, since my mother
was taken ill, been locked up, and my maid was while waiting
looking at the pictures round the room. *'Oh!'* she said. 'There
are the little dogs.'

"On the wall was a water colour drawing of three little
dogs, an Italian 'Pom' and two small Aberdeens. On the back
of the picture was written: 'The first dogs I had when I came
to Glen Tara, aged 13, Edith Brooks.' "

Albert Payson Terhune's *The Book of Sunnybank,*[5] tells of
his ghost collie—Rex, a big crossbreed dog who was almost
the size of a Great Dane. From puppyhood he was slavishly
devoted to Terhune. A spot in the hallway outside Terhune's
study door was "his favorite and only resting place." Not allowed in the dining room, the dog would usually watch the
Terhune meals through the french windows from the verandah
just behind his master's chair.

Rex was killed in March, 1916. In the summer of 1917 a friend, the Reverend Appleton Grannis, who had not been at Sunnybank for years, came for a visit. One afternoon he and his host were chatting while seated at the dining-room table. As usual, Terhune's back was toward the french windows.

Later as they left the room the minister said, "I thought I knew all your dogs, but there's one I never saw until now. The big dog with the short fawn-colored coat and a scar across his nose. This dog has been standing outside the window staring in at you all the time we've been in this room. He's gone now. Which of your dogs is he?"

Only Rex, who had died a year before, fitted this description, yet the Reverend Grannis had never seen him alive, nor heard of him from Terhune. But another friend of Terhune's, Henry A. Healy, who had been interested in the problems of crossbreeding had made a study of Rex.

One evening in the autumn of 1918 Mr. and Mrs. Healy called on the Terhunes. As they were leaving, Healy remarked, "You know, Bert, I wish there were some creature so utterly devoted to me as Rex is to you. I've been watching him as he lay at your feet. He kept looking up into your face every minute with a queer kind of adoration."

"Good Lord, man! Rex has been dead for more than two years!"

Healy frowned. "Yes, I remember now." He hesitated, then with an air of defiance added, "Just the same I would swear he was lying in the firelight at your feet all evening!"

One of the Sunnybank collies, Bruce, lived for four years after Rex's death and was the only dog then allowed in the study. During these years the dog never once set his foot on the stretch of hallway floor that had been Rex's favorite resting place. When called into the study Bruce carefully detoured around this spot as if avoiding something lying there—an act that was witnessed by many guests. Occasionally in fact his problems in avoiding this perfectly vacant spot were comical.

Although dogs seem the most frequent of animal apparitions, they must share the limelight with other creatures domesticated by man. In his book *Animal Ghosts,* Elliot O'Donnell, the British writer, offers a tale of a phantom cat as related to him by a Mrs. Louise Marlowe.[6]

Early in this century Mrs. Marlowe was visiting a friend in the small Yorkshire village of Congleton. One afternoon while driving a pony cart they stopped close to the ruins of an old abbey to pick some wild roses from the hedgerows. As the two women approached the abbey gates they saw a magnificent plump white cat sitting on top of one of the posts.

"I wonder if it would let us pet it?" Mrs. Marlowe remarked.

As they approached the cat suddenly leaped into the air and vanished. The hayfield around the post had been cut and the stubble was not high enough to conceal a cat. In bewilderment the women looked at each other. "At the time," said Mrs. Marlowe, "I was much younger, only twenty-two, and had never thought of such unearthly things as spectral cats."

Two evenings later they again drove down the same lane and once more saw the regal-looking feline on its post. They alighted, the cat looking down in a friendly way, but when they took a few steps toward it, the animal slowly faded away and disappeared, without leaving the post.

Later the two women stopped for tea in the village and told the waitress about the disappearing cat. Her only reply was a smile, but a woman at the next table inquired if it had been a big white cat.

"Good gracious sakes!" she said then. "You drove by at the right times to see Congleton's ghost-cat!"

And she went on to say that she had lived in the village over fifty years and remembered the real cat. It had belonged to a Mrs. Winge, housekeeper at the former abbey, who was devoted to her pet. When the animal disappeared she was sure it was the victim of a dog pack. Sometime later she heard meowing at the door and went joyfully to let her pet inside.

But no matter how she coaxed he wouldn't come in, just stood there and then vanished. She thought he was merely flighty, as cats are after such jaunts. But this happened night after night, until finally in bright moonlight she saw him simply dissolve away. Mrs. Winge took such a fright from the experience that she never again paid any attention to the meowing. Eventually she left the neighborhood, saying that she liked live cats and didn't enjoy being haunted by a dead one!

This, said the woman at the tea shop, had happened over forty years before, but the sight of the ghost-cat was still a well-known occurrence in the village.

Now we come to the ghost of that king of the beasts, a lion. An old lady living in Dallas, Texas, told a very amusing story of this imposing specter. Her family had lived in Northern Ireland in a huge stone house that went back to the Crusades. When her father first leased the place he was told it was haunted, but by very peaceable, quiet ghosts who never bothered a soul, and the luck of the place was so strong he'd never be sorry! Both statements proving true, he finally bought the house.

The most extraordinary of its ghosts was a lion, a large and amiable beast who padded about at unexpected moments and seemed to live in the attic. The first of the family to see him were Aunts Emily and Amelia, who came for a lengthy visitation. They had gone up after lunch to dress for a carriage ride, and as they came out of the bedroom, there was the lion —trotting quietly down from the attic landing. The shrieks of the aunts nearly raised the roof, and naturally the father and mother rushed upstairs to settle the commotion.

"A lion?" Father observed calmly. "Sure, now, it's only the harmless ghost of a poor old beast that wouldn't hurt a hair on your heads!" But the aunts' hair was standing up too straight for comfort. The ladies packed and left that very night.

The narrator was still a small child when her sister Athena saw the beast. Sent upstairs to fetch a clean handkerchief for

Mother, Athena heard something moving up above. Since family and maids were all in the dining room and kitchens, she was startled. As she looked up she saw the door to the attic stairs open and a lion step out. It yawned, stretched, and padded downward.

By this time Athena was frozen in terror. The beast looked her over, wrinkling its nose but making no sound. She clung to the banisters, too frightened to scream, as the animal passed her, proceeded down both flights, and then faded outright through the big oak entrance door below.

But Athena was hushed up by her parents and the younger children did not hear of the lion until a gentleman called on their father sometime later. While the man waited in the upstairs drawing room the maid took in a silver tray with glasses and a decanter of old whiskey, with the invitation to help himself. As she went out she failed to close the door, leaving a view of the stairs going up.

The father was delayed outdoors for some time, finally coming in just as shrieks came from the drawing room. With the mother and maid panting behind him, he dashed upstairs to investigate. The room seemed to be empty. But in Victorian fashion, a big table held the center of the room, covered by a floor-length woolen cloth. As they came running in, a corner of the cloth quivered and a terrified face peered out.

"For God's sake, man, what's up?" Taking the man's shaking hand the father pulled his guest upright.

The white-faced man could barely speak. "I kn-new you kept hounds and horses, but I didn't suppose you had a lion!" he gasped.

His host was understandably reluctant to have this story spread clear to England, whence his guest came. Quick of wit, he picked up the decanter and poured out another nip. "How many glasses of this stuff have you had?" he inquired, tilting the whiskey as if estimating drinks.

"Th-three or four," the man admitted.

Father looked stunned. "Hell's fire, man, this stuff is dynamite! You don't get liquor like this in bars. It's twenty-five years old, smooth as silk, but triple strong. Three glasses, and you see pink elephants!"

"Oh, God, is that it?" the guest cried. "I'll sign the pledge today, for I'd never wish to go through such a thing again! Plain as day I saw the beast coming down the stairs. He stood in the door and lifted his lip in a snarl, before I dived under the cloth. And the reek of the creature so strong I can smell it yet!"

As for how the lion got there, local legend said he dated back to the Crusades. Many a knight had left the region to fight for the Holy Land, and it was common enough to bring back a lion for the local seigneur with perhaps a gazelle for his lady. At any rate the poor displaced beast must have lacked that homing instinct we discussed earlier, for instead of going back at death to his native hunting ground, he'd stayed lonely for some six hundred years, haunting an old stone house in Northern Ireland.[7]

Unlike our other accounts, this tale may have been told with tongue in cheek. It rests on the testimony of one person, Irish at that! We include it as a lively and amusing grace note in a rather solemn melody.

But not all ghostly images from the past are so purposeless. In 1940 the Reverend and Mrs. Whittlesey were living in Hawthorne, California. Ruth Whittlesey was superintendent of a convalescent hospital at the time.

In March she was summoned to the hospital in the middle of the night because a patient was dying. She got into her uniform and set out. The adjoining block was lonely with no houses or street lights. As she left the lighted area a small car with two men in it careened around the corner and pulled up beside her. She started to run but the car followed slowly.

All of a sudden their big white collie Nigel raced up and planted himself between her and the car. She saw one of the men lean out and look at him before the two took off in a hurry. The dog stayed with her until she reached the next street light. Then he was gone. And only then, recovering from her fright, did she realize that Nigel had died several months before. Mrs. Whittlesey wrote, "My husband is a minister of a well-known Protestant church. We are not superstitious or overly imaginative—but we know that sometimes God moves in mysterious ways."[8]

Bayard Veiller, in his book *The Fun I've Had*, tells how his dog Penn "came back" and lightened a burden of grief. Penn was a member of the family in the warmest way. His final days were ones of intense, prolonged suffering. With heavy hearts the Veillers decided that he must be eased out of his pain. A doctor put him into his last sleep, and they buried Penn in the garden with myrtle and lilies-of-the-valley on his grave.

"Now," Veiller wrote, "here is the part I don't expect anyone to believe."

Weary from the emotional strain, he had gone to bed early. At three o'clock he was awakened by the sound of Penn barking. It was "gay, boisterous, excited." He got up and went outside. Clearly visible in the bright moonlight, racing down a hill behind the house to the garden, came Penn—tail wagging, energetic and carefree as a puppy. He ran through the garden and around the lawn several times, then vanished.

The dog was unmistakably Penn, said Veiller. Moreover, he added that he himself is not superstitious nor given to imagining things that don't exist, nor has he ever thought much about a hereafter. "I can't explain this and it wasn't a dream . . . But I'll take my oath he came back."

The next morning, before Veiller could tell his wife about his experience, she told him she had heard Penn barking during the night and had gone to the window. There she, too, had seen him romping gaily about the garden and across the lawn until he disappeared. Both the author and his wife believed Penn had come back to let them know he had entered into a new existence, that he was young again and happy, and that they must not grieve.

In 1939 the Abbey Park Museum at New Barnet, north of London, placed on display the three-thousand-year-old mummy of an Egyptian high priest, found in a rock tomb at Thebes. Prior to the acquisition, carrion crows had never been seen near the museum. But now, every morning at 4 A.M. a crow hammered the window just above the mummy with his beak for as long as four hours. Efforts by the custodian and neighbors to scare the bird away were futile. The crow simply would not be driven away!

According to one witness, the bird performed what appeared to be a ritual. "The crow perches outside the window above where the mummy lies," he said. "First, the crow bows three times to the north, then three times to the south. Next, he turns and with his beak gives three loud raps on the window." The mummy was displayed in a glass case directly below the high window and no one, man or bird, could have seen it from outside.

Father J. S. Ward, museum director, said he thought the crow could smell the scent of death. A mummy, however, has only a musty odor. There is no putrefaction and it is this process of decomposition that alone creates the smell of death.

Ancient Egyptians believed that after death a person's spiritual and astral bodies separated. The spiritual body, or *ba,* left the physical body and continued on in the realm beyond. The *ka,* which was the lower and more material part of the soul, remained with the mummified body. For this reason the tomb contained food, clothing, pots, furniture, and other things the *ka* might need in its long vigil. To shatter the mummy or tomb, or objects in the tomb, was to release the *ka.*

What is of interest here is that the *ka* in tomb paintings and statuary often took the form of a predatory bird—a crow or sometimes a hawk.

We may have here a manifestation of the same psychic force

that links tribes and families to their totem animals for long ages. Mind affects matter and matter affects mind. Belief creates its own verification in fact. Thoughts can create and we become the subjects of our beliefs. Writes Dr. J. C. Mardrus, Oriental scholar and Egyptologist, "I am absolutely convinced that they [*the Egyptians*] knew how to concentrate upon and around a mummy certain dynamic powers of which we possess very incomplete notions."

Perhaps these "dynamic powers" can operate through animals. While the alleged curse that followed the opening of Tutankhamen's tomb has been exaggerated to the point of the ridiculous, some odd events did occur at the time.

Richard Bethell, a witness, wrote in the *Westminster Gazette:* "The day was absolutely still when the tomb was opened, but as we started to enter, a miniature sandstorm arose and swept along the desert almost to the mouth of the tomb, swirled around for a moment and then disappeared. No sooner had this strange wind dropped, than a hawk (which was the symbol of Horus, supreme god of old Egypt) swept out of the east, hovered over the tomb, and then soared off into the desert. I felt a tense feeling of awe, and the urge to turn back."

And on this same day a canary owned by Howard Carter, leader of the party, was found dead in Carter's villa, killed by a cobra, the rarest snake in Egypt. The cobra was considered sacred by the ancient Egyptians.

Coincidences? Perhaps. However, any study of Egyptian archaeology will disclose that when these "coincidences" do occur, they are invariably adverse, frustrating, or destructive. When Arthur Weigall, inspector general of antiquities in Egypt, and Joseph Lindon Smith, the brilliant artist-archaeologist, attempted to raise the curse of the god Amon-Ra on the heretic Pharaoh, Amenhotep IV, by presenting a drama in the Valley of the Kings, what followed was certainly more than a series of coincidences.

Their troubles began when a rehearsal was held three days

before the scheduled performance. Twice in the afternoon the proceedings came to a halt as short, fierce electrical and sand storms came in from the desert and swept down the valley. That night both Mrs. Smith and Mrs. Weigall became ill, and both women had identical dreams of being lashed by a flail in the hand of Rameses II, creator of the Rameseum honoring Amon-Ra.

The following morning the women were seriously ill. Mrs. Smith's eyes were swollen and nearly closed. She visited an oculist who could not determine the nature of her ailment. When her condition worsened and it was feared she might lose her sight, she was rushed to a Cairo hospital.

Mrs. Weigall suffered extreme abdominal pain. She, too, was hospitalized and underwent a nearly fatal abdominal operation. Then her husband had a nervous breakdown, while Mr. Smith was stricken by a severe attack of jaundice. Of the cast of the proposed play, only the musician escaped illness, but his mother fell and broke her leg. Three members of the audience, who had arrived early, suffered serious attacks of illness.

The play was never given. The Egyptologists who had been invited—including Howard Carter and Sir Flinders Petrie—destroyed their invitations. The detailed story is told in the book, *Tombs, Temples and Ancient Art,* edited by Corinna Lindon Smith, and published by the University of Oklahoma Press in 1956.

Thought has substance, and love and hate are as material as the rays of the sun. The Egyptians of old created their gods and their gods were jealous. Several writers have pointed out that as far as we can determine, every mummy said to be bearing a curse is the embalmed shell of one who has defied the great gods.

Tutankhamen was recalling the exiled divinities, and had changed his name to propitiate them, but his efforts came too late. Thus no image of Ra in yellow adorned the bow of the boat that bore his body. No plaques exhibited the painted figures of the gods Tem, Shu, Tefnut, Seb, Mut, Osiris, Isis, Suti, and Nephthys, anointed with cedar oil. Perhaps peace did not dwell in the darkness of his tomb, only a great unrest.

The wrath of the gods does not lie like a dark cloud over the whole Valley of the Kings, nor does it stand before every tomb, invisible, vengeful, seeking to bar entry into the mysteries of the long dead. Only to the few who were heretics, rebels, who defied or offended their gods, came the arrows of their hate. And seemingly around their bodies are auras of misfortune that can release hate.

Violet Tweedale, the English writer and granddaughter of the noted Dr. Robert Chambers, tells of a mummy that shattered two plate-glass display cases in the British Museum. The account appears in her book, *Phantoms of the Dawn.*

"Those who work in museums have strange experiences," writes Henry Field of the Field Museum (now named the Chicago Museum of Natural History), in his book, *The Track of Man.* He offers the following incident as evidence:[9]

One wintry night in 1934 a guard was making the rounds when he entered the Egyptian Hall. Suddenly he was startled by a blood-curdling scream. He threw the master switch for all the lights in the hall but found he was alone. Then he blew his whistle and other guards came on the run.

The guards made a search, flashing their lights around the display cases and into the sarcophagi. Finally they checked a 125-foot case along a wall, in which a line of mummies was arranged chronologically. One of the withered bodies had fallen from its base and was lying face down on the linoleum floor inside.

Henry Field wrote that to protect the mummies from moths and other pests, the case is sealed tight and the air inside is poisoned. There is only one door into the case and it is kept locked. No living person could have entered the poisoned case. Since the museum floats on an island of concrete and there is no hard-pan on the filled-in land along the lake front, no vibration in the building could have knocked it off the base without cracking the walls. Moreover, the base extended at least four inches on all sides of the mummy.

"There is still no explanation of the scream or of the fallen mummy," Field concluded. "It is just one more example of things we cannot explain."

About the year 1880 a British diplomat, Douglas Murray, who had been stationed at Cairo, purchased a mummy as a souvenir to take home. One night a shot was heard. Murray was found lying in his bunk, dead from a self-inflicted bullet wound. His associate, who took over the ownership of the mummy, arrived in London to learn that the great Baring Bank failure left him financially ruined. He sold the mummy to a private collector of curios.

The new owner, unable to find a suitable spot in his home, gave it to Sir E. A. Wallis Budge, famous Egyptologist and curator of Egyptian antiquities for the British Museum. Then things began to happen. As two porters were carrying the mummy up the museum's stone steps, one fell, breaking his leg. A few days later, the other porter, who seemingly had been in good health, dropped dead on the museum floor.

Next Dr. Budge arranged to have the still-wrapped and sealed mummy photographed. When the negative was developed it did not reveal the face of the mummy case, but the features of an evil-looking woman with glaring eyes, very much alive. A few weeks later the photographer died of an illness that defied diagnosis.

Meanwhile Dr. Budge had read the inscriptions and determined that the mummy was the remains of Amen-Rha, priestess of Thebes. Unwrapping the body, he found it in a good state of preservation. The brown hair was of coarse texture, the eyebrows thick, the lashes abundant. The face still bore traces of paint and rouge about the arched nose and heavily sensual lips.

Now the London newspapers began to print sensational stories about the "haunted mummy" and the more imaginative visitors to the museum began attributing their later misfortunes to having looked upon the priestess in her glass case! Mrs. A. M. W. Stirling, author of *Ghosts Vivisected,* recalls visiting the museum and seeing only the empty mummy case. The authorities had placed the mummy itself in storage to end the rumors. But placed inconspicuously on view in a corner of the glass case was the notorious photograph revealing the semblance of the living face of a malignant woman, the mouth drawn back in a snarl, the eyes aglow with hatred. "I studied it for some time," she wrote, "then came away bewildered."

In 1912 an American Egyptologist who laughed at superstitions purchased this mummy. The withered body of the priestess was packed in a crate and placed aboard an ocean liner for the voyage to New York.

The name of the ship? The HMS *Titanic.*[10]

Inevitably there are incidents in this book that will be questioned by many readers. Our task has been to collect and present them from listed sources. Naturally we cannot vouch for the truth of all these reports in a world where hoaxes, lies, exaggerations, and misrepresentations exist.

Fashions exist in beliefs as well as customs. And since man in every stage of his slow intellectual progress mistakenly thinks he has found ultimate answers, theories are regarded as facts. But in time the immutable scientific truths of our generation will also join the long procession of unfashionable concepts reaching back into the past as new "immutable truths" will take their place.

Using the word "myths" instead of "theories," Professor Paul Westmeyer, in *Chemistry* magazine (January, 1965), writes: "Most people are not aware that much of what scientists 'know' is based on the myths which they have invented to help understand the relatively few things they can explain. The unfortunate thing is that most laymen and many scientists believe the myths."

And Dr. Henry Eyring, president of the American Association for the Advancement of Science, writing in the AAAS *Bulletin* (September, 1965) said: "The universe is so complex that even the widest-ranging vision is at best partial and tentative. Each generation sets itself the task of re-evaluation and re-interpretation, the quest for truth is unending."

So long as science continues to interpret life wholly in mechanistic terms, our culture will remain unbalanced and sadly wanting, and our eyes will be closed to the vast, intricate, and wonderful greater realities that exist around and within our own beings—and those of our pets.

In this final chapter, even more than in the others, each person must decide for himself what meanings lie within these riddles. There is no cut-and-dried answer that fits all the cases, for we are in ambiguous and obscure realms.

"The mystery of ourselves we place upon the Lord's Table. The mysteries of ourselves we receive," said St. Augustine. He was referring to the Christian communion service, but it applies to any vantage point. Perhaps in another and wider sense, the Lord's Table is the universe, and only the limitations of our personal radar can dull the mystery we receive therefrom.

Bibliographical Notes

I. Introduction

1. Doug Storer, *Amazing But True Animals*. Greenwich, Conn., Gold Medal Books, 1963.
2. Eldon Roark, *Just a Mutt*. New York, Whittlesey House, 1947.
3. *This Week*, March 3, 1935.
4. *Just a Mutt, op. cit.*
5. *Reader's Digest*, undated clipping.
6. *American Mercury*, July, 1953; also Sept., 1953.
7. Loren Eiseley, *The Unexpected Universe*. New York, Harcourt, Brace, and World, 1968.
8. *Tomorrow*, Summer, 1956.
9. Ronald Rose, *Living Magic*. New York, Rand McNally and Co., 1956.
10. Henry B. Beston, *The Outermost House*. New York, Doubleday, Doran, and Co., Inc., 1928.

II. Prima Donnas and Mascot Marvels

1. *Look*, June 4, 1963.
2. George and Helen Papashvily, *Dogs and People*. Philadelphia, J. B. Lippincott Co., 1954; *Just a Mutt, op. cit.; Coronet*, Oct., 1942.
3. Lewis E. Lawes, *Life and Death in Sing Sing*. New York, Doubleday, Doran, and Co., 1928.
4. *Coronet*, March, 1945.
5. Ralph H. Barbour, *The Boys Book of Dogs*. New York, Dodd, Mead, and Co., 1928 and 1948.
6. *Firemen*, National Fire Protection Association, Aug. and Sept., 1948.
7. *Man to Man*, Nov., 1950; *Cue*, July 15, 1939.
8. *Coronet*, May, 1956.
9. *Amazing But True Animals, op. cit.*; Freling Foster, *Keep Up With the World*. New York, Grosset and Dunlap, 1949; *Coronet*, June, 1959.

III. Pets Who Earn Their Keep

1. *News Bulletin*, National Geographic Society, June, 1964.
2. *Life*, May 15, 1964; *Amazing But True Animals, op. cit.*
3. Julie MacDonald, *Almost Human*. Philadelphia and New York, Chilton Books, Inc., 1965.

4. Elsie Hix, *Strange as it Seems*. New York, Doubleday and Co., Inc., 1953.
5. Elsie Hix, *Strange as it Seems,* 3rd Edition. New York, Bantam Books, Inc., 1962.
6. *Ibid.*
7. *Keep Up With the World, op. cit.*
8. *Amazing But True Animals, op. cit.*
9. *Strange as it Seems,* 3rd Edition, *op. cit.*
10. *Christian Science Monitor* quoted in *Coronet,* April, 1951.
11. *Coronet,* Sept., 1942.
12. Doubleday and Co., Inc., New York, 1962.
13. *San Diego* (Calif.) *Independent,* Sept. 21, 1966.
14. *Parade,* July 10, 1966.

IV. The Warriors and the Sleuths

1. Fairfax Downey, *Great Dogs of All Time.* New York, Doubleday and Co., Inc., 1962.
2. *True,* May, 1965.
3. *Saga,* June, 1968; *Parade,* April 28, 1968.
4. *Dansk Familieblad,* Copenhagen, Denmark, Oct. 8, 1957; *Reader's Digest,* Dec. 15, 1957.
5. *True,* March, 1957.
6. *Popular Dogs,* July, 1960; also see Leo A. Handel, *A Dog Named Duke.* Philadelphia and New York, J. B. Lippincott Co., 1966.

V. Good Samaritans

1. *Fate,* Nov., 1954.
2. New York, Harper and Bros., 1940.
3. *Fate,* Oct., 1956.
4. *Reader's Digest,* July, 1948.
5. *Fate,* June, 1952.
6. *Ibid.,* Jan., 1955.
7. *Ibid.,* June, 1953.
8. *Magazine Digest,* April, 1946.
9. *Fate,* March, 1956.
10. *Nature,* Jan., 1945.
11. *Amazing But True Animals, op. cit.*
12. *Ibid.*
13. *Fate,* Oct., 1957.
14. *Ibid.,* Oct., 1954.
15. *Ken-L-Bits,* May, 1959.
16. *Reader's Digest,* July, 1948.
17. *Fate,* May, 1961.

18. *Ibid.,* Nov., 1956.
19. *Ibid.,* March, 1954.
20. *Ibid.,* Oct., 1954.

VI. Bridges Over the Border

1. *Life,* Sept. 29, 1967.
2. *Dogs and People, op. cit.*
3. Vance Packard, *Animal I. Q.* New York, Dial Press, 1950.
4. *Fate,* June, 1959.
5. *Ibid.,* March and Oct., 1954; A.P. Dispatch, April 3, 1953.
6. Robert Ripley, *Believe It or Not,* 8th Series. New York, Pocket Books, Inc., 1962.
7. Edward D. Radin, *Twelve Against the Law.* New York, Duell, Sloan, and Pearce, Inc., 1946.
8. John C. Lilly, *The Mind of the Dolphin.* New York, Doubleday and Co., Inc., 1967; Jacques Graven, *Non-Human Thought.* New York, Stein and Day, Inc., 1967; *Life,* Oct. 22, 1965.
9. *Sea Secrets,* Vol. 11, No. 11 (3rd Series).
10. Antony Alpers, *Dolphins: The Myth and the Mammal.* Boston, Houghton Mifflin Co., 1961; Winthrop N. Kellogg, *Porpoises and Sonar.* University of Chicago Press, 1961.
11. *Coronet,* March, 1942.
12. *Ibid.,* Feb., 1943.
13. Alan Devoe, *This Fascinating Animal World.* New York, McGraw-Hill Book Co., Inc., 1951; *Life,* March 25, 1965.
14. Sally Carrighar, *Wild Heritage.* Boston, Houghton Mifflin Co., 1965.
15. Frank Edwards, *Strange World.* New York, Lyle Stuart, Inc., 1964; *Coronet,* June, 1960.
16. Leonard Dubkin, *The White Lady.* New York, G. P. Putnam's Sons, 1952.

VII. Animal Supersenses

1. *Fate,* Oct., 1967.
2. *Ibid.,* April, 1965.
3. *Nature,* April, 1941; *This Fascinating Animal World, op. cit.*
4. *Nature,* April, 1941; *Chicago Tribune* Press Service, March 10, 1964.
5. *Reader's Digest,* Sept., 1963.
6. Carleton S. Coon, *The Origin of Races.* New York, Alfred A. Knopf, Inc., 1962.
7. *Borderline,* Sept., 1965.
8. *Scientific American,* June, 1951.
9. A. P. Feature, April 16, 1967.

10. *Virginia Quarterly Review,* Oct., 1936.
11. New York, David McKay Co., Inc., 1948.
12. New York, Doubleday and Co., Inc., 1962.

VIII. Cosmic Cycles and Bio-Clocks

1. *Coronet,* July, 1959.
2. *Saturday Evening Post,* Dec. 24, 1960.
3. Michel Gauquelin, *The Cosmic Clocks.* Chicago, Henry Regnery Co., 1967; Millicent E. Salsam, *How Animals Tell Time.* New York, William Morrow and Co., Inc., 1967; Margaret O. Hyde, *Animal Clocks and Compasses.* New York, Whittlesey House, 1960.
4. *The Woman with Woman's Digest,* June, 1946.
5. *Fate,* June, 1953.
6. I.N.S. Dispatch, Dec. 1, 1942.
7. Gustav Eckstein, *Everyday Miracle.* New York, Harper and Bros., 1940.
8. *Just a Mutt, op. cit.*
9. *Frontiers: A Magazine of Natural History,* Academy of Natural Sciences of Philadelphia, June, 1951.
10. *Saturday Evening Post,* Oct. 24, 1953.
11. Quoted in Copley News Service Feature, June 2, 1968.
12. *Natural History,* March, 1966.
13. *Scientific American,* May, 1965; *Life,* May 21, 1963.
14. *Strange as it Seems,* 3rd Edition, *op. cit.*
15. *Animal I. Q., op. cit.*
16. *Animal Clocks and Compasses, op. cit.;* Ann and Myron Sutton, *Animals on the Move.* New York, Rand McNally and Co., 1956.

IX. Without Compass or Map

1. *American Magazine,* June, 1951.
2. *Fate,* May, 1959.
3. *Ibid.,* May, 1958.
4. *Ibid.,* March, 1965.
5. George Stimpson, *A Book About a Thousand Things.* New York, Harper and Bros., 1946.
6. *Coronet,* June, 1946.
7. I.N.S. Dispatch, April 5, 1950.
8. A.P. Dispatch, July 23, 1949.
9. U.P. Dispatch, June 1, 1949.
10. *Frontiers: A Magazine of Natural History,* April, 1954; A.P. Dispatch, March 23, 1953.
11. New York, Dodd, Mead, and Co., 1926; see also Capt. A. H. Trapman, *Man's Best Friend.*

X. Esp: The Gift We Share

1. Nandor Fodor, *Between Two Worlds*. West Nyack, New York, Parker Publishing Co., 1964.
2. New York, Devin-Adair Co., 1961; also see Rosalind Heywood, *ESP: A Personal Memoir*. New York, E. P. Dutton and Co., 1964.
3. *Fate,* April, 1953.
4. *Houston Post,* May 15, 1966.
5. *Magazine Digest,* April, 1946.
6. *Fate,* Feb., 1956.
7. Danton Walker, *Spooks DeLuxe: Some Excursions into the Supernatural*. New York, Franklin Watts, Inc., 1956.
8. *Exploring the Unknown,* Vol. 3, No. 3.
9. *Proceedings,* S.P.R., Vol. XLV.
10. *American Mercury,* Nov., 1944; Morton Thompson, *Joe, The Wounded Tennis Player*. New York, Doubleday and Co., Inc., 1945.
11. New York, William Morrow and Co., 1952.

XI. The Magnet of the Heart

1. A.P. Dispatch, Dec. 5, 1952.
2. *Frontiers, op. cit.*
3. Walter McGraw, *World of the Paranormal*. New York, Pyramid Books, Inc., 1969.
4. *American Magazine,* June, 1951; *195 Cat Tales, op. cit.*; Elsie Hix, *Strange as it Seems*. New York, Doubleday and Co., 1953.
5. A.P., Aug. 3, 1951; *195 Cat Tales, op. cit.;* Elsie Hix, *Strange as it Seems*. New York, Doubleday and Co., 1953.
6. Boston, Little, Brown, and Co., 1956; *Christian Science Monitor,* May 7, 1953.
7. I.N.S. Dispatch, April 11, 1945; A.P., Jan. 20, 1958.
8. *Fate,* Dec. 1963.
9. *Ibid.,* Sept., 1956.

XII. The Wizards and the Geniuses

1. Providence (R.I.) *Journal,* undated clipping; *Fate,* Nov., 1955, Dec., 1962.
2. Nandor Fodor, *Encyclopedia of Psychic Science*. New Hyde Park, New York, University Books, 1966; R. DeWitt Miller, *Forgotten Mysteries*. Chicago, Cloud, Inc., 1947; *Tomorrow,* Spring, 1960.
3. *Coronet,* Nov., 1954; Reader's Scope, May, 1948.

4. New York, American Universities Publishing Co., 1920.
5. *Tomorrow,* Spring, 1960.
6. *Cosmopolitan,* Aug., 1928.
7. A.P., July 9, 1969.
8. *Life,* March 8, 1966; *The New York Times,* Nov. 5, 1965.
9. *Coronet,* April, 1942.
10. *Encyclopedia of Psychic Science, op. cit.*
11. New York, Cambridge University Press, 1931.

XIII. The Prophets and the Seers
1. *Reader's Digest,* 1948.
2. Ivan T. Sanderson, *More Things.* New York, Pyramid Books, 1969.
3. U.P.I. Report on Soviet Studies, March 24, 1969.
4. *Encyclopedia of Psychic Science, op. cit.*
5. *Denver Post,* Aug. 26, 1963.
6. U.P.I. Report on Soviet Studies, *op. cit.*
7. *Pursuit,* Vol. 2, No. 2 (Journal of the Society for the Investigation of the Unexplained, Columbia, New Jersey).
8. *Fate,* July, 1959.
9. *Ibid.,* April, 1953.
10. *Reader's Digest,* 1948, reproduced by permission.
11. *Ibid.,* undated clipping.
12. *Spooks DeLuxe, op. cit.*
13. Quoted in *Light* magazine (England), Spring, 1969, from *The Life of Thomas Hardy* by Florence Hardy.
14. *Between Two Worlds, op. cit.; MacLean's Magazine,* Dec. 15, 1951.
15. *Mind Digest,* Nov., 1945.

XIV. Tales of the Trail's End
1. *Fate,* Sept., 1956.
2. A.P. Dispatch, early 1955.
3. *Reader's Digest,* June, 1946.
4. *Fate,* July, 1953.
5. Christina Hole, *Haunted England.* London, B. T. Batsford, Ltd., n. d.
6. *Tomorrow,* English Edition, Summer, 1956.
7. *Fate,* Feb., 1964.
8. *Ibid.,* Jan., 1961.
9. *Ibid.,* Feb., 1957.
10. *This Week,* March 3, 1935.
11. U.P. Dispatches, July 11 and 18, 1954.
12. *Our Cats.* London, Dec., 1952; *195 Cat Tales, op. cit.*

XV. Some Steps Beyond

1. *Fate,* May, 1955.
2. *Ibid.,* Jan., 1955.
3. *Tomorrow,* Spring, 1960, quoted by permission.
4. New York, Citadel Press, 1958, quoted by permission.
5. New York, Harper and Bros., 1934.
6. Elliott O'Donnell, *Animal Ghosts.* London, Rider and Co., n. d.
7. *Fate,* June, 1954.
8. *Ibid.,* Jan., 1956.
9. Henry Field, *The Track of Man.* New York, Doubleday and Co., Inc., 1953.
10. Patrick Mahony, *Out of the Silence.* New York, Storm Publishers, 1948; *Pageant,* Nov., 1945.